holden
after
&
before

Love Letter for a Son
Lost to Overdose

Tara McGuire

ARSENAL PULP PRESS
VANCOUVER

ARSENAL PULP PRESS
Suite 202 – 211 East Georgia St.
Vancouver, BC V6A 1Z6
Canada
arsenalpulp.com

The publisher gratefully acknowledges the support of the Canada Council for the Arts and the British Columbia Arts Council for its publishing program, and the Government of Canada and the Government of British Columbia (through the Book Publishing Tax Credit Program) for its publishing activities.

Arsenal Pulp Press acknowledges the xʷməθkʷəy̓əm (Musqueam), Sḵwx̱wú7mesh (Squamish), and səlilwətaʔɬ (Tsleil-Waututh) Nations, custodians of the traditional, ancestral, and unceded territories where our office is located. We pay respect to their histories, traditions, and continuous living cultures and commit to accountability, respectful relations, and friendship.

Lyrics from "Harvest Moon" by Neil Young, "Druggernaut Jug Fuck" by Agoraphobic Nosebleed, "Scenario" by A Tribe Called Quest, "Comfortably Numb" by Pink Floyd, and "Reunited" by Peaches & Herb are reprinted with permission.
Poem from *The Essential Rumi* (Harper, 1995) is reprinted with permission of translator Coleman Barks.

Cover and text design by Jazmin Welch
Edited by Catharine Chen
Proofread by Alison Strobel

Printed and bound in Canada

Library and Archives Canada Cataloguing in Publication:
Title: Holden after & before : love letter for a son lost to overdose / Tara McGuire.
Other titles: Holden after and before
Names: McGuire, Tara, author.
Identifiers: Canadiana (print) 20220206996 | Canadiana (ebook) 20220207097 |
  ISBN 9781551528939 (softcover) | ISBN 9781551528946 (HTML)
Subjects: LCSH: McGuire, Tara. | LCSH: McGuire, Holden—Death and burial. |
  LCSH: Parents of drug addicts—Canada—Biography. | LCSH: Grief. |
  LCSH: Children—Death. | LCSH: Drugs—Overdose.
Classification: LCC BF575.G7 M34 2022 | DDC 155.9/37092—dc23

For Holden, who occupies my mind,
and Cam and Lyla, who hold my hands.

"Mothers are all slightly insane."
—J.D. SALINGER, *The Catcher in the Rye*

1

They told me his body lay on a mattress in a room with a window and a brick wall. They told me he was covered, and peaceful. They told me he spoke of love that night, that he laughed. They told me he made plans for tomorrow before he closed his eyes.

The next morning, in the warm heart of summer, my son's body lay cool and slack, the scaffolding that had held up his being for twenty-one years now absent. When his soul flew, the tent poles collapsed. Only a quiet skin inscribed with language remained.

And questions.

Since then I have learned that dead children are not bound by earthly constraints. The stubborn ones disregard the limitations of oxygen and blood. I hold my son now, as I did for his breathing years, and ask him how such a beautiful choir could be so abruptly halted. From raucous, full-throated chorus to … echoes.

If I listen, if I listen very closely, he tells me. He tells me in the space just before a thought. He tells me inside the ripe combustion chamber of an idea. There is a place deeper than marrow—it aches. That is where he tells me.

Though he is gone, he is not going away. I smell Holden in the linen closet; I dream him in the pink dawn; I recognize the line of his jaw on a crowded street corner and circle the block. For me, the possibility of Holden still exists.

Once, I found him in the urgent spring lilacs at the back corner of the yard, where the rotten fence post had fallen over. I definitely see him in the electric zings of colour scrawled on concrete walls downtown. I hear him in the Neil Young song I rocked him to as a baby, "Harvest Moon."

Come a little bit closer
Hear what I have to say
Just like children sleeping
We could dream the night away

. . .

Because I'm still in love with you
I want to see you dance again
Because I'm still in love with you
On this harvest moon

He is so many songs.

And yet, my first-born child remains swirling smoke. My hand passes straight through.

There is no way to make sense of Holden's gaping absence. But I have too much love left unspent to let him be. So I dig. I assume and I sleuth and I speculate and I make phone calls. I close my eyes and wonder where it all began. I obsess. I think too much, and loop back, and zigzag like a hound on a scent. At times I see it all as if I were there.

There is memory, which is fallible, and there is also a fat file of papers in a drawer: reports, evidence, scribbled notes, emails from doctors, redacted police files, and a one-page document from the coroner's office. There are photographs and screenshots. I have trolled long nights through the false rooms of social media. I have met many of Holden's friends—fellow graffiti artists, former co-workers, roommates, acquaintances, and lovers. They grieve Holden in their unique ways while navigating their own lives in this increasingly confusing and difficult world. Some try to exonerate themselves, some slough off his death like peeling sunburned skin, others drown in the guilt of retrospect. They all hurt, but some of them helped me plaster the cracks in his story.

All of this in a futile attempt to understand how my son's footsteps led to the room with the window and the brick wall.

Though I have excavated some of the details of Holden's last year, truth is a theoretical impossibility, which makes this an imagined story. And imagination is a personal and fickle creature. The way I see and interpret the course of Holden's life is most certainly not the way others see and interpret it. The only fact is he's gone.

My son is gone, and I want him to be not gone. I still hear his voice. So I will listen to what he has to say and colour in some of the blank spaces using tools gathered along the way. Even in the lives of the living, there is so much we can never know for certain.

This is a love song to my son, who grew too old too young.

They told me his body lay on a mattress, in a room that wasn't so bad. They told me he wouldn't have known what was happening. That he was asleep when the border was crossed. Small mercy, someone said. It may have been me.

2

I lay in bed witnessing the end of Holden's life, over and over. Frosted images, blurry pictures sharpening into focus. Sensations.

That small apartment became a tableau for my turbulent mind to rest on. I travelled there easily. I could see the floor, the curtains, the bricks. The glass half-full of water on the bedside table. I smelled Holden's crusty work socks and his last slow-shallow breath hanging stale in the air. I spent a lot of time staring down at his body wrapped in a sheet on the mattress, noting the stillness of his ribcage, the callouses on his palms and the pads of his curled fingers, his sculpted arms, and his gentle, passive expression. His steel-toed leather workboots lay scuffed and stagnant, laces snaking on the bare floorboards, harbouring no ambitions.

He wasn't alone. In the bed over by the brick wall, Devon slept with the heaviness of a child. I saw the shock of pink hair swept across her damp forehead, her ivory face smooth and serene. Her chest rose and fell with effortless rhythm. One person breathing. She would wake up, and he would not. I linger in that moment.

Devon wasn't Holden's girlfriend anymore, but she kept a small locked cabinet in her heart reserved for him. She hoped the day would come when they would have a real relationship. Months later, we would speak of this heartbreak over a cup of camomile tea.

Dying—what does it feel like?

After his heart's final drumbeat, would Holden have recognized his new and unfamiliar state of being—of not being? Would he have struggled to get his bearings the same way he had when he'd walked off the plane in Paris, blinking and disoriented, during his last year of high school? He'd been taking art, history, and philosophy classes, and our family travelled to France to visit the Louvre and to learn about the thousands of young men war-dead at Juno Beach.

But Momz, where did those nine hours go? How can time just disappear?

Would he have hesitated in his cooling body for a few earthly minutes, looking around, coming to terms with his fate? Was he disappointed, angry? Did he resist?

I heard his voice.

Ah shit, really? Can I get a do over? He would have laughed, deep and throaty—Holden was often laughing.

Confusion wouldn't have been new; Holden woke up in different places all the time. He was a legendary couch surfer because he wasn't picky and because people enjoyed having him around—especially women. He had a network of obliging friends who let him crash on their sofas, spare beds, and sometimes beside them whenever he wanted. Many mornings, the first question he asked himself was "Where am I?"

Devon lived in a small apartment at the Metropole, a five-storey apartment hotel in Gastown doing its best to appear hipster, though the smell of a hundred years' worth of mould permeated the walls. In the photo of her suite that Devon sent me, I could see accent pillows and the brick wall behind the head of her bed. I could see a corner of the window and the rack she hung her clothes on. I imagined framed pictures, fairy lights, and a kettle just outside the frame. In my version of the story, she always made Holden take off his shoes at the door and put the toilet seat down.

I saw him stretched out with a pillow under his head and a thin blanket blooming with purple blossoms wrapping his body. His tattooed arms splayed by his sides, his lips parted as if he were about to say something, his eyes closed.

But how, I wondered, might it have felt for him?

∞

What the … ?

This is messed up. Something's different, and Holden has to concentrate to figure out exactly what that difference is. He's looking at the room, at himself, from an off-kilter angle. One time, a prof at art school asked him to walk around a basically naked model until he found a perspective that challenged him to see proportion in a different way. Today's kind of like that.

So fucking weird. Am I still loaded?

Physically he feels great—no headache, no thirst, no urge to puke. There's also zero anxiety, which usually rolls up pretty quick most days. No self-loathing or restlessness, either. That's a switch.

And then, another sensation ambles in, something he hasn't felt very often in the last year or so, not without chemical help, anyway. He's … the word's not quite right, but *buoyant.* There's an expansion of himself from the inside, like how he felt at birthday parties as a kid, with the candles lighting up the grinning faces around the table and everyone singing his name. It's the same kind of warm flare that ignites in his core when he's painting a big, colourful piece of graffiti.

And another weirdness: a curious vacuum, a nonfeeling, if that's a thing, a nothing that yells at him loudly, demanding his attention. Kind of like when the band at a super-loud metal show stops playing; the sudden absence of something that had filled the space completely a nanosecond before.

He rewinds, as he's done so many mornings. What the fuck happened last night?

Exhausted by the dog pile of fucked-up shit that had happened to him over the last day or two, he'd met up with Devon at the bar downstairs. He definitely hadn't been interested in talking about it with her, or with anyone, actually. He wasn't sure how he was going to get his life back on track, but he knew he could. He could turn it around if he just kept going to work. He wanted to work. Working was key.

He'd had a couple of cocktails, played some pool, and stepped out into the alley for a bump or two, nothing unusual. Then he'd started feeling sick, like he was getting the flu; his muscles ached, his hip sockets throbbed, his skin burned from the inside, and his stomach was a mess. His legs could barely hold him.

Can I stay with you tonight, Dev? I feel like ass.

You can if you promise not to hurl. You're not looking so fresh.

He raised a flat palm. I swear on the Bible.

That means a lot coming from you, mister atheist. Devon looked at the floor and shook her head, but she was softly smiling as the two of them headed for the exit at the back of the bar.

They rode the elevator up to her apartment on the fourth floor, Holden's arm a heavy collar around Devon's neck, her arm bracing his back.

Even though we're both with different people at the mo, I will always love you, Devo. Can we just hang out all the time and drink gin?

She tilted her head to knock gently against his.

Sure, Holden, we can build a house with gin on tap and raise ferrets. But we won't sell their fur. Obviously.

Obviously. His mouth had trouble with the word. Keeping his eyes open was almost impossible. I mean it, D, one day I'll get my shit together and we can try again, okay? I'll be Whole-den. See what I did there?

He leaned into her, pressing his hot, damp forehead against the cool skin of her neck. He swivelled his jawbone back and forth so his rough scraggle of reddish beard prickled her bare shoulder.

Stop it, you freak!

But she didn't pull away. Their joined reflection in the elevator's smoked-mirror wall stared back at them: Her pink hair loose and long. His head, shaved close a few weeks before, looking more like a buzz cut now. Devon pulled her cat's eye sunglasses off the top of her head, perched them on her nose, and exhaled with the patience of a kindergarten teacher.

We are BFFs all day, every day, Holden. You're just fine. What you need is a big glass of water and a good night's sleep.

Inside the apartment, dull, stagnant air. Dollar-store candles and lavender soap. Devon held Holden's shoulders from behind and marched him toward the only chair. While he mined his deep front pocket for his phone, she pulled her camping mattress out of the closet and let it fall to the floor.

Holden slumped in the chair, arms heavy, fingers uncooperative. He fumbled to set an alarm for work, leaving a hieroglyphic of greasy smears on the cracked screen, and then he toppled forward onto the mattress. Devon helped him pull off his shirt, boots, and work shorts. Sprawled out in his boxer shorts, he let out a loud, exaggerated sigh.

The relief of being horizontal spread through his aching muscles. Finally, he didn't have to work to hold himself up. Devon lifted his head, wedged a pillow under it, and covered him with the purple tapestry she'd bought in Bali.

Thanks D-Bomb, you're one of the good ones. Can you make sure I'm up for work?

She kneeled on the worn wooden floor to kiss his cheek.

Good night, you big mess. See you in the morning.

∞

I was told that just the week before, Holden had saved a man from drowning at Wreck Beach. He'd spent the day there with a group of friends, enjoying the sun, throwing a Frisbee, playing guitar. Shouts, then frantic screams had erupted from farther down along the shoreline. Holden rose from the log he was sitting on, set down his beer, and sprinted across the hot sand. He dove into the sea, swam out, and hooked the stranger under the armpits the way he'd learned in lifeguard training years ago. The man was drunk, strong, and wearing heavy jeans that were pulling him down. He flailed and clung to Holden, nearly pulling him under. But Holden was stronger. His legs became an engine under the water, interlocking gears grinding for landfall, for survival. Adrenalin electrified his muscles. Salt stung his nostrils and throat. He towed the man, kicking and coughing, through the choppy green water and whipping wind back to shore.

Finally, laid out on the sand, Holden's chest heaved with the effort of saving two lives.

∞

Devon slept on. A white square of morning glowed around the edges of the blackout curtain. Outside the window, a seagull might have screamed; the ocean was close. The small fridge probably hummed. The street below was a busy one. Maybe a truck hit its brakes, then accelerated away with pneumatic force. Perhaps someone shouted from the sidewalk. But no noise came from Holden. He had been wiped clean.

3

I had just carried the shopping bags into the house and hoisted them onto the kitchen counter. Lyla was in her room with a stack of library books, fanning them out across her bed, deciding which one to read first. It was a quietly joyful thing to put away rice in the cupboard, yogurt in the fridge, chicken in the freezer. The jumbo pack of toilet paper meant we were staying. I set a small bouquet of flowers in a glass on the table—our table, the one Cam's brother had made for us when we bought our first home. Boxes were stacked against the walls, but after ten months of living out of a backpack, the idea of possessions didn't interest me much.

The drastic time change blurred the edges of my vision, making me feel off balance. But I didn't mind the one-glass-of-wine haze of jet lag; I knew the feeling would ease eventually. This time zone was our default. We were home.

Summer had gained a foothold, bringing a dense, trustworthy blue to the sky. The thin windows at the back of the low house were flung wide open, and gentle, warm air drifted in, carrying the scent of the wild pink roses climbing the chain-link fence at the edge of the yard. Tiny green apples were beginning to appear on the gnarled branches of the old apple tree. Later, we could all sit out there in the leafy shade and relax together in our circle of pink plastic Adirondack chairs.

I felt grateful.

Most importantly, Holden was here. We'd seen him once since we'd been back and had tentatively planned for him to come over for dinner that night after he finished work. I hadn't heard from him in a couple of days, but he had a habit of just showing up. The anticipation of being able to reach over and touch Holden's face while we talked made me feel like a teenager before a date. I was so lucky. We were home, where it was safe. Everything was going to be okay.

I'd exhaled with relief that day. It was just plain good to be home. Home, where we knew people well, and where people knew us. Where we could easily read the road signs and the labels at the grocery store. Where I could look at a bottle on a shelf and know for certain I was buying cranberry juice and not some kind of vinegar. Home, where we wouldn't accidentally drive down a stairway thinking it was a street, or have to convert currency in our heads before buying mangoes. Home, where I could cultivate a new career, I hoped, as a writer. Home, where we could finally empty our backpacks, which had been stuffed and musty for nearly a year. Where I could pull on a pair of jeans that weren't wrinkled and threadbare. Where I could choose from more than three shirts. Where we could drink the tap water.

I'd been busy ticking tasks off my list. We now had phone numbers, Wi-Fi, and a rental car. We'd taken a fast trip to visit family, celebrate Canada Day, and reclaim our dog, Mocha, from my sister Janet in the far corner of the province, an eight-hour drive away. On the way back, my husband, Cam, had taken a detour to see his mother and brother—he'd be back tomorrow. He was driving the cherry-red Volkswagen Beetle convertible we'd just bought used from my sister (a car we sold shortly thereafter because I couldn't tolerate its violent degree of cheerfulness).

At eleven years old, our daughter, Lyla, was bursting with the exuberant sweetness of a summer peach. After almost a year of travelling with her parents for constant company, being alone was a rare thrill; now she could hop on her bike and set off alone to cruise the quiet streets of our neighbourhood.

A knock on the front door drew my face away from the golden afternoon. Maybe it was a friend of Lyla's, or a neighbour who'd heard we were back.

I opened the door to the dark bulk of a police officer in a bulletproof vest. I don't remember his face or his name, but I can still see his heavy black boots on the flagstones of our porch, contrasting with my bare feet on our tired hardwood floor. Lyla bounced up behind me, hoping it was someone who'd jump on the trampoline with her. Mocha crowded the doorway, too. She barked at his uniform. At the hat he was removing.

He stood there, imposing yet awkward, not knowing what to do with his hands. He asked me in a monotone to confirm my name.

Please come outside, I think he said, so we can speak privately. He gestured toward Lyla with his chin. He didn't want her to hear.

In my jet-lagged fog, I didn't suspect why he already knew who I was and wanted to speak with me. A flash: perhaps there had been a break-in in the neighbourhood, and he wanted to warn me to close the windows at night. But we were home now—how could anything bad happen?

I didn't know this was to be the last moment of peace I'd experience for a very, very long time.

Just wait here a sec, Ly.

I took a few steps out into the sunshine of the driveway. Heat rose from the paving stones, sandy grit rubbed the soles of my feet, and the sun settled on my bare shoulders. Standing in the middle of the driveway, between the lush green forest with its bubbling creek and the leafy Spanish chestnut tree, the officer held his hat to his chest with both hands, like a shield.

What happened next unspooled quickly and unexpectedly.

The quiet just before he spoke expanded and snapped back.

I should have asked for his bulletproof vest.

I'm very sorry to inform you that your son Holden has died.

I took one last full breath and dropped. A clean amputation. I curled like a fetus on the ground and felt my life jerk sideways off its axis. The earth fell away. I plummeted. And as I fell, I also rose. I could see myself writhing on the driveway, gasping for air. Anyone passing by would have thought I had been shot at close range.

The officer's voice filled the gaps in my wailing. I probably heard words and must have asked questions, but the answers landed like snow, touching me and dissolving; they were abstract, they didn't mean anything.

I'm so sorry ... no sign of foul play ... don't have that information ... the coroner will investigate ... I'm very sorry ... no sign of criminal activity ... he was with a friend ... trauma team ... can we reach your husband? ... how long will it take him to get here? ... I'm very sorry ... no, it's not a mistake ... in the morgue ... in Burnaby ... because the Vancouver morgue is full ... I don't know ... yes, I'm sure ... yes, it's true ... yes ... no ... yes.

Falling. Falling. Bottomless.

My memory of this time is fractured and likely inaccurate.

Lyla ran outside and kneeled down beside me on the flagstones.

Momma, what's happening? Her eyes stretched wide with panic. Her smooth, young face knowing terror for the first time.

I'm so sorry, Ly, it's Holden. He ... he ... How could I smash her small, simple world? I pulled her into my arms. He died, sweetheart. Your brother is gone. I'm so so sorry.

We held each other on the driveway, vines encircling, wrapping, clinging to each other. We rocked back and forth. We cried. Could someone please tell me what to do?

The police officer paced around us at arm's length, keeping a safe distance. I don't know if it was out of respect or fear. We were something wild, desperate, unpredictable. We might pull him under.

Eventually, he stood in the living room. A sentinel.

I'm very sorry for your loss. Who can we call to be with you right now?

I didn't want the police in this with us. I didn't want to be part of something that required uniforms, strangers, protocol. But Cam wasn't home.

I called him myself. I don't know what words I said. I remember it as the moan of a wounded animal.

Please!

He knew to come.

Next I called Holden's father. I'm not sure why I didn't let the police officer do it. I supposed that I felt he should hear the words from me. We had created Holden together, with love, with optimism, and we would now share the weight of utter devastation.

It's … it's … Holden. My body didn't understand breathing. This voice belonged to someone else, I could not be saying these words. I heard myself whisper. The police are here.

I had nothing left to hold on to.

My vision of this evening is obscured. The perspective is disorienting and comes back to me in shards. Each one lands with a different impact.

I called a dear friend: Can you come? Please. Right now. I need you. I didn't tell her why. Couldn't say the words.

No one in uniform. Take your hand off my back. No strangers.

Another close friend walked in saying Cam had called him, had asked him to stay with us. He was a tough construction worker used to operating heavy tools. Sullen face, downcast. I'll stay until Cam can get here. Grey eyes wet and aflame. I'm here for whatever you need. I'm just so sorry.

Somehow Holden's father was in the living room. No no no. Embrace. Surrender. Sob.

Where is Holden? Please. Where could he have gone?

My mother arrived, pale, wet, sagging. There may have been others. There were certainly others. Where is Lyla? How do I explain this to Lyla? How do I comfort her? Help me. Leave me. Stay with me. Go away. No. I don't understand.

People spoke. I heard them through a shroud, a foreign language.

Like the illuminated windows of a passing train, images flashed by. Tears. Bare feet. Vomit. Warm air, too warm. Thirst. Then dark. Cold. Lying on the rug, shivering under a blanket. Phones ringing. *Bing, bing, bing.* Car doors. Footsteps. Voices. Whispers. Water.

A blanket was covering my face. Is there a blanket on Holden's face? Curl away from it. Curl into it. Into what? It's too late for protection.

I called Cam again. Please come home. Why are you taking so long? Why are you not here? Why are you gone? Why are there so many kinds of gone?

That day, a large forest fire in the British Columbia Interior blocked the main highway, the most direct route home. Cam's brother drove with him. Many hours in the wrong direction, circumnavigating the province to find a way back. To us. To the us that was left.

Outside the car, the air they passed through was thick, ash-snowed, acrid with smoke. Inside the car, silent heat, darkness. It was almost midnight when Cam walked into our house, an older version of himself. He gathered Lyla and me into his strong arms, and we wept.

We were three now. Only three.

Please make it not be true, I pleaded to Cam. I just want it to be not true.

All he could do was sit beside me, his bones holding us both steady, and nod.

The first days, I gasped for air. The normally reflexive act of breathing now an effort. If I decided not to inhale, I could join him. It could happen easily. No inhale, no exhale, repeat. I reverted to an unrecogniz-able shape. I was no longer human. There was nothing left of me to lose.

I was a terrible mother to Lyla. I'm not sure what she did with her time. I only know I could not have been much solace. I remember her watching episodes of *My Little Pony* on the iPad, even though she hadn't watched the show for years. Something in her wanted to be younger, more innocent, to escape the moment she was in. I fear this shock has gouged her psyche in ways I don't yet comprehend. Her trust in the world, her faith in me, her ability to live fully, love fully, without fear of loss, might be decimated.

We skipped her birthday a couple of weeks later. There should have been a party. Cake, balloons, friends, and games. Our daughter never turned twelve.

It was difficult to understand where I was or where I was going. I couldn't locate any reference points to orient myself. Groundless, numb, disconnected, paralyzed, I could only lie down, as if dead myself. Whatever was left of me tossed in an invisible wind. I couldn't be any-where. I wasn't anyone.

My mind spiralled and ricocheted. I relived the moment of impact over and over and over, repelled by it and pulled toward it, reshocking my heart every time. A strange sort of autopilot operated my body: crying, sleeping, weeping, shaking, breathing. The sun rose and set.

Time lost its meaning. The collision in the driveway had just happened, and it was years ago. The cut was still bleeding, yet I had known this pain forever. I now recognized the suffering of all mothers whose children die before them—women who may appear outwardly whole, but are shattered at the core. Women of war, of famine, of fire, of injustice. Mothers whose offspring have perished through disease, miscarriage, or misadventure. Longing mothers who'd never had the chance. I understood these women in black. I was one of them. We were a multitude.

People came, many people. They must have come; it's what we do. A stark procession arriving pink eyed at the same horrible door, their quivering lips not knowing what to say. Many called and talked with Cam when I was unable to speak or to even listen. I overheard some of the one-sided conversations. I heard thank you for calling, and we appreciate that, and I'll tell her. Many more sent cards. They must have agonized over what to write. We did not starve; large ceramic dishes full of food were left on the porch. Hydrangeas and bath salts and wine. Though I do not have a clear memory of these many acts of kindness, I am certain of them. One day I will be brave enough to sift through the stack of cards in the cupboard.

What I do remember well are the awkward things said by people who didn't know what else to do, caught as they were in the glare of such complicated and enormous grief. Would you like to see my new car? It's nice to meet you. Tell me about your trip. You're going to lose so much weight. At first I was surprised by what seemed like insensitivity, but now I don't find these comments at all unusual. In hindsight, they were perfectly appropriate. We were all deranged by Holden's death.

Family members had it the hardest. They couldn't help me grieve the way I wanted them to, because I didn't want to be grieving at all. I didn't know how. They didn't know how. I was frozen and mute and absent. How do you comfort a stick?

And I was not credible. Which is to say that I could not trust myself. I didn't remember what he looked like. I couldn't hear his voice anymore. Did I hug him? Did I tell him I loved him? Before he left that morning, did I say the words? I couldn't be sure. Did he know I loved him?

One afternoon Cam brought a beautiful bouquet of flowers to our bed, where I now lived. He placed the armful of pink, purple, and white dahlias on the bedside table beside another plate of uneaten food. I didn't deserve their beauty.

Who are they were from? I asked, breath rancid, hair a woven mess.

Me. He tried to smile, but only one side of his mouth lifted. A lopsided arch. His light-blue eyes glassed with tears. Happy anniversary, babe.

Oh.

The first trimester of grief was utter brutality. Just as I had been redefined by the confirmation that I would be a mother for the first time, so did the beginning of life without that child redefine me. Some of the symptoms were the same. I was nauseated by the smell of cooking food and unfathomably exhausted. That was where the similarities ended. There was no happiness. No loosening of the vice in my chest. No tiptoeing into the freshly painted nursery to wonder what this new human would become. Then I was joyfully pregnant and couldn't wait to begin the evolution into motherhood; now I would have done anything to abort this horrible, germinating thing. Please tell me there has been some kind of mistake—that this is not his destiny.

Even when I tried to fake a smile for the sake of my daughter, the anguish persisted. I lied to her with artifice while I hardened and cracked.

In the early days it was difficult to speak or to look at anyone directly. Eye contact was an assault. Food tasted like dirt or nothing at all. My thirst was unquenchable. The sound of a camera shutter made me flinch—taking photos, once a joy, now seemed offensive. Who would want to document any of this? Listening to music was overwhelming, singing an impossibility. Holden had loved music, therefore it was banished. The act of lifting my face for a moment felt painfully vulnerable. I dropped things and left them there on the floor. A sweater, a blanket, a piece of toast. When I smashed my favourite blue teacup, its fragments jagged puzzle pieces on the hardwood, I sobbed for three hours. Anything I loved would be taken away.

Everything oriented downward, toward the bottom, the mud, the end. Standing presented a challenge. Much easier to crawl under the blankets and hide. Sadness had a pull stronger than gravity, and the only place I could comfortably spend any length of time was in our bed. It cradled me while my muscles atrophied. A friend told me of a mother she knew who, after the loss of her daughter, had taken to her bed for three years. This sounded like a plausible strategy. Through the long, hot summer and into an amber fall, I huddled under a thick duvet, fever-boned.

From bed I could see our big Spanish chestnut tree outside the window and watch its shifting shades of green. Those greens helped me find my way back to my son. Holden had loved colour. As an artist, he'd always noticed pigments, shades, intensities. He often spoke of colour. How many greens can there be, Mama? I don't know, I'd told him, when he was young and alive and we walked in the forest together and sun speckled the fluttering leaves so they seemed to be lit from within. Let's count them! And we did. Mossy-rock green, thirty-six; pickle green, thirty-seven; Shrek green, thirty-eight!

I watched the light subtly shift as the days changed from bright and crisp to velvety and vague. I lay there for hours, days, weeks. Warm cups of tea arrived, cold ones were taken away.

I stayed in bed so long I disgusted myself.

I'm pathetic, I said to Cam.

No, he said, you just haven't let yourself have a break from this.

And his endorsement made it easier to move. I went outside and sat on one of the pink plastic lawn chairs. There were bugs and roses. The apples were fattening. The grass had turned sun stiff—it poked the bottoms of my feet. I could hear children playing in the park across the street. Cars travelling on the highway. No other life had stopped but mine. And his.

At times I would lay a flat palm against my chest to check for a rhythm, for any sign of warmth. I became a brittle shell; one tap from a tiny hammer and I would have disintegrated into dust and blown away. And I wouldn't have resisted. I wouldn't have missed myself at all. I was less than a thought. What was left of me weighed nothing. The crater where my heart had once thrived was filled with cold sludge. If I were to fall into the ocean as I scuffed along the grey edge of the seawall, crying behind my sunglasses, I would surely be dragged to the bottom like a sack of rocks tossed over the rail of a ship.

From what I could recall of morning sickness, it swooped in at predictable times. I remember, while I was pregnant with Holden, running from the radio studio down the hall to the bathroom to vomit my oatmeal while Whitney Houston sang "I Will Always Love You." She was dead now, too.

By contrast, mourning sickness, as I'd come to think of it, came rampaging in, full throttle, like a bomber on a midnight raid. No warning, no reason or order. Books about grief and loss materialized on my beside table. Apparently there were stages, but any progression of healing that the books suggested sounded like bullshit.

Denial, isolation, anger, bargaining, depression. Acceptance. These tormenters didn't stand in line waiting their turn. They ganged up on me, crushed me in the dark hours. How did anyone survive this?

I need everyone to go away (isolation). If I text his phone number maybe he will answer (denial). I am furious at him for what he did (anger). It's my fault for having been away for so long (bargaining). I abandoned him, I'm horrible (depression). I have failed at my most important job and deserve to suffer alone (isolation). I will never again experience any form of joy (depression). If I keep a bed made with his sheets, will he come back (bargaining and denial)? Why didn't I … If only … Maybe I could … (more bargaining).

I kept roaring (anger) around a desolate cave of my own creation. And I didn't want anyone in there with me. I wanted to rant alone (isolation).

Mother and son. Getting familiar with this new arrangement.

Former me had been very good at completing assignments and solving problems through sheer will. I could be counted on to get things done. I'd brandished an abrupt personal style: bring it on, I can handle it. Suck it up, Buttercup, had been one of my favourite expressions.

But the death of my child was a riddle that refused to be manipulated into submission. There was no way to finesse the fact of Holden's death. He was gone (acceptance).

The memorial service was held and the legal business tended to—there wasn't much. Flowers wilted in vases of stinking water, the banana bread had long been eaten, and there I was without him. That Holden was gone was the only thing I knew.

I aged a century that summer. I became an old woman—foul-smelling, weak, and wrinkled. I didn't give a shit about my hair, though I never had much. I got winded walking up a single flight of stairs.

It took me a long time to be able to leave the house. In the early days, the outside world was a harsh landscape, too bright, too loud, too overwhelming. Obviously, it could not be trusted.

When I finally gathered the strength to venture out for more than a walk, I took Lyla to a gymnastics class so she could forget her sad heart and live in her limbs for an hour or two. While I watched her tumble and roll, the woman sitting beside me where parents waited in straight-backed chairs along the wall leaned closer. She pointed out a small girl with tangled hair swinging from the parallel bars, then a boy, maybe a year older, smiling with arms wide while he did his best to balance on the beam. I have four children, she said, how many do you have?

That summer I was unable to speak much at all, let alone to a stranger. Speaking had always been easy, the one thing I could do well. Not anymore. My voice had vanished along with my son.

One.

I felt repugnant for not saying two. But that may have led to other questions I was not capable of answering. I ran outside to sob in the parking lot.

In some ways, I died the day Holden did. Once a confident and articulate person, I had become a scared and uncertain one. The woman who climbed mountains, went scuba diving, and travelled the world with no map had become too terrified to go out for a cup of coffee. The one who was fun at parties and could always be counted on to keep the dancing, jokes, and conversation flowing was now the silent, broody figure in the corner. That fortunate soul who had been the mother of two was now the demoralized matron of one.

I began to think of grief as a physical place. A bleak wasteland lined with barbed wire and riddled with hidden landmines. A no man's land, a waypoint between the woman I'd used to be and the one I was to become. I was passing through an uncharted borderland dividing the territory of who I was before the police officer knocked on our door and the new country I would plant my flag on. I was a mother whose child had died before her. A refugee dumped in a new world I did not wish to inhabit.

So, rather than hurry to start over in a place where I didn't speak the language or understand the customs, I chose to stay a little longer in that desolate mourning zone. I chose to remain in the bottomless sadness with my son rather than walk into a new world without him.

4

By the time Holden was about three, his father and I saw our family life and the future in vastly different ways. We tried counselling, and there weren't many arguments, but as our fundamental differences became more and more clear, the tension in our home morphed into a loud silence that wasn't hospitable or healthy for anyone. With a feeling of tremendous failure on both our parts, we separated. Holden's dad found an apartment downtown, and I kept the house we had rented near the university. I hired a student to look after Holden while I went to work early each day at the radio station. Every weekday morning, when he woke up, I was already gone.

If you want to wake up the city, you have to beat them to it, I'd say, holding his immaculate face between my palms and windshield-wipering his wet cheeks with my thumbs.

From Monday to Friday, the babysitter poured milk on Holden's cereal while he perched on a kitchen chair, swinging his legs. While I sat in the dull thud of the soundproof radio studio, I imagined her spitting on her hand to flatten his spiky blond hair. She helped him tie his shoes and strap on the ladybug backpack with his carrot sticks and juice box inside so he could wait on the bottom step for his dad to pick him up and walk him the three blocks to preschool, where he learned about letters, colours, and shapes. Things he already knew.

The house was big, with a brick fireplace, rattling windows, and shiny wooden floors he could slide across in his socks. His bedroom was painted blue, with puffy white clouds on the ceiling. He slept under a sunny day of robin's egg and cumulus.

The dining room was completely empty, just a dim chandelier dangling from the ceiling and cracked paint on the walls. I had no dining table, no candlesticks, no silver salt and pepper shakers. Instead, we collected big boxes and taped them together to build a fort. We cut out a door and windows and drew flower boxes under those windows with crayons. Holden wrote his name in big red letters on the rough brown cardboard above the door. Inside, we put pillows and blankets, some of his favourite books, his collection of toy trains. Thomas the Tank Engine parked in his own special corner.

On a summer long weekend just before Holden's third birthday, he and I took a trip on a "real live train." Before we got on board we inspected the engine and the rails, then got in our seats to watch houses, trees, and mountains fly past the windows. We ate cheese and crackers on our fold-out tables. Two hours later the train pulled into the station in Pemberton, a small potato-growing town, where my friend stood waiting on the platform. We would pick strawberries and play touch football. We would gaze up at the towering, jagged face of Mount Currie, drink cold beer, and duck swooping hummingbirds while the children swung on swings, slid down slides, and chased each other around in sweaty circles.

Shortly after we arrived, I looked out my friend's kitchen window and saw a man standing shirtless in the heat. He was wielding a chainsaw to carve log benches for the firepit at that night's Canada Day party.

Who is that?

Tell me about it, my friend said. That's our tenant, Cam.

He was strong, athletic, and possessed of an adventurous spirit—I could tell by the way he moved. His grin and glacier-blue eyes emanated mischief and light. That afternoon I discovered that he was kind, patient with children, and soft-spoken. And when his rough hand held mine that evening, I felt both electrified and safe.

Back in Vancouver, alone after Holden had fallen asleep, I dragged a chair across the kitchen floor to take down the cigarettes hidden in the cupboard. I twisted the old lock on the back door and stepped onto the porch to smoke and talk to my sister Janet on the phone.

It makes my heart hurt, I told her. I mean, the babysitter's a nice kid, and Holden seems to be doing fine, but I feel horrible that he wakes up with a stranger five days a week.

Why don't you move in with me?

Are you serious?

She was.

Holden and I moved across the water to North Vancouver, and my sister cared for Holden while I worked. He woke up with family every day. Janet's backyard was full of tall cedars and pines. Her two dogs, Milo and Sadie, filled the house with motion. Every morning Janet played Neil Diamond loud. She made Holden hot chocolate whenever he asked and Eggs Benedict every Friday. He loved her.

Every second Sunday evening, his dad would bring Holden back home after their weekend together, and I would fill the bathtub. He made sculptures of aliens with the bubbles and put on swimming goggles to float on top of the warm water, stretching his toes to touch one end of the tub, the other with his fingers. He could almost reach both ends at the same time. I would sit on the floor of the bathroom, leaning against the smooth white edge of the tub, and ask him to tell me all about his weekend.

We went to Granville Island and played at Kids Only, which is totally full of toys. We watched a guy play Red Hot Chili Peppers on a Chinese guitar. We fed the geese.

The blond strands of his hair slithered between my fingers as I washed them.

I love you infinity, I would say.

I love you infinity, he would repeat.

Some mornings, when I was leaving for work before there was any daylight at all, the sound of my keys would wake him, and he would slide out of his bed and run to the front door. He would stand between me and the rest of the world in his red spaceship pyjamas, trying to block my way with his small body, his arms bracing the door jam. I would drop my bag and coat to kneel on the rug so we were face to face, then I'd gather him up. With his arms locked tightly around my neck, I could smell his sleepy breath and feel his body jarred by crying.

Don't go, Mama.

Holden, when do I come back?

After work.

That's right, and how do you know?

Because you always do.

Exactly. You're very smart. And what do you do if you miss me?

I can look in the photo book, or go sleep with Auntie J, or call you on the phone.

You've got it. Now let's get you tucked back in. It's still nighttime, buddy. You need a big sleep so you can play with all of your friends at school.

I don't want you to go.

I don't want to go either, but I have to work so we can have money for food and clothes and Pokemen.

Pokemons.

Right.

I took his small hand in mine, and we walked together down the hall, back to his bedroom. I tucked the blankets snugly around him in an attempt to reassure him that he was contained and would not fracture. A cast on a broken bone.

I will be waiting when you finish school. We can go to the playground for as long as you want. Will you be super helpful and feed the dogs their breakfast when you wake up?

Okay, Mama.

But it wasn't okay. It was devastating. Holden constantly longed for one parent or the other. This daily act of division pecked a hole in his centre. His young heart didn't know why it hurt, just that it sometimes did. The erosion was slow and immeasurable. He was a sunny child with many friends who was always singing. He was also a cracked jar that could only hold so much water.

Cam and I spent two years in a long-distance relationship, commuting and getting to know each other. Our values aligned, and we became very committed to one another. We bought a small house together in North Vancouver and got married. The three of us embraced the comforting patterns of school, work, and daily family life. We enjoyed beach summers and ski-slope Christmases.

Holden travelled back and forth between his two homes. We loved and cherished Holden, but in that place where security and comfort were supposed to reside, he developed a chronic abscess. Later, with the stirring of adolescent hormones, the wound became restless. It began to fester and pulse. That was when the first shots of his personal civil war were fired. Holden's need for closeness was equally balanced by the necessary survival instinct he had cultivated to detach at all times. Nobody was getting in, so nobody could leave in the night. This apartness became Holden's default. He began to feel normal in the abnormal, to feel secure in the insecure. At least it was familiar. He'd become accustomed to drifting back and forth between his two homes, always somewhere between wanting and deserving, between his birthright and his reality. You could say he shared custody of his own happiness. With whom, he couldn't tell you.

As a young teenager, Holden learned that beer, weed, graffiti, and loud music could push the restless feelings away, but they always came back. And every time, it was a little more confusing. He wanted to be with people as much as he wanted to be alone. He was an ache, wrapped in tough guy, wrapped in a comedian.

Of course, this is only my theory. Holden probably couldn't have told you why he felt what he felt, or did what he did. He just felt shitty on the inside sometimes, and if you looked at his life from the outside, it didn't make sense.

5

Before I was grief-dredged, hollowed, and scoured, I was a talker. I was a broadcaster who hosted a daily morning radio show and all kinds of live events. I could speak to just about anyone about just about anything: celebrities, musicians, world leaders, writers, public figures. Robert Redford, after one interview live on stage in front of thousands of people, sent me a personal note on monogrammed stationery to say that he'd a great time with the lively discussion I had crafted. He said that I probed in interesting ways, improvised with unexpected responses, was funny, and knew how to add just the right amount of irreverence.

Lively, funny, irreverent—these words did not belong with me anymore. But at one time, they had. My radio career had begun with a two-year program at the local technical college, where I learned to edit copy with a thick, black pencil and to tear newswire paper using the sharp edge of a table. This was in the pre-digital, analog '80s. We had full access to the on-campus studios; my classmates and I experimented, making imaginary radio shows for pretend audiences. When I graduated, I could slice audiotape with a razor blade and enunciate by touching my tongue to the inside of my front teeth. I was twenty-one, and the things that deeply interested me were Tears for Fears, cold apple cider on ice, black-and-white photography (because I thought it made me seem mysterious and artistic), and the long houndstooth coat with thick shoulder pads that I'd purchased while living in a London squat the previous year.

My first real radio job was pressing a button that controlled a huge reel-to-reel machine that spun the wheels of tape imprinted with old radio plays like *The Shadow*, *The Green Hornet*, and *The Twilight Zone* that only graveyard gas station attendants and insomniacs would hear. The button had to be pressed once every fifteen minutes, and if I didn't load the reel correctly, threading the tape around the correct pins, pulleys, and tension bars, it would spool out onto the floor like a tangled ball of wool, and the radio station would go silent. This dreaded silence is called "dead air," and it happened to me only once. After that, my heart thudded as the end of each segment drew near.

But the anxiety was worth it. The darkened studio with its insulated walls thrilled me. So did the bright-red *ON AIR* light, the intimidating microphone with its grey marshmallowy cover, the glowing audio monitors' bouncing needles, and the overflowing ashtray. Stepping into the studio and closing the heavy door after me was like walking out into the muted hush of a fresh snowfall. All unnecessary noises were held captive within the sound-baffled walls. It was the coolest place I had ever been. It felt sacred.

Those first few years, I said yes to any opportunity the program director offered, even the ones that scared me. I flew around in a Cessna 152 of questionable safety, reporting on traffic jams; I drove brightly coloured radio station vans to parades, fun runs, and festivals; I hosted a multitude of charity events. I put on a white-leather jumpsuit and rode a motorcycle to the racetrack. I spent a great deal of time giving away tickets to Tom Petty, Fleetwood Mac, or U2 concerts. I went "on location," which usually meant sitting under a tent in a parking lot, handing out stickers and hot dogs. I stayed up all night running recorded programming of other announcers—older, more experienced broadcasters, mostly men, who were at home sleeping.

I pushed other buttons, the ones that played Led Zeppelin and the Rolling Stones while the morning men did the talking. Soon I started asking for more. I began doing interviews, gathering research, writing segments, offering to fill in on short notice whenever anyone was ill. I would work any time of the day or night, sometimes multiple shifts on the same day: morning show producer, afternoon traffic reporter, evening charity event MC. One morning I came home from an all-night shift and cracked a beer while my roommate applied eyeliner for her job downtown at an investment firm. She raised an eyebrow and shook her head.

Really? Beer for breakfast?

But for me it was a shift change. I probably went back to the station a few hours later to do something else. I played second base on the station's baseball team, I skied on the promotional ski team. I don't remember ever making coffee for anyone. The sink in the staff kitchen was always full of horribly stained cups with cheesy slogans on them. *Vancouver's Best Rock! Top Dog Radio! The News You Need When It Matters!*

In the late '80s, commercial radio was a highly creative medium filled with idiosyncratic characters who each brought their own brand of style, and the vast majority were men. On the FM side, the "jocks" chose which songs to play during their shows, as well as the topics they wanted to talk about. That was why people listened. On-air person-alities were celebrities with fan followings who could drive up ratings and, therefore, profits. I found it maddening that DJs were forbidden to play two female artists back to back. If you heard Pat Benatar or Heart, it would be at least half an hour before you'd hear Chrissie Hynde. On the AM side, talk radio focused on issues, opinions, intellect. The AM hosts influenced politics and policy—they were loud and powerful. They made big money and had big egos. Once, a morning host took me for a ride in his long-nosed Jaguar, and I remember thinking that the car had likely cost the same as my parents' house.

The newsroom and on-air studios were filled with cigarette smoke, dark humour, and dirty jokes, which was fine with me. These people were sharp, opinionated, unrefined, and impatient to the point of being rude. I spoke a similar language. The club was very clearly designed for the old boys, but for some reason, they allowed me access. I had found the place where I belonged. Simply being present, eyes and ears open, taught me more about broadcasting than I could ever have learned in radio school. Everyone worked too much and slept too little. There were parties, substances were ingested, affairs were fairly common. I never slept with my co-workers—except for the one I eventually married, a man with a deep voice who made me laugh.

My first official on-air gig came one New Year's Eve with the silent and terrifying flash of the studio hotline ringing. Our program director was legendary for causing palpitations with these phone calls. If the hotline was ringing, you were in peril; you were definitely going to be yelled at, and you might even be getting demoted or fired. That night, the boss slurred something about how terrible the prerecorded New Year's countdown show was.

Sounds like shit, I think he said.

I can do it live, I may have said.

Have you ever been on-air before? he asked, ice cubes rattling in the background.

Yes, I lied.

Okay, kid. Go for it.

And he hung up.

I lowered the microphone close to my face. It smelled like cigarettes and something metallic. When I pulled the black leather headphones over my ears, a trail of drugstore cologne followed them. Probably Polo.

The midday guy bathed in it. I pressed a small, square, illuminated button. The red *ON AIR* light glowed above my head, and the room fell silent. It was the most exciting moment of my life to date.

In 1991, when I was twenty-seven and freshly married to the deep-voiced man, radio was still unpredictable and exciting. It was also cut-throat. I accepted an offer to fill in on the morning show at a brand-new pop-music radio station while the female co-host enjoyed her two-week honeymoon. I did my very best to sound like sidekick material. The day the co-host returned home with her Mexican suntan and her new husband, she was fired, and I was given her job. It felt like I had just stolen someone's boyfriend. A boyfriend I'd secretly desired very much. I was ethically bewildered and professionally elated.

Though the job was considered a supporting role, the morning time slot received most of the attention and money. A top morning show guaranteed financial success for the whole radio station. Gradually I started creating and contributing my own content and expanding my footprint on the show.

When Holden was born two years later, I vacated my on-air chair for maternity leave. Staying at home with him for a full year gave me time to figure out what kind of mother I wanted to be. I read mothering books. I breastfed. We played classical music. We used cloth diapers and drank filtered water. Holden chewed on non-toxic, wooden educational toys. Organic baby food wasn't yet available in jars; I made it myself and froze it in ice-cube trays.

At Holden's first birthday party, our families had a picnic at the local park. Holden dug his pudgy fingers into the blue icing of his cake and smudged his first taste of processed sugar across his face.

When it was time to return to the morning show, I discovered that I had been replaced by the person who had filled in for me. I couldn't be angry, but I could threaten, in a strongly worded letter from a reputable lawyer, to sue. With the settlement, I was able to stay home with Holden for several additional months. While his father was at work, Holden and I ventured out together to swimming pools, libraries, parks, and playgrounds, and he made his own small friends. He took his first steps inside the Vancouver Art Gallery, striding away from me toward a giant abstract painting that captured his interest. Though I cherished the extra time with him, I itched to get back to broadcasting. I watched the radio landscape closely, waiting for the perfect position to poke its head up above the waterline.

In early 1995 one of the top morning shows in the city was looking for a female co-host. I went to so many interviews that I ran out of different pairs of shoes to wear to them. There were meetings, test shows with the male co-host, focus groups, and undoubtedly much backroom consultation. Before "manifestation" was a buzzword, I taped a sign onto our fridge declaring that the job was mine. At last, the offer came.

Here's how those days were different: When I accepted the job, the president of the multimillion-dollar family-owned business sent me a handwritten letter of congratulations for landing such an important major-market position. He welcomed me into his broadcast family and wished me a long and successful career with his company. And that was exactly what happened.

I hosted the morning show for nineteen years, with two different men in the chair opposite me, while a multitude of talented support staff came and went. I was given equal airtime and eventually, after several years of negotiating, was paid equally, too. The original family company was eaten up by a larger one, which was eaten up by an even larger one. By the time my tenure was over, my fellow employees and I would be identified at head office four thousand kilometres away not by our names or our faces, but by our own unique seven-digit codes.

One Tuesday morning, a man wearing what were possibly twelve-hundred-dollar Gucci running shoes poked his head into the studio and asked my co-host and me to come into the boardroom for a minute. Being unexpectedly invited to the boardroom at 9:00 a.m. on a Tuesday is never a good sign. He slid plain brown envelopes across the table toward each of us.

I took my teacup and the framed picture of my children and left the building forever. From the corner of Robson and Burrard, I called Cam with the news. Next, I called Holden.

Are you serious? I have a job and you don't? That's a good one, Momz.

By the time I arrived home twenty minutes later, my phone had been wiped of all company content and my email address no longer existed.

By then Cam and I had been together for eighteen years. For the last few, he'd listened to me complain about how the radio industry was morphing in a direction that bothered me. We went to a restaurant that looked across Coal Harbour to the glimmering Vancouver skyline, and I drank two margaritas before lunch.

As the tequila reached my extremities, I began to feel less angry and more relieved. Yes, I was exhausted from waking up in the dark for so many years, but I'd also been having a crisis of personal values. I had talked with friends about what I called "the velvet rut." On air, I hawked orange juice and laser hair removal to finance my yoga and meditation retreats. This was hypocritical on many levels, because while I complained about corporate greed, globalization, overconsumption, and capitalism over tapas and pinot noir, I also very much enjoyed our lovely home, the dental plan, and seven weeks of annual vacation. Surely I could find something more ethically aligned to do with my one precious life.

This sudden change in circumstances helped me do what, until that point, I had not been brave enough to do myself: leave. It would give me the space and time to figure out what was next. Lyla was ten, and Holden was twenty, working and living with roommates. We had options.

We could have stayed put. I could have started working in radio again. Offers arrived. But I had already said out loud more than once that retirement is wasted on the old. We should take a break from the middle of our working lives, I said, to explore the world while we're healthy and mobile.

Before Lyla was born, a radio station engineer with thick glasses had come to our house and built a very basic studio next to the laundry room in our unfinished basement. Six weeks after her birth, I was back hosting the show from home while my co-host and producer were downtown at the radio station. I could hear my family waking up and starting their day above my head. Ten-year-old Holden jumping down from his top bunk to brush his teeth. His spoon clanking against the edge of his cereal bowl. Cam did everything but feed Lyla; when she was hungry, he would tiptoe down to the studio and silently hand her to me. I would sit in my pyjamas and headphones, nursing her while I read the day's news, wrote scripts, introduced songs, and interviewed guests.

That was why I also framed our planned year of travel as a delayed maternity leave, a chance, eleven years after her birth, to be with Lyla for a dedicated period of time, just as I'd had with Holden.

For twenty-eight years, my radio work had been structured around constantly marking the time, minute by minute, so Cam and I decided to travel slowly, without much of an itinerary. We would stay in small, out-of-the-way places and absorb regular life, rather than hustle through marquee tourist destinations with a checklist. We would study languages, learn customs and history, we would surf, hike, and scuba dive. We would homeschool Lyla as best we could. We would take recommendations from locals and see where the path led us. I would write a blog as we travelled. We were free.

Holden's plan was to stay in Vancouver and continue building his own independent life, as young adults do. Sometimes he lived with roommates, sometimes with his dad. He had a few different jobs—warehouse worker, art store clerk, pressure washer, landscaper—and always manage to squeeze by. I felt there was some value in the struggle, something to be gained through figuring things out on his own.

Cam, Lyla, and I arranged to leave Vancouver near the end of summer, and we got together with Holden as much as we could before then. As much as he'd let us. We enjoyed some warm, laughter-filled family lunches and dinners. A few weeks before our departure, he and I met downtown for a movie he wanted to see, *The Grand Budapest Hotel*. After the film, we shared butter chicken at an Indian restaurant. He wore a grey thrift-store cardigan over a death-metal T-shirt.

I remember him slicing the air with his hands as he spoke, and the resonance and confidence of his young man's voice when he declared how much he loved the sophistication and irony of Wes Anderson's work. I remember the red Steve Zissou–style toque we gave him. I remember the black arcs of paint under his short fingernails against the white polyester tablecloth, the dried-hay wisps of new whiskers sprouting from his chin, and how his hair was long enough to poke out from under his backward baseball hat and trail down the sides of his neck. I remember how when he smiled, his left eye closed a little bit more than his right. I remember loving him so much that my heart thundered at the sight of him, and my eyes swelled with tears.

Or maybe that's just happening now.

Another day, Holden and I went to the Vancouver Art Gallery to see the Douglas Coupland exhibit *everywhere is anywhere is anything is everything*. We wandered together through the tall rooms looking at bright colour-block paintings and elaborate LEGO sculptures. I took his picture in front of a large canvas with vivid geometric lines slashed across it. Holden didn't like having his picture taken. He slouched. And now I can see him shaking his head and hear his deep voice saying, Why mom, just why? We laughed a lot.

When I look at the photographs from that day, I search for warning signs I missed. Did I, in the excitement about my own new phase of life, ignore something critical about his? Did I disregard clues a good mother should have been attuned to? Did I fail to interpret danger in his expression, in the way he flicked his fingers while he stood in front of that painting, or in the way his arm hung so heavily across my shoulders when a tourist took our photo together in front of the giant replica of Coupland's head covered in chewing gum?

I will forever question our decision to leave, to abandon Holden for so long. Would the same thing have happened if we'd stayed home? Would my proximity have made any difference? Surely if I'd been nearer to him, I would have sensed the trouble coming to a boil and intervened. If I'd stayed home and paid attention, would he still be alive?

Maybe. And maybe not.

I missed the last year of my son's life. A year I am now attempting to reconstruct—with flimsy building materials.

Time may move in only one direction, one fine, uninterrupted line, but memory is fluid; it follows no rules, and it can be cruel.

6

We had an unspoken agreement when Holden started high school: I would knock on his bedroom door and wait in the hall for the *I'm not naked* signal before entering. C'mon in! But one night, I didn't wait. I tapped five quick pecks with my fingernail on the hollow wooden door and walked in. From the top bunk, Holden exhaled loudly into the darkness so I would think he was asleep, then rolled to face the wall.

Other parents had told me that when their kids hit grade nine, they seemed to be orbiting the dark side of the moon, so at first I'd blamed hormones for Holden's change of character from bright to grey. But after a few months, I became concerned that his new behaviour was more than a bad mood. Online chat rooms were just becoming popular with teens at that time. Though I felt conflicted about invading Holden's privacy, I was worried enough to sometimes look through his browsing history on our family computer. Which made me more worried. Getting mental health advice from other angry teen boys was not the best life strategy.

Are you all right? My hand reached up to find him, fingers settling in the trenches between each rib. He was getting so thin. I jostled him back and forth, not completely sure whether his crying or some kind of nocturnal animal call had woken me.

Holden shifted away from me, closer to the wall, and exhaled again, more loudly than necessary.

He and Cam had recently painted the walls of his room forest green to cover the Caribbean blue and tropical fish he'd grown out of.

Goodbye clownfish, goodbye angelfish, goodbye dolphins, goodbye buried treasure, he'd said with the paint roller in his hand.

Are you awake? Are you crying?

I'm fine, go back to bed. His words caught on something.

You don't seem fine to me. What's up?

∞

What's up? Good question. Holden's been wondering the same thing for a couple of months. He asked around on Nexopia, but those geniuses didn't have any answers. How can he tell her what's going on when he has no idea himself? All he knows is that he feels really sad sometimes. For no reason.

His bed shakes when she steps up onto the bottom rung of the ladder.

It was Lyla, he says. She must be thirsty.

Maybe it's because he jerks off a hundred times a day or eats too many Ichiban noodles—those flavour packets are full of weird chemicals. Maybe the blue hair dye travelled up his follicles and turned his brain blue.

He thinks the strange, sticky sadness that sometimes jumps on him started about the time he pierced his ear.

Sit perfectly still and I'll poke it through for you, his mom said.

He took a deep breath and held it. He clamped his eyes shut.

You're going to feel two pops. Ready?

Two? Why two? he asked through his teeth.

Front layer, back layer. Your skin is pretty thick, you know.

Gross.

He was sitting on a stool in their kitchen, elbows propped on the counter, chin on his fists, offering her his naked ear.

Don't worry, I've pierced lots of ears. All of my friends in high school had three.

Pop. Ow. *Pop. Ow!*

That's it, you're done. Let me just put the back on. She smiled at him. It looks nice.

Holden hopped off the stool and ran to the bathroom, leaning close to the mirror to get a good look. What his mother hadn't told him was that after the two pops, his ear would feel sizzling hot and pinched, as if a snake had bitten it, whatever that felt like. But the little golden ball on his burning red earlobe looked so cool that he didn't care how much it hurt.

Until he got to school the next day and Cole called him a fag.

Dude, left is right. Cole laughed, pointing to Holden's ear. And right is wrong.

What?

That's the gay side. Are you trying to tell me something?

A wave of nausea passed through him. The instant the lunch bell rang, he sprinted to his bike and raced home. His mom was in the kitchen with her hands in the sink. His little sister, Lyla, was sitting in the middle of the kitchen floor surrounded by pots, bowls, and old yogurt containers.

Well, hello there! I didn't know you were coming home for lunch today.

Wrong ear. His chest heaved. Wrong ear. Do it over.

Not sure what you mean, bud. Slow down.

I only have eleven minutes to make it back for third block, can you switch it to the other side?

Your earring?

This is the gay side. Can you take it out? Please. Right now.

One soapy hand clamped to her mouth. She turned to the window. Was she laughing at him?

Sure I can, just let me get the stuff from the bathroom. She dried her hands on her jeans and stepped around his sister.

Hurry.

Pop. Pop. The stab hurt even more the second time, maybe because he knew what to expect. But the burning that followed was strangely satisfying. It filled him with a buzzing kind of energy. His mom dabbed the new piercing with a cotton ball drenched in rubbing alcohol. A cold stream dripped down the side of his neck. He liked the sharp smell of it.

There you go. She kissed his cheek.

Thanks, Mom.

Der you go, dodo! said Lyla, who had been watching closely with a wooden spoon in each hand. She banged an overturned frying pan for emphasis.

Thanks, kiddo. Holden spread his fingers like a spider over her sparse blond hair. He bent to kiss the top of her head before running out the front door to resurrect his bike where it had fallen on the front lawn just three minutes ago. He took his time getting back to school.

Holden had tried to let his mom know that something was bothering him. A couple of weeks ago, he'd written about it on the computer in the basement and left the page open so she would see it when she did her usual spying through his stuff while she pretended to be doing her work.

Lately I have been feeling an uncontrollable sadness. I don't know what is causing this. But I feel lonely and insecure. The need to be around people I like is gone. Sometimes I feel that I am the only human being on earth.

That Sunday, when he came in from playing road hockey in the lane—he'd bagged a hat trick, two top shelf, one five-hole—she'd held up a piece of paper. What's this? Her round face seemed more pale than normal. The two deep lines between her eyebrows looked like the number 11. Can you tell me about this?

She blocked the hallway with her body so that he couldn't pass.

But on that day he'd been feeling fine, great, even. Oh, that? He grabbed the printout from her hand, pretending to look at it even though he already knew what was on there. Just some song lyrics. It's for a school project. He'd swerved around her as if he were still playing road hockey, hurried down the hall to his room, and closed the door before she could ask any more questions.

Now, curled in his bed in the inky black, he feels the thing grow bigger inside him. He can't hold it in. A yelp jumps out of him, sudden and scared, like a dog whose foot just got stepped on. Once the gush starts, there's no stopping it.

What is it, honey?

I don't know, Mom. Tears and slime coat his face. He's crying pretty loud now. Making faraway noises. Mournful and distant. Animal sounds. I don't know.

She doesn't say he needs to be quiet or he'll wake the house. She doesn't remind him that she has to get up at 3:00 a.m. for work. She doesn't say anything at all, which is how Holden knows this is serious shit. His mom always has too much to say. She can use ten sentences where one would do the trick. His mother is very into her own opinion.

Can you please come down? she whispers. I can't get up on that rickety bunk with you. It'll collapse.

She locks her grip around his wrist like they are two characters in a cartoon and he's dangling off a cliff over a raging river. Like she is the only one who can possibly pull him back up to safety.

No. I can't move.

Yes, you can. I'm right here. Come down to me, Holden.

Her voice is morphing in the darkness. Now it holds more than just fear; there's an offer of comfort mixed in. Like the marmalade-orange light that oozes under the door from the bathroom nightlight. It's enough to get Holden to turn his face toward her.

Just put one foot on the ladder, she says.

He heaves his leg over the railing and flails his foot around in the dark until his toes make landfall on the top rung. Cool metal.

That's it, you've got it. She never lets go of his wrist. Almost there.

Once Holden reaches the bottom of the ladder, he steadies himself, his bare feet on the black and white geometric shapes of the carpet. When they did the new paint job, they also got rid of his old rug, the one with the train tracks and railway stations all over it. He'd played on that rug for hours, for years, with his trains—Thomas, Emily, James and all of their friends. He'd delivered packages, greeted passengers, hummed to himself.

Holden turns, his vision adjusting to the dark. His mom braces his shoulders, staring into his face, but he's unable to meet her eyes; his chin drops. In the pale-grey light, he looks down at his bare chest. He used to be a fat kid. Used to be embarassed by the way his hips hung over his bathing suit at the pool. Now he's bony.

You're shivering. Hang on a sec, his mom says.

She lets go of his arms to pull the quilt down from the bunk, then she drapes it over him like she used to when he was little and the quilt was warm from the dryer.

You always liked to be wrapped up tight. We called it the sausage roll. Remember?

Holden nods. Pressure bulges in his throat. Can a person choke on their own sadness? Her arms are around him now. He can loosen his fists and let go of some of it, just a little. She's holding him up. And down. It's possible that she's preventing him from floating away.

Behind her in the faint light, he sees the other wall. The black one, the "signature" wall. He and Cam painted it with special chalkboard paint to complete what Cam called the "teen hangout effect." Holden's buddy Amin, who shares the same ideas about what's funny, christened the chalk wall by drawing a giant dick with hairy balls on it. After they laughed themselves stupid for about half an hour, Holden tried to erase the image, but the faint outline of a schlong was still visible, so he turned it into a cartoon dog by adding eyes, ears, and another nostril.

All the colour's gone, he says.

Your room is so grown-up now. It's a big change.

No, Mom, all the colour is gone. I can't breathe. His knees buckle.

She catches him. Then leads him by the hand down the hall and across the smooth wooden planks of the quiet, dark kitchen, where the clock on the stove reads 2:14 in red letters, and out into the quiet freshness of the backyard. The cold grass feels like small electrodes zapping the bottoms of his feet.

His mother's fingers wrap his wrist. Is she taking his pulse? Her head is bowed as she leads him across the lawn. The white SpongeBob pyjama pants he gave her last Christmas kind of glow ahead of him, a beacon to follow. They walk toward the hammock in the deepest corner of the yard.

∞

On summer days we would swing in the shade to cool off, but that night the leafy cover offered a different protection. We were safely hidden from the questions of the stars and the interrogation of the streetlights.

I climbed into the hammock first, the same way you would get into a dinghy—low and slow. Holden and I had learned about stability when we took sailing lessons together and managed to make it from Eagle Harbour all the way to Bowen Island for ice cream.

All aboard. I tugged gently on his arm. He lurched forward, elbows, knees, Adam's apple jabbing at the world. The hammock rocked and jerked until the turbulence subsided. I tucked the quilt around him and held him as tightly as I could. I tried to contain him so he would feel safe. So he could release whatever he was holding, whatever was happening inside him.

It's okay, love. My fingers traced his wet cheek. You'll feel better in the morning. It's okay. Let it go.

I cradled his neck so he could surrender the weight of his head. His sobbing lost some of its fury and gave way to halting gasps, then diminished even more. His breathing slowed, and the crying trickled to a stop. I could feel him softening, relaxing, absorbing my warmth. I exhaled, Holden exhaled, and his symmetrical breathing told me he was finally able to allow himself to sleep.

A bruised purple-blue surrendered the sky for another night, giving way to timid yellow. I stayed awake, holding my son, not knowing what else to do, while the stars slowly disappeared.

When Holden died, a fragile hush came over our house, as though the air might crack if anyone spoke too loudly. Very much like when the children had been born, people came and went in a tender stream, not staying long, bringing with them flowers, food, and emotions. A month or two later, Sean, the close friend we had shared our sailboat with, a tough ex-cop who always packed a broad smile and a dirty joke, delivered something else: a cardboard banker's box. He had retrieved it for us at the coroner's instruction from the warehouse where the Vancouver Police keep evidence.

Maybe just put that away somewhere for later, he said, arching his bushy eyebrows at Cam, who sat at the kitchen counter with a cup of strong coffee in the ceramic mug he'd chosen in Italy. The one souvenir he'd bought on our trip and carried for months in his pack, wrapped in a T-shirt. Sean had worked in homicide for years and understood the collateral agonies of a death in the family. He knew from experience that opening the box was a bad idea. He also encouraged us to request a full autopsy, advice which, months later, I'd wish we had followed.

My first reflex was to tear the lid off and see what was inside. Or rather, what of Holden was inside. Was there something that would lead me to him? I was desperate for some kind of clerical error that would make Holden's death untrue. Some kind of glitch in the system that would void what had happened and allow us to hit reset. I flipped open the lid and saw that the box was filled with brown paper bags and envelopes of assorted sizes, each with a detailed label. My chest contracted.

I sucked in a breath and held it as if I were about to dive underwater. These objects were all that was left of him.

Cam and Sean eyed each other, their lips whitening with pressure.

Passport, one of the labels said in official type, followed by serial numbers and dates. I guessed he must have lost his driver's licence and needed to carry his passport for ID.

Bank card, declared another.

Keys.

Cigarettes. Wait, cigarettes? Another new habit I hadn't known about.

Socks.

Holden's last personal effects lay on the kitchen table. The earthy smell of him rose into my nostrils. I could see the corner of his black backpack and his workboots at the bottom of the box. I closed my eyes.

Are you sure you want to do that now? From across the top of the box, Cam's rough fingers stroked my hand. I mean, maybe you could just think about it? For a while?

Cam knew better than anyone what digging through the contents could do. He was the one who held me while I pressed the sheets Holden had last slept on to my face and sobbed. He knew the triggering effects of certain songs on the radio, of photographs, of a bagel with peanut butter. He could never be sure when a cup of tea was no longer just a cup of tea. When a cup of tea became Holden drinking a cup of tea at our kitchen counter the last time we saw him. When a book became a mistake I'd made, or a leaf falling from a tree became a small blond boy jumping through a pile of crunching orange and red on a joyous fall day. More than simple brown envelopes, each object held power, each one potentially a fresh slash with the sword. These items *were* Holden. They were the closest thing to being with him, and being with him was agony because he was always being taken away. His death repeated, over and over, with every dead thing.

It's dangerous to love something so much. More of you can be stolen.

I nodded, and Cam gently closed the box, coaxed it from my reluctant hands, and took it down to the basement, where he placed it on a high shelf in the storage room with the camping gear and Christmas decorations.

I wanted and didn't want to look. I wanted and didn't want to know.

Months later—I wore sweats, so it was probably fall—on a day when I was alone in the house, I crept down to the storage room and reached for the box. I sat on the cold cement floor with the box between my knees and opened it. There were the brown paper bags, there were the labels.

T-shirt, blue.

Work gloves, brown.

Foil.

Tucked in the corner under his backpack, wedged behind the heel of one of his dusty workboots, was an envelope the size of a paperback.

Samsung mobile phone.

I snatched the envelope, slammed the box's lid closed, and ran up the stairs before the pungent, stale-dirt scent of Holden's work shirt and socks could sabotage my plans.

Upstairs in the kitchen, heart hammering, I slid the phone out of the envelope onto the counter. At first, I didn't touch it. The screen was cracked in a splintered web, but not shattered. I saw the thick, greasy smudges of Holden's fingerprints all over it. Likely the last thing his hands had touched.

And then I could see his hands, how the fingers of his right hand curled in a loose claw ever since his accident with the knife. How his knuckles widened and his fingernails were chewed close. I saw the paint, the raw hangnails, the soil.

But the phone was not my property—it was his. Was I betraying a trust by looking at his private information? Or was this knowledge now mine? Transferred to me, as his next of kin, with the rest of his worldly possessions? What if I found out things I didn't want to know? I would definitely find things I didn't want to know. I poured myself a glass of water from the tap and downed it. I braced myself, grabbing the edge of the counter. My arm muscles contracted. The word "ethics" flashed somewhere and was quickly overruled.

This was a way to find out.

I picked up the phone. There were worn stickers on the back, a red one that said *LAYOUT* and a small blue one that said *ACAB*. I'd have to look those up.

I pressed the power button, and the phone vibrated, chimed three times, and buzzed to life. So easily revived.

Where to look first.

I wanted to see him.

Photos.

Not familiar with Android, I stalled, searching for the right icon. I tapped. The screen filled with a gallery of colour. The last picture Holden had taken was of a concert poster stapled to a telephone pole advertising a heavy metal show at Pat's Pub on Hastings Street, July 3. Something the shape and size of a fist lodged low in my throat.

July 3 was the date printed on Holden's death certificate, the day whose sunrise he did not live to see. But he had wanted to hear some live music that night. I scrolled, and a spur of sharp glass shaved the edge of my thumb. The shot before that was of a forested trail: blackberries, salal, ivy, and dappling light. The one before that showed that he had been up on a hillside, looking out over the ocean, with cobalt islands rising from the sea along the horizon, the sky a brilliant shade of blue. The next was of a golden grassy road long forgotten by cars. It looked like the view from Wreck Beach near the university. The photo was time-stamped a week before he died.

Looking at Holden's photographs transported me through time and space. I could be where he had been, see what he had seen, get some sense of his mood. These photographs were not dark and destructive; they were bright, beautifully composed, and calm.

I felt the heat of summer on my face, smelled the sea, and the warm pine sap. I heard him laugh. Saw him rake a hand through his scrub of hair and tug on his auburn tassel of beard. I smelled his breath.

Oh, there was the arc of the highway overpass—he must have been painting graffiti. And there was the rushing Capilano River—he had been close to our house, he was almost home! I saw another forested trail—he'd been hiking or at least walking in the forest. The next picture showed a distorted, almost time-exposed image of his face surrounded by leaves and refracted sunbeams filtering through a luminous green canopy. His last selfie. His last documented green.

Any conflict I felt about opening his phone disappeared. During the last weeks of his life, Holden had been in nature, he had been in motion, looking for beauty and finding it. He had been creating it. For the first time in months, I thought of my son with something other than sadness. My tear-streaked cheeks rose in an unfamiliar arc. He had lived.

I began sending the photographs to myself. My own phone came alive vibrating on the counter, *buzz, buzz, buzz,* messages coming in from Holden, Holden, Holden. It's him, he's alive, wait, there's been a mistake. Wait. There he is. There.

What else could I excavate from Holden's phone? Could I piece together what had happened the year we'd been gone, and the days and hours leading up to his death? Could I find out who had been involved? What had been involved? Could I uncover what had really happened?

I knew the phone company had cut off Holden's account about two months before he died. After that, I guessed he must have used Facebook messenger to communicate with people.

Looking through his private messages would be akin to reading his diary or his personal letters—another line to cross. But I was free to look at any time through his many personal sketchbooks and papers in the basement, so I rationalized that reading his texts wasn't much different. I had looked at his Facebook page from my own computer to read the messages of condolence from his friends and to look at his older posts, but I had never thought to open his profile on his own device and read his private messages. These conversations could be the black box, the record of what happened before the crash.

I launched the familiar blue Facebook app. This, I thought, would fill in the blank space, the unaccounted-for hours on the last night of his life. I'd be able to tell who he was with, what his frame of mind was, whom he spoke to, where he went. I would at least know more about what happened. I would know if he was happy.

The app opened, and his page came into view. I clicked on the messenger icon, and blurry words began crystallizing. Anticipation and hope rose in me, inflating my chest. I could find my son here. This would explain everything.

Then the entire screen faded to smoke, and letters appeared: "Account Inaccessible. This account has been memorialized."

It felt like strangulation. My son was dissolving into vapour, again. His last communications would not be mine to see. Memorialized? What did that mean?

I emailed Facebook explaining the situation, pleading for help. The next day I received an automated reply saying that Holden's account had been memorialized on the direction of a close friend or family member and could not under any circumstances be reverted back to active status, nor would they, under any circumstances, provide any additional details. This procedure, a Facebook bot declared, would keep the account "secure."

I hadn't given Facebook permission or instruction. I asked around, but nobody in our family had done it, nor had any of Holden's friends that I talked to. Could some kind of intrinsic algorithm have triggered the slamming of the gate? Too many RIPs, too many keywords of condolence? Or had someone made the request to protect themselves? The string I was following, the one pulling me through the mystery of Holden's death, was rudely snipped.

I consulted a lawyer who specialized in intellectual property. After some research, she advised that there was no point trying to fight Facebook; there wasn't enough money in the world for that. Her laughter fluttered awkwardly.

So I gave up and added one more cruel devastation to the long list we had suffered and would continue to suffer.

Down in that storage room in the basement, I had my son's books, his artwork, his report cards, his high school diploma, his teapot, and his video games. I had his vast music collection, his workboots, and his tie-dyed underwear. But I still had no knowledge of his last few hours. Not because Facebook couldn't provide that closure, but because they refused to.

Later I found out that Facebook has a provision for users to appoint a legacy contact, which allows for access after death. But show me a twenty-one-year-old who thinks he is going to die.

8

One of Holden's friends, an artist he stayed with when they worked on projects together, told me that Holden had seemed lost that summer, that he never knew when to stop, never wanted to go home. His evenings typically started with alcohol. Booze had a way of softening and hardening Holden at the same time. His drunkenness often overrode his best intentions and sometimes brought out the darkness and the antagonist in him.

I don't think Holden considered himself an alcoholic, but he drank nearly every day during the last year of his life, and being a drinker was a big part of his identity. At one point he scrawled *Drunk for a Year* on a mailbox and posted the photo on Instagram.

I wondered how much of Holden's alcohol abuse was hereditary and how much was cultivated. Heavy drinkers lay in graves on both sides of his family, social consumption was common in our home while he was growing up, and getting drunk on the weekend had been standard practice for me as a teen and as a young adult. If I was honest with myself, ·I had to admit that every truly dangerous thing I'd ever done was after too many margaritas. Once, several tequila shots in, I'd thought it a fabulous idea to climb onto the roof of a taxi speeding down a pot-holed highway outside of Puerto Vallarta, terrifying my friends and the taxi driver. I'd thought everyone was overreacting—I knew what I was doing. Chill out, people. Relax.

So who was I to delineate the boundary between entertainment and destruction?

I didn't drink at all while I was pregnant with Holden, but I did have a few Stellas and glasses of Chardonnay during the year I breastfed him. I wondered if I'd imprinted his young DNA with some kind of comfort marker for booze in his bloodstream.

When Holden was fifteen, I decided to teach him how to consume alcohol responsibly. He'd already been watering down our vodka so much that it froze in the freezer. I had done the same, raiding my parent's small liquor cupboard behind the kitchen door and pouring fingers from each bottle into a jam jar to share with my friends. One of us was always vomiting in the park. I didn't want to green-light underage drinking, but I wanted him to have more knowledge than his posse of hormonal skateboarding buddies could offer.

The two of us stood in the small kitchen at the back of the old house, which we called the Mustard Pot because its paint job reminded me of Grey Poupon. It was an old duck hunting cabin, and the previous owner had lived there for more than sixty-five years, from birth through retirement. Giving the house a cute name did not make it cute, however. The floors sloped and gave us slivers, the windows shivered in their frames and let in the wind, most of the walls were painted varying sad shades of yellow, and when you sat on the toilet in the only bathroom, your knees pressed against the daffodil-yellow bathtub, leaving indentations in your kneecaps. Layered under everything was an undefinable smell, a combination of second-hand clothing store and leftover soup. In the front entryway, the beige carpet was worn through almost completely.

I had loved the street, and Cam and I planned to renovate the place into a cozy family home, but once we moved in, we learned that the foundation was shot, and the wiring was a fire hazard. When we looked inside the walls to check for insulation, all we found were a few newspapers from 1928.

You can't polish a turd, Cam said.

The house was bulldozer material, but it would take us years to save enough to rebuild. In the meantime, we didn't want to waste any money on upgrades or repairs, so the drafty, lopsided Mustard Pot became our home. I burned many pine-scented candles.

In the kitchen, Holden stared down at the linoleum, which wrinkled over the floor like an elephant skin. He kicked the ripples with the toe of his shoe and nodded his head so it would look like he was listening intently to me when, in fact, he was chewing the inside of his cheek, trying not to laugh. We were both pretending that he was new to the topic of alcohol. I watched him massage the hinge of his jawbone with his fingertips.

I know you guys are getting into this, so you might as well know the science. I poured some apple juice into a shot glass and held it up in front of his face. This is one ounce. Then I poured the juice into the bottom of a water glass and filled it up to the top with water from the tap. If you mix this much alcohol with juice or Coke, you can have one of these per hour, up to about three or maybe four in total for the night, and you'll be fine. More than that and you'll be drunk and sick. And stupid. I held the glass up again. You won't have a very good time.

Okay Momz, I got it. One per hour. Thanks for the pro tips.

When Holden hugged me, his chin rested on the top of my head. He had surpassed me in height when he was thirteen, and in the two and a half years since then, he'd grown another eight inches at least. I held him tightly and spoke into his chest. Please be careful, Holden. Just take it easy. You can have a good time without getting plastered.

The Mexican taxi careered across my memory.

I know, Mom. I will.

I tried to make eye contact, but he turned away quickly and thumped down the rickety stairs to his room in the basement. The story he told me later that night didn't add up. I don't know exactly what happened, but I know the end result.

∞

Holden doesn't like lying to his mom; it makes him feel devious. But he does it all the time. He's got a bottle of Jameson stashed behind the books on his shelf. There's a second bottle in the old chimney pipe beside his bag of weed.

He texts Amin, who replies instantly.

Skate park shenanigans?

Fuckin' rights. 10 mins

Through the thin floorboards above Holden's head, he hears the sound of knocking and the familiar scrape of the dandelion-yellow front door that barely clings to its hinges.

Helloooo, anybody home?

Grandma!

He's guessing that Lyla, who's exactly ten years younger than him and pretty much creates her own electrical current, has just leaped from the fourth step into Grandma's arms. She pulls this move with him, too. That kid thinks she can fly. And she trusts someone will always catch her.

Holden doesn't want to babysit his little sister anymore these days. She's good times, but not on a Saturday night. So here's Grandma with her pyjamas in a bag so Mom and Cam can go to Mom's office Christmas party, even though it's February. Upstairs, his mom is going on about how much of a scam it is to have a Christmas party in February. Complete bullshit, she says, and Grandma laughs.

From his bedroom downstairs, there's a direct air vent to the living room, so he can hear their voices clearly. This is how he listens to Mom and Cam arguing about him after he skips class, rolls his eyes at Cam, or sneaks out to spray paint. Cam thinks Holden needs to "feel the repercussions of his actions," and his mom thinks he needs "a sense of personal responsibility," whatever the fuck that means. He is their number one topic of conversation. They'll go on and on about him for hours until Cam bails and goes for a bike ride. It's pretty funny, actually.

His mom is still ranting. A huge, multimillion dollar company trying to save a few bucks on the bottom line, so we have to have a winter holiday party—he imagines her air-quoting the "winter holiday" part—when the rates are lower, instead of a Christmas party in December, like the rest of the western world.

He mentally high-fives her. Stick it to the man, Momster.

Holden! His mom opens the door at the top of his stairs and calls down to him. Grandma's here, come up and say hello.

He stashes the bottle back behind his growing collection of Ernest Hemingway and Douglas Coupland novels and clomps up the arthritic spinal column of stairs into the kitchen.

Hey Grandma, how's it hangin'?

I'm just fine, dear. Oh, you give the best hugs, Holden. How are you doing?

When Grandma laughs, her cheeks jump like bouncing balls, and her small green eyes sparkle.

Good, thanks, G-ma. All good, just heading out skateboarding with Amin.

Well, you have a good time out there, and be careful on that thing.

She rests her warm, papery palm against his cheek for a second, then gives it a couple of soft little smacks.

Cam comes down from upstairs, yanking on the collar of his shirt with one finger. He opens his eyes extra wide in a way that says he'd rather not be wearing a tie. He's freshly shaved, and his hair is trimmed close. He buzzes it off himself with electric clippers. Cheaper than going to the barbershop, he likes to say. Number four, down to the wood. He thinks it's priceless every time he says it.

How do you like the monkey suit?

Crisp, Holden laughs, and he means it.

When Holden was younger, before Lyla was born, Cam had taught him how to ride a bike. A purple one called the Little Missy that they got at a garage sale for three dollars. He and Cam would ride bikes together all over the neighbourhood. They'd made up their own secret names for different trails: the Peachy Leechy, the Broncin' Buck, Lemon Jello. They'd go for hikes down to the river while his mom was working and take a sailing trip together every summer.

But after all the fights and lectures lately, they just don't get along anymore. These days, when Cam launches into the ever-popular speech about disrespect, entitlement, and ungratefulness, Holden just goes somewhere else in his mind until it's over. Tolerance is a two-lane highway. It's not like Cam is Holden's real dad or anything, anyway.

He used to call Cam "Papa," but not long ago switched back to calling him by his name. The first few times he did it, Cam's disappointment was obvious in the way his shoulders slumped and in the sound of his exhale, like a truck releasing its air brakes, but lately, all Holden notices when they talk—which isn't all that often—is thinly veiled resentment.

Thanks, Cam says, shrugging. Hey, keep it on the rails tonight, kiddo.

Cam grabs Holden by the shoulders and pulls him close for a hug. Holden lifts his arms to hug back, but it's awkward; the timing is off, and the embrace is over before it has a chance. Cam has no illusions about what "skateboarding" means. He knows Amin doesn't even own a skateboard. If Mom's an optimist, Cam's a realist.

The Jameson burns as it descends, its bitter taste stinging his tongue, rising into his nostrils. Every swallow warms Holden and takes him a little further away from the feeling of weighted dread he can't explain. He gets lighter and lighter as the sky gets darker and darker.

Just vunn ounze. Holden's doing an impersonation of his mother from earlier, but in the voice of a German drill sergeant. You can haf vunn ounze per owah. Holden takes another swallow and slides the nearly empty bottle across the graffiti-covered concrete to Amin. Or you vil be drunk, und sick, und schtoopid.

He and Amin are sitting in the biggest and lowest bowl of the skate-board park, their backs pressed to the cement.

You know why this is called the toilet bowl? Holden asks.

I can imagine. Amin's dark eyes are curtained by his even darker wavy hair.

Because it looks like one, obviously, Holden says, but also because when you crash and burn in here, it feels like shit.

Their throaty laughter swirls around them in the toilet bowl.

Though they've already finished the joint, the flame from Amin's lighter continues to blink on and off in the thickening darkness. His white running shoes tap incessantly on the concrete. Amin's always nervous, but Holden doesn't know what about. Overhead, dark branches poke into view like gnarled witch fingers.

Whatcha wanna be when you grow up? Holden says, his mouth losing traction on the words.

Fuck off.

I mean, not that I care, but I gather we're supposed to care. Do you care?

Not in the fucking least.

We have the entire planet to consider. All of it. With the worldwide freaking web there are just way too many options. We could literally go work on a yak farm in Kazakhstan if we wanted to.

You'd be a great yak farmer.

Rancher, you mean, Holden says. Technically, yaks are range animals, they don't grow from the ground. So, I'd be a rancher, not a farmer. In Kazakhstan.

I stand corrected. You'd be a rancher. A Jolly Rancher.

I think I liked it better before, when our choices were, like, doctor, firefighter, or dolphin trainer.

Dolphin trainer would be rad.

It freaks me the fuck out.

Are you afraid of dolphins?

No, you idiot, the future. The future freaks me the fuck out.

Why are we even having this discussion, butthead? Amin's voice slurs. He bites at a loose piece of skin on his thumb, then pulls his hands inside the sleeves of the soccer jacket he's worn every day for the last three years.

Amin and Holden have known each other since they were about six years old. They both have divorced parents, a love of heavy metal, an undying loyalty to the Canucks, and a deeply fucked-up sense of humour. They go to different schools now. Holden was flunking out of Baywater last year, so even though his dad was against it, his mom transferred him to a private school across town, where he is basically force-fed his history and biology homework like a veal calf. It turns out you really can buy a high school diploma.

Holden turns to Amin, who has slipped down to the bottom of the bowl. All anyone at Laurel Ridge talks about is which freakin' colleges they're applying to even though grade twelve is two goddam years away.

They all want to be rocket scientists and lawyers and captains of fucking industry.

So you'll have friends in high places, Amin says.

Well, they're high, that's for sure. I mean, at Baywater there's weed, but kids at Laurel have everything. One day I saw a couple of seniors doing lines of coke on the sink in the bathroom.

Did they have to hold their neckties out of the way? Amin rolls toward Holden and gives him a shove.

Dude. Pretty much.

Amin drains what's left in the bottle and yells, Nectar of the fucking gods! He attempts to fling the bottle up out of the toilet bowl and onto the grass, but it explodes against the concrete edge—a loud shattering cracks the quiet, and chips of glass rain down on them.

You fucking feeble idiot! Holden yells. What the fuck?

Fuck you, I didn't mean to.

There are some things you just don't fucking do, and smashing fuck-ing glass in the skate park is one of them, fuckwad shit-for-brains.

Whatever, douchebag.

Some things actually matter, you know. Asshole. Holden rolls close enough to kick Amin in the side.

Jesus, back off. Loser.

Amin kicks back, and then the two of them are wrestling in the sharp splinters at the bottom of the toilet bowl. At first, it's casual, but Amin clips Holden on the cheekbone with a sharp elbow, which makes Holden mad, and things get hot. Amin breaks free and rolls away. He scurries up and out of the bowl. Holden jumps to his feet to follow, but his shoes slip on the shards of glass. He doesn't have enough momentum to chase Amin up the side, and he falls, hard, into the bottom of the bowl.

Darkness.

On the couch in the living room Holden cradles his forehead in his hands. Grandma's quiet is worse than any yelling could be.

Sorry about this, Holden says. It's the preemptive strike he learned years back: whether you did anything wrong or not, just apologize and get it over with. Big time saver.

Grandma pulls the collar of her robe tight to cover her chest. Well, I'm sure you won't do that again. She pats his thigh.

I won't. *I probably will.*

Holden stands, ready to retreat to his room in the basement.

Not so fast, mister. Let's just wait until your parents get home.

Parent. He drops back onto the couch and stretches out. Grandma pulls the blanket down from the back of the couch and tucks it in around his legs. Her breath is sleepy and old, same as the house.

He wants to tell her that he's not a horrible person. That he wants to be one of those kids who plays on the soccer team and writes essays for the school newspaper and makes his bed. He wishes that were him, he really does. It would make life so much easier. For everyone. But that's just not him. He always ends up doing the wrong thing or being in the wrong place or making the wrong decision. Every time. Don't ask him why. He wishes they'd cut him a little slack.

Grandma hands Holden a bowl. In case you're sick again. She winks at him.

It's the smooth metal bowl they use to make oatmeal chocolate-chip cookies. He sets it down on the bile-coloured carpet. He'll never feel the same way about cookies again. He fingers the marshmallow-sized lump on his forehead.

Does it hurt? Grandma asks.

Does what hurt, the fact that he's so confused and scared of life that he never wants to come out of his room? That basically the only time he feels the slightest bit happy is when he's painting graffiti, which is illegal, so basically he can do what makes him alive and be a criminal, or spend his whole life doing things he doesn't like, which makes him a hypocrite?

Nah, it's okay, he says, staring up at the ceiling.

His grandmother's feet, in red slippers with flowers stitched all over them, are propped up on the coffee table. She presses the redial button on the phone in her lap over and over, then gives up and replaces the handset in its cradle, exhaling in a way that says this is more than she signed up for.

They both flinch when the phone in her lap rings.

∞

Cam and I stood in the rain outside the hotel, the balls of my feet bruised and swollen from dancing in what I called "big girl shoes." I pulled out my phone to call a cab—what I saw on the screen sent a wave of panic sweeping from my stomach to my teeth.

Mom, what's going on? Why did you call me seventeen times?

I called you seventeen times because Holden's had an accident. He fell at the skate park. The ambulance attendant brought him home, said he's been drinking.

Oh my god, is he okay?

He's got a pretty big bump on his head, but he's fine.

We're getting in a taxi.

All right dear, see you soon.

When Cam and I burst in the front door, Holden swung his legs down off the couch to make room for me beside him. Cam hovered silently, shaking his head and stroking his jaw with his fingertips.

In the lamplight, I held Holden's face between my hands and stared into his eyes.

I'm fine, he said. His face was cool. He wouldn't meet my gaze.

What happened?

Nothing. I just fell and smacked my head. Some lady called the ambulance. She didn't need to.

I swept the hair off his forehead with my fingers to get a better look at the mauve egg hiding there.

I'm glad she did. What the hell, Holden? We just talked about this.

Cam disappeared upstairs, opting out of the co-parenting good cop / bad cop thing for tonight.

I didn't drink that much. Really, Mom, it just has a weird effect on me. Amin drank most of it.

I don't give a rat's ass about Amin.

I hadn't cared for Amin since the time he'd come to the door late one night, red-eyed and jittery, looking for Holden. I told him Holden was in bed and that he should go home and sleep it off. That was when Amin called me a stupid cunt. The next morning I told Holden Amin had looked deranged, that he was a bad influence. What I didn't know was that Amin's younger sister had just tried to jump off of the Lions Gate Bridge after her boyfriend broke up with her. The things you find out when it's too late.

I looked past Holden at my mother.

I'm sorry, Mom, I kept my phone in my hand until after ten o'clock, then I figured Lyla was sleeping and Holden was probably home, so I put it away. I didn't know you'd been trying to reach me.

She nodded.

I gave Holden a one-armed hug. Why don't you go down to bed. I'll come check on you in a little bit. The blanket peeled off him as he stood, a snake slipping its skin. Take the bowl with you just in case.

I'm sorry if I upset you, Grandma.

That's okay, dear. All's well that ends well.

I heard Holden's heavy footsteps descend the wooden stairs to his bedroom.

Look, my mother said, parting her robe to expose a series of electrodes taped to the loose skin of her chest in several spots. The doctor has me doing a stress test, so I've got these gizmos all over me.

Oh my god, Mom, why didn't you tell me?

Well, I didn't think it would be a problem. It's registering my pulse and blood pressure for twenty-four hours. I'd say tonight has been a pretty good test of the old ticker, wouldn't you?

Our laughter cracked the tension.

If you can survive teenagers, you can survive anything, she said. Her voice was softer now than when we first arrived home.

You should know.

I remember when you kids were his age. I didn't get much sleep for quite a few years there. This too shall pass, darlin'. Don't you worry. This too shall pass.

The floor of the Mustard Pot creaked under her gentle footsteps as she padded across the carpet in her red slippers. At the door to the spare bedroom, she turned back to me.

By the way, she said, he didn't even have a skateboard.

9

Holden's phone was a shovel I could use to pry the ground, to dig him up. If I could find out how or who, maybe I could get closer to why. And if I knew why, I could rest. I could let him be.

At night, in bed, I didn't have to rationalize my behaviour. When the house was silent, I let my grief send out exploratory tendrils. I let the sharp edges of the broken screen scrape at my fingertips the way they had scraped at his. Perhaps I could fall, like Alice, through this magical piece of glass and find him in another realm.

Cam slept beside me with his dependable breathing. After nineteen years of his iron-cast protection, I trusted his steadiness to hold my head above water. I could risk my own sanity because I knew he was anchored, his mind and body were sound, and he was holding my hand. When I sank, he braced. He never asked me to hurry, to get out of bed, or to make sense.

I'm here, babe, he said, while I convulsed under the weight of the weeping. I'm right here.

He suffered, too, I'm sure he did, but only one of us could wade in completely.

I know the mistakes I've made, Cam said one day. I could have done so many things differently. The laugh lines at the corners of his glacier-blue eyes were now joined by deeper creases across his forehead and the ones bracketing his wide mouth. He must have done his weeping in private. In the shower, or the car. I never asked.

Cam quietly stood guard while I tried to undeath my son, the small blond boy he had welcomed into his heart without reservation nearly twenty years before.

At two, three, four in the morning, I scrolled through the texts on Holden's cracked Samsung. I created lists of his text messages and their corresponding names and numbers. I scoured his contacts for someone to blame. Names like Seabass; Jane's girl I think; Shaner-feel-mode; Awex; carlatron.

I noted with a stab that my phone number was listed as Tara. I wondered when I had ceased to be Momz. Maybe when I'd refused to replace a third broken phone, or when I'd stopped paying his phone bill, telling him shortly before we left on our trip that he could handle it himself.

If you can afford to party every weekend, I had said, you can afford to pay your own phone bill. Another line I wish I'd never drawn. If I'd just found the grace to pay forty dollars a month, maybe I'd have been able to reach him. Or maybe he could have called for help. If I hadn't been so righteous.

Any conflict I felt about the invasion into Holden's private life was outweighed by my obsession with discovering what had happened. I was learning to translate his innuendo, speak his slang, crack his code. I discovered a language that was Holden's alone.

> Supdo, I wavy wizzem bars,
> No skillz I tell Udis.

I transcribed everything I found into a notebook. I created phone logs and cross-referenced them with the text messages. I overlapped these with his emails and his Facebook and Instagram posts. I connected faces to names. I created a rough calendar of the year noting what I thought were Holden's relevant activities.

Fall

- We were away
- People I've never heard of
- Looking for work
- Got a job at the art shop
- Spent all the money he made

Winter

- Short phone calls in and shorter ones out
- All night long
- Struggled to work
- Kept seeing Doc D
- Mental Health Centre
- Harder drugs,
- which he regretted
- Court dates
- Legal aid

Early Spring

- Brighter mood
- A desire to work
- Optimism
- But the short phone calls continued
- In out in out

Late Spring

- Long calls at 3:00 a.m.
- Maybe going back to Montreal
- Getting paid = lots of alcohol
- A tax return meant even more
- More time with his dad

- Vows to stay sober
- Phone cut off

I wanted to know who he was talking to and what was important to him. Who he was doing drugs with, who he was getting them from? Who did he spend the most time with? Who did he like? Who did he pretend to like? Who did he love? Who did he tolerate? I was a private eye building a case with rudimentary forensic investigation skills. Reconstructing a composite year based on slim threads. I filled in the many dark spaces with guesses, then I cantilevered bridges between the guesses with more guesses. I was a fabricator, manufacturing a fiction for myself to believe. I just wanted something to stand on.

Some things I found out: Holden had multiple circles of friends. Some were old friends, some brand new, some just wanted to paint trains. Holden loved trains, wanted to paint trains, paint anything, and play music, mainly guitar. Bass guitar. He never said mean things about people to others. He wasn't racist or sexist, and he did not discriminate. He was not solitary or self-isolating. He desired the presence of others. He was funny—very, very funny. He understood irony and used it like a jousting stick. He wanted privacy. Everyone wanted to party. He went to a lot of parties. He went to the beach. He worked. He slept on many couches. He didn't sleep enough. His friends were funny, too, and generous. Some were concerned about him. One helped him get a job. Some were disappointing and unreliable. He was disappointing and unreliable. At least once, he overdosed and was revived—likely twice. After one of these overdoses, someone badgered him to drop acid with them, even after he refused. Someone wanted to buy drugs from him. Holden didn't sell drugs, he said, but his "lady friend" did. He was living with her. They fought. He moved out. He cut ties. He moved on easily.

I invaded his private correspondences and found that Holden could be by turns impeccably polite or disgustingly crude. He used perfect grammar when sober and made glaring, almost intentional mistakes when he was not. As if his drunkenness took away his affection and respect for words. He liked women. A lot. He was always looking for a booty call. He was a good flirt. He sent song lyrics, poems, and YouTub

> Relax. Stop being such a drag,
> I was only with you for the sex
> and the beer.

He got excited about live music shows. He would invite people to go to these shows with him, whether he knew them well or not. He looked at porn. He would often drop away and leave people hanging. He sent himself messages and reminders.

> Show up, it's important!
>
> Go home, don't mess this up!
>
> Go to the doctor!

He was often depressed and anxious. He was often optimistic and philosophical. He shared the truly intimate details of his life with only a chosen few. Not the few I might have thought.

Through Holden's last winter, he made many short phone calls at ungodly hours: a few seconds, then a call back. A few more seconds. A drug deal? At the same time, Devon was a constant, day and night. Some very long calls to Audrey in Montreal. I read apologies from Jenna, thoughtful discussions about addiction and withdrawal with Yuki. I found jokes and invitations. Fear, failure, and confusion lived alongside honest effort and kindness. I found evidence of creativity and happiness, too.

He was trying. As best he could, he was trying. He wanted to live. He'd wanted to live well and healthy, but it seemed he either didn't know how or refused to allow himself that pleasure.

I contacted as many of these people as I could. Some spoke with me, some refused. Some were clearly struggling with their own mental illnesses and addictions. Some remained in deep denial or just wanted to forget about it. Some met me at coffee shops, in graffiti-coated rail tunnels, or on street corners. Some never showed up. Some cancelled with excuses. I forgot I had to move today. My boss won't give me the time off. I'm sick. Some blocked my calls and Facebook messages. What were they afraid of when the worst thing had already happened? Unless, I imagined, they were somehow complicit.

More than anything, I wanted someone to blame. Someone other than Holden, whose chain of responsibility dead-ended at my feet.

Speaking to Holden's friends gave me a convoluted way of speaking to him. Being with them gave me a way to be with him. Their stories were golden gifts wrapped in shining paper. Even when they were unflattering and frightening. Hearing about how Holden moved through the world via the memories of his friends was a form of resurrection. The brave ones told me the truth, and in telling his truth, perhaps found something of their own. Some of them absorbed Holden's death as a cautionary tale and worked hard to change. Some let his passing bounce off them and continued on their own oblivious, self-destructive paths.

But the ones who did show up—the ones who came to our home, who stepped across our police-stained driveway and through our door as a form of pilgrimage—were the bravest of all.

Claire arrived one rainy night, chilled bones and sorrow in the porch light. Her hair hanging in thin wet clumps, her eyes small caves. Behind her, out by the road, I detected a tall silhouette, a watercolour shadow.

Come in, I said, it's a terrible night.

I just needed to come, she said, her voice a faint rasp, and tell you I knew him. I knew your son. Her black fingernails fluttered to her mouth, wings of dirt and paint.

Would you like some tea?

No. Thank you. My mom is waiting. Her hand reached for the doorknob. She reminded me of a trapped animal. I could tell she had something important to tell me. How could I convince her to stay?

Were you his girlfriend?

She turned back to me. No, not really. Her voice was so frail I strained to hear her. We mostly got drunk together and painted. We both liked to wreck stuff. She laughed, and the laugh morphed to crying, the crying to sobs. Her long arms swaddled her birdcage torso. I wondered if she saw Holden's face in mine the same way I saw his raw youth and his struggle in hers. I saw her possibilities, too.

I just wanted you to know. He was kind to me. She looked at her dirty shoes. A dog bit my face. He bandaged it, and he stayed with me all night until he had to go to work. He spray-painted his name on my sofa. She risked a quick glance at me. I kept it—the fabric, not the sofa. I'm going to put it in a frame.

She stopped talking, and neither of us knew what else to say. She smelled of wet leather and cigarettes. Mascara melted down her cheeks. She shook. I wanted to hear more, I didn't want her to leave. Her being here, this gesture, felt like a ritual. I needed to make some kind of offering in exchange.

Please sit down, I'll be right back.

I wanted to give her something to help plug up the leaks, some kind of token for the gift she had just given me. I went to the bedroom, dug in the bottom drawer of our dresser, and ran my hand through a stack of his clothing. The smell of Holden rising with the fabric.

Here. It's not much, just something to say thank you. For coming. I handed her a pair of his boxer shorts.

Claire gasped and buried her face in black cotton. I watched her inhale a kind boy on a sofa who cared and waited and watched over her till dawn. She was an earthquake.

You look so cold, are you sure I can't make you some tea?

Thanks, but I have to go, my mom's outside. She stood and walked like an injured bird to the door. Then stopped. Something else, she said, it's important. Your son … She wiped away snot from her face with the back of her tattooed hand. He was amazing. I have never met anyone smarter. And … She paused, her bony fingers on the doorknob again. And. I'm going to do better.

The women Holden knew were laden with guilt and responsibility, the men—who were not yet men—with denial and justifications.

Why didn't you tell us? I asked more than one of his close friends over the phone in the days after his death. If you knew he was doing heroin, why didn't you tell us?

Slow, hollow replies crawled through the phone.

I don't know.

I didn't know how to reach you guys.

I guess I just felt like it was his decision.

He wouldn't have listened anyway.

Yuki and Lina came on a cloudy day when rotten apples littered the grass outside and a T-shirt wasn't enough, but a sweater was too much. Yuki round-faced, small, and stout in boy's jeans, Lina skeletal, barely holding up her clothing. They stood in the kitchen across the counter from me, fingers interlocking, in the same place Holden had last stood. Yuki told me about her own recovery from heroin addiction and how Holden had asked her for advice and help. But it was Lina, a former girlfriend he'd written poems for in high school, who was inconsolable, her collarbones rising gulls. She folded over the back of a kitchen chair like a thrown coat.

We were with him, she said. That last afternoon. I'm so sorry. I was right there. I could have done more. I keep going over and over it. But I wasn't sure. I wasn't sure about what I couldn't see. She sobbed, and her eyes were raw pink. But I didn't move to comfort her. I didn't want to silence her. I wanted to hear everything I could of that last day.

What would have happened if we didn't let him go? Lina whispered, and her legs gave out. Yuki caught her with a steadying arm. Lina's eyes pleaded with Yuki for some kind of reprieve. Pleaded with mine for some kind of forgiveness.

I gripped the edge of the counter and wondered the same thing. What would have happened if you hadn't let him go?

Lina was no longer in our kitchen, eyes drowning, grey sky back-lighting her tangled crown of peroxide dreadlocks. She was sitting in an old car on a summer's day with her thin, pale, arm reaching for Holden through the window, hovering in the soft warm air. I can still see him going away down the ramp to the SeaBus, she said. She blinked and bowed her head. There was something off in the way he was walking.

I used these fragments and intermittent whispers as wood and nails to construct conversations, to erect whole situations. Holden was resuscitated in the scenarios I built in my mind, as if I were standing beside him. I imagined him, phone in hand, receiving messages and sending his replies. I could see him walking, painting, plugging the matte-black electric guitar we'd given him into his amp with a distorted click-hum; standing in the crowd at a metal show; sleeping. I could hear him laughing, feel nervous adrenalin for him when he got in a fight, laugh with him when he made a clever joke. It didn't matter to me that it was all fabrication. I was reliving the last year of Holden's life. The year I had abandoned him. The year I let my selfishness override his need for guidance and compassion.

Holden and I had agreed to speak via Skype every Sunday while I was travelling, but it didn't end up happening often. He was rarely available, and his avoidance frustrated me. I was angry when I should have been understanding. I made declarations when I should have been asking questions. Instead of asking why he didn't feel like talking, I got frustrated with him for not making more of an effort to connect. According to my Skype call log, during my ten months away, I had tried to reach Holden more than fifty times. I heard his voice less than twenty.

Through court documents, I discovered that one of his police altercations involved a domestic dispute: a loud argument, threats. He had some kind of weapon in his pocket, which turned out to be the small wooden baton he carried for protection when he painted graffiti. He was taken to jail for the night.

This was in the winter, during the month we'd spent in Seychelles and Mauritius, when Holden had lived with Jenna. She was older, a barista who made him eat vegetables and, I later found out, sold drugs as well as coffee. Though I've never seen Jenna, I've spoken with her on the phone. I pictured her with long dark hair, severe horizontal bangs, and teeth straightened by six years of braces.

When he was released from lock-up the next morning, Jenna tried to apologize.

Holden, how can I say sorry
when you won't talk to me?

He froze her out.

All good. Nothing to apologize
for.

He didn't live with Jenna for much longer after that.

Something about the dates on the timeline I'd constructed didn't make sense. Why would Holden have called legal aid the day *before* he was arrested for disturbing the peace? I checked again and caught the glitch. His police and court records showed that he was due to appear in Provincial Court on a different charge the next morning: destruction of property. This meant graffiti. It would have been his third charge of vandalism and very likely would have had him worried.

His father and I had been to court with Holden on his first graffiti charge, when he'd been warned the judge would go easy—initially—if he showed remorse. She had instructed Holden to write an essay about what his life would be like with a criminal record. His biggest concern at the time was that he wouldn't be able to go to music festivals in the US with Amin anymore. I imagined him writing a poem instead, as a subtle form of resistance.

I've met the judge, she's a joke. Write an essay about how your life would suck with a wrap sheet. Oh snap, no more Rock the Bells? Let's reconsider. Graffiti is not a crime, it's an art form. *And* a jerk-off drag race to the coolest place not on the map. Remember, I am a teenage male with basement self-esteem and a shame frigate of unknown origin. Maybe I write my name big to make up for how small I feel, in relation to the rest of the universe. Tags are not legal names because that would reveal too much. Too much hole, too much dig. Coward. And I might get busted. Again. But when I press that nipple, that white cap, with my middle finger and those subatomic particles of redblueyellowwhiteblack fly, some of my hatred flaps its wings. Life is inflated by hostility. If I had a record I'd deserve the blue beat down I got last week. Just for saying Lay off, officer, he's already down. Each one of us is a small enemy waging a small war with ego. I am a child starting a schoolyard fight over vertical real estate. I mean, it's a Dumpster, Chuck. I rolled your piece, you buffed mine. Burn, dis, stab, punch, die— acrylic and oil-based threats. It's all toys down here, and I am a pink baby looking for love on a cement wall or slow-rolling railcar. Guys have died for a throw up. Cracked a skull. Right leg left on the tracks. How I seek to spend my time may depend on how much time I perceive myself to have, a theory I learned in philosophy class. Does the fact that I have very little regard for my own safety indicate that I will live forever, or not long at all? Irrelevant, Your Honour. But I'll take it eaze, cuz I just wanna fly.

What could he and Jenna have fought about? What would have made him so enraged that the police were called? What do couples fight about? I researched the most common reasons for relationship disagreements: commitment, jealousy, money, sex, substance abuse.

Lying in the dark somewhere between asleep and awake, my mind composed possible scenarios. Two figures walk hand in hand along a wet sidewalk, neon signs above splashing their faces. They smile.

∞

Jenna and Holden stroll together down Granville Street. The cadence of their strides matches the ambient music spilling from a retro diner. A bus splashes past. Then another. On their way from bar number two to bar number three, they pass groups of high-heeled clubbers and huddles of street kids with sleeping bags and dogs. Jenna and Holden are optimistically drunk.

The rain has finally stopped, and the normal piss-and-weed undertone has been exchanged for a clean, green freshness. Jenna wears a long Aritzia coat and running shoes. She's not particularly tall or thin. She has no piercings, at least not on her face. She walks with the posture of a former dancer.

I've been thinking, she says.

That's encouraging. Holden squeezes her hand as they pass a donair restaurant, its slab of meat spinning and spitting in the open window. Their bodies bounce off each other, and their grasp pulls them back together. First time for everything. He winks at her.

Seriously, Holden, I'm almost thirty. I'd really like to have a kid before I'm a senior citizen. Can we at least talk about this?

Dude, I'm twenty-one and not exactly fatherhood material. I mean, I do have the dad bod, but I don't even have a job. How the fuck would I take care of a family?

That stuff always works itself out, I'm not worried. Look, you're smart and we care for each other. I've been saving all the side hustle cash. We're living together already. So why the fuck not?

Because no, that's why not.

At least give me a reason.

Holden plants his feet on the sidewalk and turns to face her. He stares into her eyes and speaks methodically. Look, my parents broke up when I was two and that fucking sucked, okay? If I wanted to see my dad I had to wait till Wednesday. Two Christmases, two birthdays. I don't want to have a kid and never see it. All right? And why the fuck do you always bring this up when we're having a good time?

He turns and strides away from her down Granville Street.

Because you're happiest and therefore most receptive when you're buzzed, she says to his back.

He stops and turns. Oh, so you're trying to manipulate me when I'm intoxicated. Nice. That's a cold bitch thing to do.

Jenna hurries to catch up. She grabs his arm.

Now you're just being an asshole.

I *am* an asshole, when are you going to figure that the fuck out?

What if it's too late? She stops walking.

He freezes. His flushed face now ashen. He places one hand on each of her shoulders and walks her backward until her shoulder blades are pressed against the darkened glass of an out-of-business clothing store.

Is it? Are you pregnant? Jesus fucking Christ. Holden runs the fingers of one hand through his hair, grabbing big handfuls and pulling. Are you fucking kidding me?

What if I am?

Holden presses her against the glass. Tell me! He's louder now, heart thudding in his chest. Tell me the fucking truth for once, you conniving cunt!

A group of young women walk by in too-tight dresses.

Hey, leave her alone! One of them pulls out her mobile phone. Let her go, I'm calling 911. Another films.

Mind your own business! Holden yells at the group of women. Jenna, tell me.

Stop it, it's my decision. She tries to wriggle free.

Holden feels a strong hand on his shoulder.

What's going on here? A uniformed police officer pulls him away from Jenna into the middle of the sidewalk.

Fuck you, it's private. We're fine.

Doesn't look fine to me. Young lady, are you all right?

Leave us the fuck alone! Jenna shouts.

When Holden shoves his hands into his pockets, he feels the small carved club he carries when he goes painting.

Go away, we're just talking.

The stick is in his hand.

You're coming with me now. The officer takes the stick and pulls Holden's hands behind his back to cuff him.

Are you fucking kidding me?

$$\infty$$

The vision brought me fully awake. What if there was a baby? If Jenna had been pregnant, there could be a child. Holden's child. I sucked air as though I'd been sprinting. How could I find her? I couldn't disconnect from the feeling that it was possible. That there could be a small descendent of Holden in this world. A grandchild. A niece for Lyla to love. I saw her as a girl. A smiling girl with loose blond curls just like his sister's.

10

Travel was always a priority. The longer the trip, the better. After high school, I spent over a year backpacking. When Cam and I got together, we saved what we could to go where we could. Our first home was full of garage-sale furniture, but we always found a way to camp and ski. Experiences over ownership was a philosophy we agreed on.

Both kids knew that when they turned sixteen, I would take them on a trip. Holden chose New York. Our relationship had been swerving back and forth from warm-close to distant-fraught, and the step-parent situation between Cam, Holden, and me felt like I was being pulled apart by two strong, stubborn horses. The pressure-filled school year was finally over, and I wanted a few days alone with Holden to simply have some fun away from the frequent tension at home.

Visiting New York would also give Holden a way to explore a little bit of an art scene he might feel some connection with. I didn't care whether or not he went to university, but I wanted to help him find something to engage with on his own terms. Something to give him a spark and a view toward what his future could include. Motivating Holden to do pretty much anything was like trying to sculpt a handful of Jello. He rejected any form of authority or direction, and his style of communication was to agree verbally—Yup yup yup sounds good, I'll get right on that!—then completely disregard everything that had been discussed and do what he'd originally been planning to anyway, which was to sleep, listen to music, or play video games down in his room.

Mainly we went to New York for the same reason most people do—to experience all of the energy the city has to offer. From my perspective, it was a wonderful trip, but when I replayed scenes of those five days, I wondered what the city and our time together may have looked like, felt like, and meant to him.

∞

A layer of ripe-garbage smell hangs over everything, and the sky, what he can see of it, is oily gold, like it's been painted with a coat of melted butter. Holden's never experienced this kind of humidity before. Sweat expands across the back of his T-shirt, and his jeans are stuck to his legs. He sees fire escapes and brick walls, Dumpsters in alleyways, and rusty lampposts along the edge of the street. As they walk, he imagines tagging each object; his hand moves involuntarily, as if he's writing his name in the air in glossy white lines. He can even see the letters dripping as he and his mom continue on their way: *RuleR, RuleR, RuleR.* He inhales the fumes and the noise of New York City and realizes he's smiling. His shoulders are relaxing. The electric buzz inside his ribcage has been turned down to a three.

Holden tries to look up at the skyscrapers without tripping over the cracks in the sidewalk. They landed at JFK less than two hours ago, and already they're "out exploring."

Why do you always have to walk so fast? You're like a freakin' squirrel.

Holy shit! His mom stops abruptly in the middle of the wide sidewalk. She's looking up at the black awning above their heads. It's Birdland! She turns to him eagerly, but he has no idea why this place is significant. We have to go in! Every great jazz musician in the history of the world has played here. She pulls on Holden's arm.

Dude, we can't go in, it's a bar. He takes a step back from her, toward the curb, as if she's just asked him to help her to rob a bank.

How do you know? She shrugs. Maybe we can. Come on, let's try.

This is what he loves-hates about her. Always trying to weasel her way in. She doesn't "pay attention to the rules," which is what she's always telling him to do.

The doorman waves them through with a bored nod. Before Holden can process what's happening, he's sitting at a table in what appears to be a jazz bar–restaurant combo. Waiters in jackets are delivering plates of food and trays of drinks. Instruments and music stands clutter the stage. Most of the people at the other tables are old and Black. He feels very not old, and very not Black. It's awkward and a bit exciting at the same time. I mean, he's in a club in NYC. And he's not even sixteen yet.

He leans back in his chair and looks around, hands resting loosely on his thighs. Yup, he's the youngest person here by like, a hundred years. He's incredibly uncomfortable—damp clothes, stiff chair, awkward silence. His mom is grinning at him from across the table. He forces a weak smile.

The waiter sets down two glasses of beer down in front of his mom, because there's a two-drink minimum, and by "drink" they mean the dreaded alcohol. A fresh Coke fizzes in front of him, which is fucking ironic considering he's rarely allowed to drink the devil's sugar water at home. In his life he's probably consumed more beer than Coke. He's also eaten more zucchini muffins than chocolate cupcakes.

It would be so much better to be older. If he was older, one of those beers would sit in front of him, and he could signal the waiter to bring him another without anyone telling him he couldn't. But someone else, as usual, is calling the shots. He can't wait to be old enough to be in charge of himself. Then everything will be so much easier. If he was older, the lady eyeballing him from across the table, her face tinted a faint orange by the thin strips of neon above the stage, would be younger, more interesting, and they would probably be getting shizzled.

Maybe he would lean toward her, elbows on the table, closing the space between them. Maybe she would tilt forward, too, laughing at his hilarious banter.

There's something extremely distressing about going to your first bar with your goddamn mother. Completely and fundamentally wrong. Shouldn't a man's first trip to a bar be cooler than this? A milestone—like his first fuck. Something he can look back on later with pride, something he can brag about to his friends. It should not be sprung on him like a carjacking. This is so messed. His face hardens, and the familiar prickle and buzz begins to flare under his skin. He looks around, trying to figure out a possible escape. How can he stop this before it goes too far?

Maybe we should just go to Times Square, Momz? he says. Can't we go look at the cheesy lights? Can't we just go have a burger and call it a night? I'm tired.

We're here now, honey, we don't have to stay long, she says.

They've missed their chance. The band has taken the stage and is counting in a song he recognizes from his dad's CD collection, but can't quite peg. He will in a second, though. It's close. He can almost grab the title from the air just above and to the right of his mom's head. He's always been able to see music. As a little kid he could identify all the different instruments in the songs on the radio.

That one has violins and a saxophone. Do you hear the trumpet, Mama?

No, I don't. Mom would look over at him from the driver's seat. But I'm sure you're right.

Music has always been clear to him. Easy.

The dude on the stand-up bass is running an incredible riff, and even though the drummer is leading the rhythm section, he's working the snare beautifully from just a slight shade behind everyone else. Classic backseat driver. The music envelops Holden and seeps into his muscles.

The wall behind his mom's head is filled with framed, signed portraits. He recognizes a lot of them: Parker, Mingus, Holliday, Davis, Fitzgerald. They've all performed on this stage just a few feet away. She's right, it is fucking amazing. He picks up his Coke, takes a sip, and there it is—he knows the song the band is playing. "Take Five" by Dave Brubeck. Nailed it.

His mom slowly surveys the room. Then she exhales, leans forward, sets her hand purposefully on the white tablecloth, and slides one of the glasses of beer toward him.

What the heck, she says, looking over her shoulder to check if anyone saw her.

Holden laughs out loud. He picks up the glass and is about to take a sip.

Wait! She raises her glass and holds it out toward him. Cheers! Happy almost birthday!

They drink as the band segues into Thelonious Monk's "Body and Soul." He gets that one in the first few notes.

Holden's glass is empty long before hers. The music continues and another beer arrives, then another. Soon the neon lighting seems less offensive, the chair less hard against his back, and his mother's voice less abrasive in his ears. He watches the band, noticing how all of their limbs are moving in rhythm, elbows jerking, knees rising and falling, heads bobbing in unison. They pass around the lead, communicating in subtle gestures. He can see the layers of music overlapping as the musicians work together to build something more beautiful and substantial than any of them could make by themselves.

The hostile vibration inside his ribcage drains away like spaghetti water through a strainer. Another beer and it becomes less work to smile back at his mom. She's sitting there watching the band, her fingers keeping track of the beat on the tablecloth. She softly grins to herself, and her head dips in time with the beat.

Maybe the trip is a good idea for them after all. All that fighting with her and Cam about the homework thing, and the pot thing, and the girl in his room thing, and the stealing booze thing, the sneaking out to paint thing, and the cops thing. He feels an involuntary surge of affection flood his chest. His mom tries so hard, but she doesn't have a fucking clue. She doesn't know him, and he can't explain himself to her, so there's always a space between what they both want and what they each have.

Clapping and cheers fill the void left by the fading vibration of the melody. The musicians tenderly set down their instruments and walk off, like construction workers at the lunch whistle.

Coffee break for the band, his mom says. Have you had enough? We can go any time.

Sure, he says, though this seems like a good place to stay for a while.

She pays their tab with a green hundred-dollar bill, and when the waiter brings the change back, she hands Holden a twenty that looks to him exactly like the hundred she just paid with.

Here, in case we get separated. Not that we will.

He tucks the twenty into the front pocket of his jeans. *Separated?*

He follows her out through the club, down the red-carpeted stairs, through the heavy double door, and onto the street, where it's not quite dark. A hint of azure drapes across the chunk of sky he can see.

Do you think you could find your way back to our place if you had to?

They're not staying in a hotel. Some radical professor lady who Mom and Cam met at an Italian restaurant in Paris offered them her apartment. I mean, why you would go to an Italian restaurant in France, he has no idea. Apparently the apartment is rent controlled, which is a rare and noteworthy thing. From what he remembers, the building looks exactly like every other apartment on the street. Brown bricks, cement steps with wrought iron railings, black front door.

Sure I could.

Good. How would you get there?

I would … He looks left and right, up and down the street. I would … He has no fucking idea. Well, it's on 72nd Avenue.

It's on 75th Street. At Amsterdam, she says. You could take the subway to 72nd Street and walk from there. Remember that, 75th and Amsterdam.

Got it, 75th and Amsterdam.

But don't worry, I'm not letting you out of my sight.

So, just like at home then. He laughs.

Yes, just like that. She laughs too, only bigger. She slips her arm through the bend of his elbow and they walk, linked together, toward the artificial glow of what he presumes is Times Square.

∞

Over the next few days we explored all we could of Manhattan. We spent hours at the MoMA and accidentally snuck into the Museum of Natural History when we were looking for a bathroom. Holden did a very funny impression of a raptor in the dinosaur exhibit. We threw coins to buskers, photographed graffiti, ate hot dogs with grilled onions and mustard on the street corner while steam from the subway grates snaked up our legs. We checked out the view from the top of the Empire State Building at night, when low woollen clouds doused the night sky and the never-ending city lights below us looked like a blanket of stars—as though the whole world was upside down. We got discount tickets for an afternoon performance of *Billy Elliot* on Broadway, where I cried because sometimes it's hard for parents and children to *see* each other.

We shopped for knock-off handbags and T-shirts at the Canal Street markets—Holden bought one with a young Fidel Castro smoking a cigar and another with Jeff Bridges as the Dude from *The Big Lebowski* in an Andy Warhol pop art style. We went to a basement comedy club in Greenwich Village, ate kite-sized slices of pizza, then accidentally ended up in Harlem at 1:00 a.m. because we hadn't noticed that our subway line stopped its regular service at midnight. We went sailing on the East River with a group of gay hairdressers who insisted on giving us beer after beer after cold beer, until a sudden, powerful electrical storm struck, and we had to turn back. We all put on rubber-ducky rain slickers and howled with laughter while lightning crackled and warm rain drenched us—we never did get to see the Statue of Liberty. Instead, we ran from the pier through the ankle-deep-flooded streets, hair dripping, until we could flag down a yellow cab, then back at our apartment, soaking wet, we ordered chow mein, and Holden tipped the bicycle delivery boy the twenty dollar bill he had stashed in his pocket for an emergency.

I noticed that he always seemed more optimistic and open—happier—after he'd had a few beers.

The next afternoon we made a pilgrimage to the Dakota. Mid-July sun filtered through the majestic elms lining the path across the street in Central Park. We sat side by side on a bench, and I sang one of my favourite Lennon songs, "Jealous Guy," into Holden's ear.

Flowers, candles, and poems scattered the ground at the centre of a mosaic that formed the word *IMAGINE*.

Could you imagine living here? I asked him.

I actually don't think so, Momz, it's all just way too much.

His neck was bent over as though it didn't want to hold up his head in the heat anymore. I was close enough to inhale the earthy smell of his thick pelt of sweaty hair. His face was flushed in an expression that showed approval and disapproval at the same time. He didn't want to disappoint me, but he was exhausted.

We had one more day to spend in New York: Holden's sixteenth birthday.

∞

Happy birthday to you, happy birthday to you …

Holden wakes up on their last morning in New York to his mother singing over the hum of the air conditioner from her bed on the other side of the one-room apartment. He's sleeping on the couch in the corner. He can feel a rectangle of sunlight coming in through the window, warming his feet. Now she's hovering over him, finishing her song.

Happy birthday, dear Holden, happy birthday to youuuuu!

She kisses his cheek. You are officially sixteen years old, she says. Wow, sixteen years, how did that happen so fast?

Go away.

This city feels kind of like a video game where he has to pass all the levels, but—shocker—there's always another level. He'd thought maybe he could live here one day, as most artists aspire to at some point or another—or maybe that's a cliché? But anyway, now he doesn't know if he could handle it. What he wants to do is sleep. At home. Alone. He wants to be in his room in the basement, in the dark.

Did I ever tell you about when you were born? His mom rests her hand on his back.

Only a thousand times. Holden pulls the thin blanket up over his head.

What does a sixteen-year-old want to do on his special day?

He wants her to stop fucking talking. Sleep.

You *have* been sleeping, come on, it's noon. I've been waiting for you to wake up for three hours. I've read every piece of paper in this place.

Did you know that in Sweden they're burning bunnies for fuel? TIME magazine.

I don't want to do anything, go by yourself. He covers his eyes with a bent arm to fend her off.

I'll let you vandalize the landmark of your choice.

He knows it's pointless, she will never leave him alone, so he begins the uphill march of willing himself vertical.

They walk to a stationery store.

You can pick out whatever you need, birthday boy!

He chooses two white paint markers. One thin line, one fatty. They take the subway to the Fulton Street station, and when they emerge into the light and heat of the afternoon, there it is, the Brooklyn Bridge. They walk along the boardwalk. Just before the first square stone tower that holds up the swooping cable, Holden stops and spreads his hands flat on the thick iron railing. It's warm. Rows of rivets and layers of paint bubble under his palms.

This is good, he says.

What should I do? his mom asks.

Just stand right there and cover me. He pulls out the thicker of the two pens from his back pocket, gives it a shake, and hunches over the railing. The river flows by below his feet as he scrawls *RuleR 09*. It's small, but it's there. He looks up at the skyline of the city and nods his head with approval. He's just tagged the Brooklyn fuckin' Bridge.

Can I take a picture of that? she asks.

If you want to.

That afternoon he tags a mailbox, the back of a newspaper stand, and the plywood cladding around a construction site. The more he etches his mark on the city, the more settled he feels in his skin. He grows taller and breathes more easily. Graffiti for him is the opposite of kryptonite. He writes *Don't Sad? Be Smile!* on the wall inside a subway station. His mom stands beside him watching for security guards and doesn't say a word. When they arrive back at the apartment, Holden runs up the four flights of stairs.

11

Why are you doing that to yourself? Cam's voice drifted over from the far side of our king-size bed. A vapour trail of exasperation loitered behind his words.

Doing what?

But I knew what he meant. Curled and tangled in our rumpled duvet, clothes musty, hair unbrushed, morning breath though it was night, I was rereading *The Catcher in the Rye*.

Hot, fat tears gushed over my nose and cheeks, overflowing my ears, soaking my pillowcase. It's possible that I was making noise.

J.D. Salinger's words, the gorgeous dialogue and the vivid scenes, raked my heart raw. And yet somehow this scouring felt satisfying. It was a useful kind of pain, like the soreness deep in your back muscles after a day of early-spring gardening. Reading the book felt right. As right as a table with three legs can feel. Seeing Holden's name on the pages felt important.

The last time I had read *The Catcher in the Rye* was when I was five months pregnant with Holden, twenty-two years ago. I'd taken shelter under a quilt then, too. My mother and I had made it from scraps of bright fabric we'd found at a garage sale, woven squares of soft pink, teal, and buttercup all anchored in a grid of black. I'd lain, expanding with life, under a checkerboard of pastels.

The night before, I had been jarred awake by a searing ripple of cramps low in my belly. I'd reached down between my legs and caught a gush of deep-red blood in my fingers. At the hospital, with my feet braced in cold metal stirrups, a disinterested night-shift doctor informed us I was having a miscarriage, and there wasn't much he or anyone else could do about it.

I disagreed.

Back at our apartment in the early dawn, I called in sick for work, burrowed under that quilt, and propped my hips up on stacks of pillows, afraid to move. I devised a recipe of gravity, prayer, and positive visualization to persuade the universe to let my body hold on to our baby. I stayed in that position for four days.

A close friend who had been a punk rocker in college before becoming a high school literature teacher had sent a paperback copy of *The Catcher in the Rye* when she heard we were planning to name our baby boy Holden. Maybe she sent it as a warning flare. A shot across the bow. A cautionary tale.

I see that now, of course. I see so many things more clearly now.

Our story was supposed to be a joyful one: our love would last forever and the child of that love would be called Holden. Not for the literary character, but after his paternal grandmother, Margaret "Peggy" Holden. Pegs, an accomplished dancer with a sensational set of gams, had been a boisterous nightclub singer in the heyday of Elvis, the clean-cut, wholesome era of the Mickey Mouse Club and the cinched-waist skirt suit with matching hat. Miss Holden's razor-sharp wit, sailor's tongue, and zesty laugh made her the North Star in every room she entered. Her children adored her, and friends often gathered around her, telling stories and pouring drinks. Pegs was one of the most entertaining people I had ever met. Once I watched her bend over in the kitchen and light a fart on fire. She howled as the blue flame licked the back of her flowered leggings.

Our child's name was a tribute—it wasn't supposed to be tragic.

I'd hunkered down in bed, *Catcher in the Rye* balanced on my pelvis, willing the baby to grab hold of me. While engaging my core and reading some of the more agonizing passages, I began to worry that choosing the name Holden might be a mistake. It weighed too much. Anyone who had read the book—which was basically anyone who attended high school in North America—would envision a delusional teenager in a hunting cap at the mention of the name. The kid in the book was just too sad and confused. Loveable, smart, and funny, yes, but also becoming mentally unhinged and largely oblivious to it. Perhaps hanging the Holden tag around our baby's neck was unfair. Too complex, too dark. He wasn't even born yet. Perhaps he never would be.

But we were too young and too optimistic to take heed. We knew better. The rules didn't apply to us.

The bleeding eventually slowed, then stopped, and soon I went back to work and forgot about the anticipatory terror of losing someone I hadn't met yet, but already loved deeply. How was I to know the reprieve was simply a delay tactic?

Around the time the ultrasound showed that we would need two hands to hold him, we briefly considered other names. We liked Henry until we heard a woman screeching the name to her husband with an upward inflection: Henreeeeee! I tried Elliot on for size, calling to an invisible child in the next room. Elliot, it's time for dinner! Elliot, will you come here, please! But there was no substance to it. Our child would be Holden. After his grandmother. And he would inherit her humour, her wit, her warm, loving nature, and her magnetic charms along with her name.

Twenty-two years later, after the death of that child—and his namesake just three days before—I was again sequestered in bed, and I felt compelled to read *The Catcher in the Rye* again. I had no idea why. Somehow the novel appeared in my hands. Seeing the familiar letters of

Holden's name printed on the pages made my heart lurch and bellow. I loved the beautiful, anguished, deeply flawed young man in the story. I loved his irreverent way of talking too loudly. I loved his habit of insulting people without noticing, of spending his money on strangers, of walking around all night, soaking wet, trying to figure himself out. I loved Holden Caulfield.

More than that, I understood Holden Caulfield. I wanted to hold his hand while he avoided going home to his rich, detached parents after being kicked out of boarding school again. I would have helped him face the disgrace. I'd have wrapped him in a blanket and made him a bowl of soup. Taking a cab and booking into a cheap hotel with Holden Caufield felt like spending time with my own son. And that didn't seem crazy to me at all.

Honestly, babe, why are you torturing yourself? Cam lay on the other side of our bed, waiting for an answer. I hadn't noticed the rainstorm on my face, tears dripping from the sagging skin along my jawline.

I don't know, I whispered back across the duvet, and flung the book across the room. I don't know why I do anything anymore.

The paperback skidded and spun on the floor, wedging itself in the corner. It was almost touching the stack of Holden's books that I had unpacked from another box in the basement. Kerouac, Hemingway, Burrows, Wolfe, Thompson—the classic reading list of the disillusioned adolescent. I had marked the box in black sharpie: *Holden—take these when you move out.* On the side of the box, I had drawn a smiley face, and he had drawn a cartoon figure with a bulbous nose and a halo.

What else could I do to continue my relationship with my son?

I booked a session with his psychologist, had lunch with his doctor, convinced the police and the mental health clinic at the hospital to release his private records. Every night I begged for dreams in which he would explain it all to me. I consulted mediums and clairvoyants.

One of these mystics, who charged me $350 USD to talk to me on the phone from Memphis, said that our angels (I hated that word, I could almost hear Holden scoffing, *Angels schmangels, Momzerz*) often communicate with us using physical signs, earthly symbols. Holden might let me know he was with me by placing dimes or white feathers in unusual places for me to find. The snake oil tasted delicious.

But a dime with the Bluenose on one side was a symbol that made sense. Holden had had a traditional-style tattoo of a schooner in full sail on his arm, like a sailor or a pirate would have.

I began finding dimes. My fingertips landed on a dime in the bottom of the kitchen sink while I was elbows deep in hot soapy water. I found a dime under the Christmas tree. Dimes clinked in my pockets on many occasions. Lyla found them, too, in her bed, in her school books, on her bedside table. My sister Janet, who had spent years caring for small Holden, often found dimes on the logging roads where she walked her dogs. She took pictures of them and sent them to me.

I also found downy white feathers. Rolled inside my yoga mat, in my hair, and often between my feet when I looked down. One day, white feathers fell in a swirling snowfall while I walked on a trail near our home. An eagle had killed a seagull in its high nest. I stood alone, snatching white feathers from the air, stuffing them into my pockets, crying and talking to the barren branches.

Hi, Holden, I miss you, I said. I love you. How are you? Please tell me how you are and what you're learning.

These were pretty much the same things I'd said to him while he was alive.

More and more, I talked to Holden inside my head. I would tell him about his sister, his friends, and the world. Trump is president. I know, it's ridiculous. I asked him how I was supposed to heal. How could I best move forward? What did his life mean? How about mine?

I wanted him to be alive. I wanted to talk with him. I wanted him to talk. I wanted to give him a voice. I could do that on the page. I began to ask Holden if it would be okay to write about him. I asked specifically if he wanted to tell his own story, in his own voice. I asked if he thought that telling his story, or at least my interpretation of some of the things that had happened in his life, might help create a better understanding of people struggling with drug use, a greater empathy for their humanity.

Thousands of people were dying of overdose, mostly of a powerful drug called fentanyl that was poisoning the street supply of heroin, but also from all kinds of prescribed opioids and other adulterated drug combinations. Very few people begin using these drugs because their lives are wonderful. And I no longer saw substance users as criminals, or statistics, or strangers. I saw them as someone's child, who needed help. As human beings who deserved dignity and kindness.

I needed Holden's permission.

I knew I was in the dark about the most intimate parts of Holden's life, including his drug use, but I told him that I would have to be honest about his struggles with his mental health, his substance abuse, and his choices if I were to write his story at all.

Holden, is it okay if I write about you, even though you're not around to clarify or defend yourself? If you say no, I won't do it. I promise. I don't ever want to hurt you or embarrass you or betray your trust in any way. I won't exploit your death. And I would never want to profit from your sacrifice. Are you open to the idea of me writing your story as best I can?

I promised Holden that even if he gave me the go-ahead to write, I wouldn't publish anything unless he approved of the end product.

I waited for an answer.

None came.

I walked and read and meditated and bored myself shitless with Netflix and I kept asking. I attended 187 yoga classes during that first year. Gentle gatherings filled with grandmothers and nature sounds where I mostly stayed hunched in child's pose while tears drew maps of sadness on the sky-blue yoga mat Lyla had given me for Christmas.

I waited for some kind of direction.

Nothing.

I wrote a poem. I wrote a sentence, a paragraph. I filled a page.

Nothing.

When I spent time writing about Holden, I transported myself into a delusion that I imagined was his mind. And while I scribbled words I imagined were his, I felt a jagged anxious crackling between my ribs. It was a feeling I had never experienced before, which made me wonder if this was how he'd felt all the time, as though he were somewhere he didn't belong, a trespasser. My writing was becoming a kind of portal to a place he had never been, a place of my construction, which felt like a corruption. Was it possible to injure him with my thoughts? Was I causing him more pain in order to relieve some of my own? Was I losing my mind?

I felt internal and external resistance to writing publicly about Holden. The idea of breaching his privacy was extremely uncomfortable. He had long before asked me to stop talking about him on the radio. But he wasn't here, and I felt strongly that his story was an important one to tell. As a compromise, I built parameters. I would try to portray only the parts of Holden's life that connected with mine or some mode of witness. I had no idea how to do this.

Perhaps it would have been easier to forget about him altogether. Like soldiers did with the horrors they had witnessed in war. Never mention it, push it down, pretend it didn't happen as a way to survive. Turn sullen and grey. Cry alone.

But that was impossible. Holden's shadow clouded my every waking moment, and some of the non-waking ones, too. His voice spoke inside my head—he would not let me stop.

One day I noticed *The Catcher in the Rye* lying in the corner of our bedroom where it had landed several weeks before. The famous story of the other lost Holden in whom so many readers saw themselves.

I lifted the book from the scuffed hardwood. Where had I left off reading the night that Cam had accused me of torturing myself? I thumbed through the worn pages, past scenes of the Holden Caulfield I could picture so vividly. Holden in his dorm room, Holden riding in a cab across New York City, Holden sitting in a dark bar with some questionable company, Holden trying to ice skate and impress a date at Rockefeller Plaza.

Then I found it, mid-chapter, the place where I had stopped reading that night. Page 151.

And there, resting neatly in the valley of the book, among pages yellowing and dusted with the years, was a single pure-white feather.

12

Holden's trying to sleep in his usual spot at the back of the school bus, his legs stretched out under the seat in front of him. Whenever he's in a moving vehicle for more than ten minutes, he falls asleep. He considers this a superpower, not a problem. The buttons of his school shirt are undone to show off his black Cannibal Corpse T-shirt, and his striped necktie is yanked loose, as it often is, with no regard for symmetry or rules. His school blazer is rolled up and shoved between his head and the window, but the jacket keeps slipping down; every time the bus hits a bump, his head whumps off the glass. His fingers rise to touch the silver ring in his right nostril—blatant disregard for the Laurel Ridge school uniform policy. But not really. Seniors are cut a little slack when it comes to the uniform. He's just finished day three of his final year of high school.

Holden's phone vibrates in the pocket of his itchy grey pants. He wipes the drool off his cheek with the sleeve of his shirt and flips it open.

Yo.

Hey man, it's Michael. I'm having a party tomorrow night. Kind of a back-to-school thing. Can you make it?

I no longer attend your peasant school. Remember?

I'm aware, Michael laughs, but it'd be great to see you, bud. Everybody's going to be there. Just come.

Okay, I'll think about it. Thanks, dude.

Holden and Michael have kept in touch since his mom transferred him to the expensive private high school after it became apparent he was flunking out of Baywater two years ago for not giving a shit. Something about his 31 percent in math—slightly higher in science—and several unexplained absences. Laurel Ridge would help him, as everyone kept fucking repeating, "live up to his potential." And maybe that's true. It appears he's likely to graduate in June.

On Saturday night Holden goes to Michael's party, because what else is he going to do? It's raining too hard to go down to the rail yard and paint. Even he's not that much of a diehard. It's a decent party. Cool to see some of his old friends again. Michael, Cole, and Kyle are easy to be around. They hang out in the kitchen having a few beers. These are the guys Holden grew up with, the ones who came to his Slip 'N Slide birthday, his laser-tag birthday, his Spiderman birthday. They played so many games of road hockey in the garage Cam built that they called it the Garage Hockey League. Even took a team photo that Holden still has on his bookshelf, right between his CD collection and his guitar.

Remember the GHL? Kyle says.

How much freakin' time did we spend out there taking shots on each other? Holden can hear the thwack of a tennis ball against plywood. And now the only shots I take are whiskey, he says. He drains his beer and crushes the can between his hands, making a caveman grunt.

What a beast. Cole laughs, putting his arm around Holden's shoulders. I've missed ya, bud.

I miss you guys, too.

These are the people he belongs with. The ones who are chill and not obsessed with "life planning," like the kids at Laurel who only ever talk about their GPAs, early acceptance, and scholarships. Some of them actually walk around with fucking SAT flashcards.

After a while the music gets cranked, girls dance on the deep-blue carpet in the living room, and Holden spots a bottle of rum among the empty beer cans and red plastic cups on the counter. He grabs the neck of the bottle and takes a long pull. He's not sure where Michael and the crew have gone. Something about beer pong in the basement.

Holden opens the fridge and grabs the first beer he sees. It's not his, but he doesn't care. Beer, pens, and umbrellas are universal property. Holden raises the beer to a large kid with short hair and a tight jewel-green T-shirt that says *Baywater* across the front. This guy has a neck like a telephone pole.

Holden slaps him on his muscled back. Hey, you like Kerouac?

I haven't heard any of their songs. I mostly have country on my iPod, the kid shouts over the music. Are they any good?

The music gets even louder, the lights lower. Girls are dancing with each other in the living room. Holden leans against the counter and scans the swarm of bodies. A circle is forming around Chelsea. It looks like she's about to take off her top, because Chelsea always takes off her top eventually. A huddle of green T-shirts surrounds her. They are all laughing like idiots and chanting.

Take it off, take it off, take it off.

Chelsea is so wasted that she thinks this is flattery, that she's the most original idea to ever happen. Like when girls make out with each other for the guys to watch. He silently thanks Katy Perry for that one. She doesn't understand they are mocking her for their own amusement. She's trying to strut and pose in her bra like a fashion model, but is mostly tripping over her own feet.

Holden hears a low voice shouting, Who's a naughty bird? Work with me, work with me. Dylan's pretending to be a fashion photographer as he snaps shots with his flip phone. They're all killing themselves laughing. Then Holden's pocket vibrates, and he opens his phone to see what's up.

It's from Dylan. A picture of a basically topless Chelsea. Dylan's sending photos to every guy at the party. Holden's mood starts to shift and darken. This is not cool. Why don't any of her friends yank her out of there? They don't even seem to care.

He slides through the crowd and grabs Chelsea's wrist. He puts his arm around her bare shoulders and basically drags her into the bathroom and wraps her in a towel.

What the fuck, Holden! What are you doing? she yells. She has dark rings of makeup under her eyes and sparkles on her cheeks.

Holden doesn't even like Chelsea that much, but he can't help thinking of his sister and how somebody needs to look after these girls, because they don't know how guys are.

You don't understand, he says.

Chelsea shoves him against the door.

Mind your own business, Holden. You think you're so much better than us.

What the fuck, you're welcome.

All he can do is shrug and leave her standing in the bathroom staring into the mirror.

He knows he can be an idiot sometimes, but humans really disappoint him in general. "Better than us?" What did she mean by that?

Whenever he's upset, music helps. He cuts through the crowd dancing in the living room and over to the iPod dock to scroll through Michael's tunes. Pretty horrific list. Bruno Mars, Lady Gaga, and dear god, Ke$ha. Eventually, he finds some Drake, which is not ideal but better than nothing, and taps play. Then he lines up an old Eminem track to go next, the thought of which prevents his head from exploding.

The deep carpet feels spongy under his feet. How many hundreds of hours has he sat on this rug playing video games and Beyblades with Michael?

Holden looks across to the kitchen, where Michael, Cole, and a few others have returned. They're leaning up against the cupboards, talking and laughing. Holden takes a run at it and slides across the kitchen floor in his socks. It's brighter here. He doesn't even bother explaining what just happened. He's sure they all have the pics on their phones anyway, and now Chelsea will never get a good job in her life because her tits are all over Facebook.

After midnight, the music drops from a nine to about a four. Holden helps Michael throw red cups and pizza boxes into a big black garbage bag. He says goodnight to Michael's parents, who've been up in their bedroom the whole time. It's still raining when they funnel out onto the street. Holden stands with Kyle, the quietest of his friends from the road hockey days. Kyle kicks the toe of his sneaker against the curb over and over and over. He's a drummer, so that makes sense. They walk together down the hill toward home, faces angled against the diagonal rain.

Holden shakes his head, and drops of water spray off his hair like a lawn sprinkler. He stumbles sideways. His feet don't meet the road when he thinks they are going to. How much rum did he chug?

Did you get the pics of Chelsea? Kyle asks.

I just delete that shit. Well, first I look, then I delete, Holden says. Fucking Dylan. How will the human race ever advance?

Whoa, someone's been paying attention in biology class at fancy-ass school. Did you get an A in natural selection?

Actually, I got a B-, fuckface.

At the bottom of the hill, under a streetlight, he sees the morphing silhouette of a huddle of bodies. Holden hears laughing and raindrops tapping on the shoulders of football jackets. As they pass the group, Holden gets a whiff of wet leather. Those jackets always smell new.

You think your shit doesn't stink? What are you even doing here?

It's Dylan, of fucking course. The irony is that Dylan doesn't go to Baywater anymore, either. He graduated last year and is apparently in university now. On some bullshit scholarship, probably.

Well, I live here, Holden says, and Michael is my friend, and he invited me to his party. And then, because he can't help himself, he says, What are you doing here, getting some tutoring?

When Holden hears Kyle whisper, Oh snap, he realizes that probably wasn't the best thing to say, but he's drunk enough not to care.

Dylan slurs, Just because your parents are loaded and you can afford to go to that rich snob school, you think you own us? Well, you don't, dickhead.

Holden is about to tell Dylan that his parents aren't rich—they keep telling him they've drained their retirement fund to send him there—when the first blow lands, heavy as a bag of sand against the side of his head. His vision warps into a strange kind of slow-mo. His skin tingles, but his arms won't move the way he wants them to. They hang useless at his sides. He attempts a feeble roundhouse kick he learned in tae kwon do when he was ten. The kick misses Dylan completely. Dylan pounds on his back, on both sides of his head, his ribs. Holden's arms are lifting now, he's able to bear hug Dylan's torso and bury his face in slick leather. One more solid punch in the gut knocks Holden down. Are the boots next? He closes his eyes, pulls his knees up as best as he can.

He hears a car pull up, doors slamming, an engine revs, tires squeal. Then it's quiet. Just Holden curled on the road with raindrops smacking the pavement and blood surging in his ears. He opens his eyes to see Kyle standing over him, looking tragic, not saying anything. It's totally normal for Kyle not to say anything.

He's gonna be sore tomorrow, Holden grunts.

Kyle helps him up. Once Holden's standing, a blast of adrenalin forces its way up his spine and down his arms to his fingertips. He instinctively runs in the direction of his house half a block away. He tries to burst through the yellow front door, but it's locked. His chest and knees slam against the wood, and he bounces back onto the porch.

Kyle is walking toward him across the front lawn. Need a hand?

Really, dude? Like you were so much help.

He sits on the curb under the big trees in front of the Mustard Pot. Pine needles poke through his jeans, pins in his ass. Big raindrops plunk down on him from the branches above, and the fucking street light keeps glowing its fucking hazy moon through the mist.

$$\infty$$

A thud followed by a muffled yell woke me up. Something heavy had slammed against the front door, shaking the exhausted panes of glass. I got up, ran down the stairs, and pulled back the web of lace curtain. I could make out what I thought was Holden and someone else under the trees out by the road. I pulled on my slippers and ran out into the rain.

Holden, is that you? What's going on? I heard a big bang.

Sorry. Couldn't get in. His voice was hoarse.

Oh Holden, what did you do with your key this time? I squatted down to better see him in the dark. He stared down at the road. It's pouring rain, come inside and get to bed. Hang on, are you drunk? Wait, are you crying? Oh my god, are you hurt?

Kyle shifted nervously from one foot to the other. I turned to him.

Please tell me what happened here.

I don't really know. Sorry, I gotta go. I'll call you tomorrow, bud.

Kyle turned and walked away. His footsteps flittered on the wet pavement in an even, diminishing rhythm.

Okay, what happened? I placed my hands on Holden's knees. He shuddered and shook his head. Rain mixed with tears on his face. I could tell he was very upset; his knees were jackhammering. His breathing came in jagged gasps.

I urged him to come inside, but he wouldn't move. Cold rain ran down the back of my neck. His, too, I supposed. I shifted to sit beside him with an arm across his shoulders. The neighbourhood was silent. Not even the hum of cars up on the highway. We sat.

I'm freezing, can we please go in now?

I helped him stand and guided him up the stairs and through the yellow door. The warmth inside was a relief, and the old house smell that normally annoyed me seemed comforting.

I hugged him until he pulled away.

Are you hungry? Can I make you something?

No thanks, Momz, I'm just going to go to bed.

Good idea, I'll make you some pancakes in the morning. I love you.

Night. Love you, too.

∞

Holden thumps down the creaky wooden staircase to his room in the basement. He takes in the unfinished walls, low ceiling, and cement floor. Yeah, he's such a rich kid. But there's no reason to fix anything up because they're going to tear this house down and build a new one. That's what the parentals have been saying for years, anyway.

Holden drops onto the end of his bed. The night replays in his head, even though he doesn't want it to. Shotgunning beers, downing rum, the whole weirdness with Chelsea—so much for chivalry. The kitchen party. Maybe some comments were made, maybe he was drunker than he thought, maybe he still is. Though he's completely still, the inside of his body rocks and sways like he just got home from a sailing trip.

It's so fucking frustrating to not belong anywhere completely. Not the old school, not the new one. Not the old friends, not the new ones. Not the jocks, not the band geeks, not the goth metalheads, although they have the best weed. Not at this house, or at Dad's apartment downtown. He's always moving back and forth. Always getting shit from one side or the other. People are always judging him and telling him what to do. Always.

Holden looks into the mirror on the wall. Snot runs from his nose like two viscous worms, and his eyes are bloodshot. His lip is swollen, there's a big bruise on his cheekbone, and the sleeve of his favourite sweatshirt is nearly ripped right off.

Looking good. He gives himself a thumbs-up in the mirror.

On the shelf Cam made for him, the blue one that perfectly fits all of his CDs and books and his CD player and the aquarium that used to be full of water before he forgot to feed the fish and they all died, Holden sees the jackknife Grandpa bought for him.

For Holden's seventeenth birthday, Grandpa had taken him to a photography workshop, and then they went to Mountain Equipment Co-op, which is Grandpa's favourite store because it's full of outdoorsy stuff like snowshoes and kayaks. Grandpa really wanted to buy Holden a bike helmet.

I will never wear a bike helmet, Gramps, Holden had said, and Grandpa seemed confused. Just for kicks, Holden pointed at the biggest knife in the glass case where they kept the compasses and underwater watches. But I'd love that bad boy, he said.

Grandpa didn't flinch. We'll take that one, please, he said to the clerk, and he seemed to be smirking. Holden couldn't believe it.

The knife has a long blade and a camouflage handle. It's probably for skinning a deer. He didn't even show the knife to his mom for a month because he thought she'd take it away for sure, like she did when she found his big glass bong and his stash. But to Holden's shock, she said he could keep the knife if he promised to be very careful and never take it out of the house, which is probably a good general philosophy, because if he'd had that blade with him tonight, he might have taken it out and made sushi out of that big dumb shit, Dylan.

Dylan. The fight. Holden relives the strikes, re-smells the leather, and again the cold rain seeps into his clothes as he lies on the road. The car speeds away. Again, rage thumps in his temples. Again, a churning, pulsing pressure inside Holden's chest cavity. The knife is in his hand. He opens it just to see the huge blade. It clatters to the floor. Fuck. Holden leans over to pick up the knife and smashes his head on the corner of the shelves, in the same place Dylan hit him. Fucking fuck. He grabs the knife handle, stands up quickly, and stabs it as hard he can into the wall beside his sputtering reflection in the mirror.

The pain is instant and searing. So penetrating it shocks Holden into alertness. The tip of the knife is stuck into the wall and a fine red line is rising diagonally across his fingers. He sits down on the end of his bed and stares at his palm. Blood begins to flow from deep cuts across each finger, warm and wet. Large drops of deep red grow bigger and bigger on the white carpet with the black swirls. Holden watches the thick viscosity of his own blood. The floor starts to look like a Jackson Pollock painting.

$$\infty$$

Drifting off for the second time, I heard another thump and another shout. I went to the kitchen, opened his door, and called down to Holden in the basement.

Hey, are you okay? I heard more banging.

It's okay, I just cut my finger, I'm gonna put a Band-Aid on it and go to sleep.

The timbre of his voice wasn't right. He sounded resigned, as if he'd given up on something.

Cut yourself? What do you mean? I switched on the lightbulb that hung over the stairs and went down to his room. Blood was streaming from his hand, pouring onto the carpet. So much blood. An adrenalin tide surged. What happened here?

I don't know. The knife slipped, I think.

His eyelids were half closed, his head at half-mast.

That stupid knife. Where are your shoes?

I'm sorry, Mom. I don't. I don't know what happened.

I pulled him up the stairs. In the kitchen, I reached for a clean tea towel and wrapped it tightly around his hand.

Cam had just returned home from a sixteen-hour day volunteering as a mechanic at a mountain bike race and was sleeping soundly. I yelled up the stairs to him. Hey, can you start the car, Holden's hurt. We're going to Emergency!

I wedged Holden's wet shoes onto his wet feet while blood continued to drip from his fingers across the pale-yellow kitchen floor.

13

Shorter, heavier days tempered the light filtering through the chestnut tree outside our bedroom window. Delicate moss green diluted to a muted grey. The low sky brooded, and so did I. Dampness plumped the air. I was bored of lying in bed, and Holden wasn't coming back voluntarily, so I had no choice but to get up and search for him. I needed to sniff the ground where his scent was still warm, go to the places he'd gone, talk to people he'd talked to, listen to his music.

It wouldn't be the first time I'd gone out looking for him on a cold, wet night and brought him home.

On some level, I understood that my behaviour could be considered unusual. I didn't care. I remembered hearing about pregnant women eating dirt. Motherhood can make us savage. I was willing to think crazy, wade into crazy, be crazy to reach back, or down, or through and touch him.

I became a detective. Retracing Holden's steps, investigating the places I imagined would offer me new details about him. Beaches, lakes, government offices, darkened nightclubs, greasy back alleys. I knew it was impossible to outrun my own shadow, but could it be possible to grab a corner of his and pull?

I drove to East Vancouver, to the first basement apartment he'd shared with a couple of co-workers from Hysteria, a clothing and tattoo shop on Granville Street. I had thought this basement suite with the filthy kitchen floor would be an opportunity for him to learn some practical life skills, some independence and momentum, but instead it had cut the lines and set him adrift.

In the lane behind the house, my tires skidded on gravel, and the car clunked into a pothole. This was where I helped him unload his bed and his laundry basket. This was where I handed him his reading lamp and warned him not to burn candles in his windowless bedroom. This was where I deceived myself about the real danger. Candles were not the issue.

The tall, narrow house looked even more pathetic than I remembered. As if the rotten wall shingles could blow off in a moderate wind, leaving it naked. How could I have left him here? I was angry at a house.

I climbed out of the car and gathered my scarf closer around my neck. A low-rise apartment building stood across the alley, its balconies filled with rusted barbecues, broken children's toys, ripped tarps, and empty bottles. Beside it, a dark-green Dumpster covered in graffiti leaned up against the cinderblock fence. Could his fingers have touched this metal? None of the tags looked familiar, but I always had to check. To me, they were footprints in melting snow. I took photos of all the tags that bore any resemblance to his style, just in case. The language was so cryptic that I could never be sure. I texted the pictures to Luke, who could tell me whether Holden had done them or not.

Nope. That's another guy.

Nope, that's just ugly.

Yup, that's Sef Daddy!

At the end of the lane, an open lawn invited me closer. I walked across the dormant grass and through a stand of skeletal trees. Wet wind whipped my hair, and strands stuck to my face. I moved, not knowing why, toward a large divot in the distance. This was the park Holden had told me about, the place he had gone to lie on the grass and look up through the branches at the sky.

Just chillin' in the park, he'd texted, and I imagined him lying there, swaths of clover surrounding him, bees circling low over the ground, painting patterns—buzz here, buzz there, and gone. I imagined him happy in his body.

Deserted benches, swings, and a slide stood waiting for children and a drier day. I was drawn toward the concrete indentation of the skatepark with its pools and troughs and always toward the graffiti. I walked to the edge of the largest bowl and stopped. A blast of colour against the grey concrete shocked my frailty. The electric current in my chest and arms increased its wattage. I began to process what the bold letters and swirling words of the graffiti were shouting.

Holden. RIP.

Sefer Forever.

Holden.

Deser.

RIP HOLDEN.

Red, blue, purple, white, black.

I fell to my knees on the cold wet ground, and a rush of sobs gushed from my throat. He'd been here. This place was so significant to Holden that his friends had returned to inscribe his name. His real name— because now he could not be arrested.

I knelt on the grass and wept. Mud oozed between my fingers, soaking the knees of my jeans. With a rampage inside my chest and tears streaming, I scanned the jumble of modern-day hieroglyphics.

And then, there was Holden, gliding over the undulations of concrete on his skateboard, big shoes, clothes hanging loose, his eyes clear, the curve of his cheekbones lifted in a smile. There he was, young and happy with his *Skateboarding Is Not a Crime* T-shirt fluttering, his blond hair poking out from under his helmet.

The downpour drew its pattern on my back.

Leaves fell from the tired chestnut tree, grey-green lichen crawled along her branches, and the rain never stopped. Shallow pools reflected silver clouds across our driveway. A constant dripping thrummed outside our bedroom window where the gutter had come away from the roof on the day, a few months back, I'd yanked the Christmas lights down and left them in a tangle on the front lawn, spitting, I fucking hate fucking Christmas. Christmas lights were for happy times. For family.

Five of Holden's T-shirts lay in my bottom drawer. I slid it open and ironed my hand over the white shirt, now stained yellow under the armpits, with the image of Fidel Castro smoking a cigar. I pressed the soft cotton to my face and breathed deeply. It must have been washed since he'd last worn it, but I was sure I smelled him between the threads. I took off my own faded T-shirt and pulled his over my head. I looked at my reflection in the mirror and saw his face, not mine, rising from its neckline.

He is hours into sixteen, no real sign of trouble. No loud bells ringing. We are in New York scouring the street markets in Soho. We are riding the steaming subway late at night. We are running for a cab in the rain. We are slowly wandering the airy white-walled rooms of the MoMA, and he is standing there, feet planted, staring at a large geometric painting, rubbing his chin with his thumb. He is holding a burger in both of his hands, and the juice is dripping onto his plate. His face is gentle, his hair thick, soft, and shining like metal in the July sun of 5th Avenue. The dark shadow of brand-new whiskers spreads across his upper lip. His hand is in mine, and we are walking through Central Park singing John Lennon songs.

During the dark empty hours, all I could see was the lighthouse of my mistakes flashing error, error, error. I relived every parental wrong I had committed. None of the rights. The rights didn't count for anything, because my child had died, and the most basic job description of any parent is to keep them alive. All I could hold was the litany of faults I had committed. The times Holden and I slapped up against each other and bounced farther apart. The moments of impact when I couldn't find the right words for what my heart wanted to say. The impatience, the assumptions, the anger. The distance, both physical and emotional.

But the biggest one was the hardest to bear. I would never forgive myself for missing the last year of his life. This shame covered me in a second odious skin. Shame is pride turned inside out.

I wanted to collect all of my mistakes in a huge fishing net, haul them up onto shore, and burn them. I'd know better now. I'd be more resilient, ask more questions, insist on answers. I'd stay close. I'd be kinder. Hindsight can be a motherfucker.

This can't go on, Cam had said after one of the more volatile fights with Holden. He'd brought a group of loud friends and a Tupperware salad bowl full of pot into the house late one Wednesday night. When I screamed at him that he couldn't have drugs in the house and didn't he care about what he was teaching his little sister, he'd pushed his stoned and belly-laughing friends into his closet, shut the door, and grinned at me.

He's making you into a wreck. He needs consequences, Cam had said. I didn't know what to do, and that indecision paralyzed me. Infuriated and helpless, I felt squeezed between my son and my husband. When would we cross through the turbulent river of parenting and land safely onto the far shore of camaraderie? When could I simply be his friend?

At the epicentre of the power struggle, around the time Holden was finishing high school and at his most eye-rolling and insolent, my hair fell out in thick clumps, and I broke out in an angry pattern of hives. Red welts bloomed in my armpits, across my stomach, and up my shins. I would claw at my legs all night, as though I'd walked through stinging nettles, then get up at 3:00 a.m. and drive downtown to the radio station, where I performed public cheerfulness for a living.

Eventually, Holden went to live full-time with his father.

I kept seeing my son's body and the markings on it. The indelible map of his journey through time, and the intersections significant enough that he chose to emboss evidence of them under his skin.

What about a tattoo, is that a stupid grief cliché? I said to Laureen, the oldest of my three sisters, when she called one evening. I've been thinking of getting a replica of something he had.

It's not stupid at all. It's symbolic. I'll get one with you, she said. I've been considering getting one of Holden's graffiti pieces on my foot.

Then I'm descending the stairs to his bedroom, cupping my hand over the meaty muscle of his deltoid, gently rocking him back and forth.

Good morning, love. Time for school. He rolls toward me, shirtless, blinking. And there above his right nipple, in inch-high black, fluid script: *us and them.*

What's this? I point, surprised.

Oh yeah, I got a tattoo.

I see that, I sputter. When?

A while ago.

Well, let me have a good look at it, then. Us and them. Do you mean, like, Pink Floyd "Us and Them"?

Sort of. And just, people who are with me and the ones who are against me.

I hoped I was *us*, and wondered at times if I was *them.*

I closed my eyes and again witnessed his body evolving from sixteen to twenty-one, thickening, distilling, hair growing like dark grass in the cracks and divots, moss in the hidden places. Muscle. I saw the classic Sailor Jerry–style schooner in full sail on the tender skin of his inner arm, a flower blooming across his outer forearm, scrawled text on his thigh dripping black blood down over his kneecap. A dagger pierced the flesh of his bicep. An hourglass, and a circle of recently pulled bloody teeth surrounding a pair of pliers, the kind barroom dentists with whiskey anesthetic would have used to yank a rotten molar. Words, too, in a stylized font: *You're born, you do shit, you die.*

Another fight had erupted when I first saw that one on his arm.

Really, Holden, you're born, you do shit, you die? How completely ridiculous. I thought you were more articulate than that. Do you really think you're going to be happy with You're born, you do shit, you die on your body when you're forty?

I'm happy with it now, he said faintly, before leaving the room.

I never asked him what it meant to him.

I opened my eyes, looked over at Holden's framed photo propped on my desk, and attempted to gauge his expression. It was the last photograph I had of him. We had taken it together a week before his death, standing in the kitchen. What had I missed in those eyes? What were you thinking, Holden? What did you want the world to know about you? You're born, you do shit, you die?

I opened my laptop, typed in the words, and hit return. Instantly, several site descriptions stacked in a tall column on the screen, each referring to Agorophobic Nosebleed, a heavy metal band with many YouTube videos. Holden's tattoo was not a life philosophy, necessarily— it was lyrics.

I clicked on one of the links. The song was called "Druggernaut Jug Fuck." Charming. I winced at the images on the band's album covers. Cartoon renderings of skeletons, faces contorted in agony, bare-breasted women bound with ropes and chains.

I clicked another link and began reading the lyrics.

Fuck burning a church
Let's burn down schools and wildlife preserves
Killed a baby bear with a hunting knife
You're born. You do shit. You die

My breath came in barbed sips. The skin of my face contracted. Why would Holden have wanted these horrifying words, relating to more horrific images, engraved on his body? He was not an abusive person. Violent at times, but never toward women. That I knew of. I thought he respected women. He had a sister. This revelation didn't make any sense. A cold sensation twisted low in my abdomen.

I searched the band's name to try to find out more about them. Wikipedia told me that Agoraphobic Nosebleed (or ANb) was a drum-machine grindcore band from Springfield, Massachusetts, formed in 1994. "The band is known for the brevity of its songs. The album *Altered States of America* features 100 songs (including one hidden) in just under 22 minutes, with many songs of 5 seconds or less, and the longest song being only 1:45."

Songs under five seconds?

Alarmed, a little nauseated, and suddenly very curious, I clicked on the band's Facebook page. I needed to understand why this music was attractive enough to Holden that he would tattoo the lyrics on his arm. I decided to contact the band.

> Weird message for you. My son had a tattoo that said, "You're born, you do shit, you die." I never realized what it was until now. He passed away recently, and I am trying to learn as much as I can about him. Can you please tell me about your band and what the lyrics of that song in particular might mean to your fans?

The next afternoon I received a reply:

Not a weird message at all. Thanks for getting in touch. The
answer might be a little strange, however. A lot of our band's lyrics
and imagery could be described as satire (see Jonathan Swift's
A Modest Proposal), somewhat offensive for the sake of being
coarse, which is somewhat in line with the aesthetic of the music
itself. I'm quite sure your son was aware of this and not taking any
of our lyrics or artwork at face value, but rather enjoying
their absurdity. It's all a bit juvenile and puerile, but it's fun and
energetic. That's just the best way I can explain it.

We hope we gave him some happiness. Sorry for your loss.
And any further questions, please feel free to ask.

Scott/ANb

Scott Hull was the band's guitarist. He seemed very polite and
well-spoken for a man with another band called Anal Cunt.
I wrote back:

I appreciate your response. I'm pretty sure Holden would have
been aware of the satirical nature of your music. He was brilliant,
but also self-destructive at times. His favourite poem was "Howl"
by Allen Ginsberg, if that gives you an insight. He died of an
overdose. It was an accident. Naturally, we are broken-hearted.
I'm following all the clues I can find.

Thanks for your openness. I'm sure you gave him a bit
of amusement or maybe even happiness, who knows?

I'm going to read *A Modest Proposal*.

He replied:

"Howl" was my favourite as a youngster, too. Alongside *Naked Lunch* by WSB. Good luck on your journey. Please get back in touch if we can help. ☺

I called several shops to see if Holden had been tattooed at any of them. I asked around and found out that he had some artist friends he had met through his job at Hysteria who would do his ink for beer. Not a surprising arrangement. I connected with a few tattoo artists I saw on his Facebook page, but none of them remembered doing the scroll on his arm that I was wondering about. The word ran from his elbow to his wrist in an inverted orientation so he could read it clearly when he looked in the mirror: *courage*.

I wanted to take something Holden had had on his flesh and engrave it on mine. I wanted to archive the story of his skin and its markings onto my skin, as though a writer could begin a sentence on his body and finish it on mine.

A young woman answered the phone at the Window. I heard a softness behind her voice.

Could you tell me if my son had any work done there?

We can't really release that information, I'm sorry, she said.

I understand. It's just that, I'm his mom, and he died … I started to cry. And I really want something the same as he had. As a tribute.

I'm not supposed to, but hang on a second, I'll check for you.

Holden's name was on record. She couldn't tell me exactly what image he'd had done, but said the amount he'd paid indicated it was likely something simple. Maybe a line drawing or script, which was exactly what I was looking for. I made an appointment.

Thanksgiving weekend, Laureen and I walked in the rain down the cold sidewalk of Seymour Street. Above us, graffiti pulsed from the walls.

We both wore flip-flops, as if we were on our way to get pedicures, not permanent markings.

Inside the tattoo shop, the ceiling was crisscrossed with pipes and air vents. Black everything. Loud music. Holden had been here, he had stood on this concrete floor and thought about what he wanted inscribed on his arm. A strange vibration began flowing through my limbs, a low-grade motorized current. If this buzzing feeling were a colour, I'd have said it was traffic-cone orange. My legs began to shake. I scanned the lobby for a place to sit down.

My sister and I took a seat on the retro leather couch. We flipped through binders full of images—headless, naked body parts scratched with ink on every page. Leafing through pages was easier than looking into each other's eyes or talking about why we were there.

When Holden died, our families did their best to console and hold us. A most difficult job. I'll always remember Laureen, after driving eight hours from her town with my two other siblings, crawling into bed with me and saying, This is not your fault, he was only trying to feel better.

How's it going, guys? I'm Stin.

The tattoo artist dropped into a deep lounge chair and leaned back. He was large, yet somehow delicate at the same time, and thoroughly decorated, with a salmon swimming across his forehead just above his eyebrow, tribal markings on his temple, and a warrior in profile on the side of his neck. I was impressed with his level of commitment.

Stin's manner was professional. He fanned out a few sheets of paper on the coffee table. His fingers were loaded down with silver skulls and antlers, his ear lobes stretched wide with the same kind of plugs Holden had worn for a while. I remembered telling him his ears were going to look like cat sphincters, a memory that oddly made me smirk.

I made some stencils based on the photos you sent me, Stin said. What do you think?

Can you tell me about your name? I asked. Stin, it's interesting.

Justin's my name, I just chopped it up.

Laureen leaned forward, elbows on parted knees, surveying the samples. She held herself royally and considered her options.

This is the one, she said, dragging an image toward herself with a fingertip. It was a replica of one of Holden's graffiti pieces. I had taken the photo myself shortly after his death, standing with his friend Luke in the blackberry brambles at the back of our local grocery store, when I was frantic to preserve any visual evidence of Holden's existence.

For me there was looping cursive. Stin had replicated the script I had sent him and printed *Holden* in different sizes. I chose a sample and held it against the top of my bare foot. Did I want to see his name every time I put on socks? Every time I went to the beach, or did a downward dog?

Perfect, I said.

We followed Stin up the stairs to the loft area, where padded massage tables stood in a row. Laureen went first. I tried to distract her, but I wasn't much help. I disappeared into my own thoughts of Holden lying on one of these tables.

How are you doing? I asked her two hours later.

It really fucking hurts, she said, her hands balled into fists.

Yes, I agreed. It does.

By the time her tattoo was complete, my sister had wet streaks lining her smooth face. And on the top of her foot, a replica of Holden's graffiti was permanently engraved. SEFER in silver, outlined with yellow and black, against a grey cinderblock background.

All done, Stin said. Be right back.

Thank you for doing this, it means a lot to me, I said to my sister.

It means a lot to me, too, she said. It's really cool, isn't it?

We hugged each other.

You ready? Stin was back at his workstation already, trimming the stencil with small surgical scissors.

My shoulders shuddered silently. Holden had been here, but now I didn't want to be. Not for this reason. A pulsing pressure knocked against the inside of my sternum. It would have been easy to vomit. I climbed up onto the table, and he held the word Holden over my bare right foot, trying out different angles.

How about like this? He lined the letters up along the sharp crest of bone.

Sure. I lay back on the table.

This area can be quite painful, he said. Not much flesh.

Laureen gripped my hand like a birth coach.

Stin began injecting ink under my skin, and I closed my eyes.

The sensation was unlike any pain I had ever felt. Different from a broken bone or a migraine or labour pains. Not really a pain at all. The throbbing ache behind my heart was far more painful than anything physically happening to my foot. Instead, a searing heat pricked into my core. I envisioned an ancient craftsman in a leather apron gouging worms of writhing putty from clay. A sculptor with hammer and chisel. Granite. I would be the gravestone he'd never have. His name etched onto the ridge of my foot would proclaim, Holden. Holden. Holden. He existed. He mattered to me. He was once inside my body.

I thought of all the tattoos Holden had inked into his flesh, the beautiful ones and the ones I didn't understand—what they may have meant to him, the significance they held.

And then my body was gone. I flew through time. I was feeling what Holden had felt. Experiencing what he had experienced. The burn and sting. Perhaps on this very table. Doing what he'd done where he had done it. We were together. For that fleeting moment, the curtain between us dropped and we were joined, fused in an ethereal arc.

There was no table, no sister, no ceiling. There was only the shimmering energy at the tip of a needle. What is, melding with what was.

14

It's actually kind of awesome how much blood one little towel can absorb. By the time Holden and his mom get to the hospital—usually a ten-minute drive, but they get there in like six because it's 3:00 a.m. and she's blowing through intersections like they're rollin' in a fire truck—the entire cloth is plump with brilliance.

That's me, he thinks. I am full of red. I am spilling out into the world. I'm all over the freakin' place. I could fill a sink. If I was a shade of paint, the label on the top of my can would say *Red All About It.*

Keep pressure on it!

Her voice arrives to him like she's at the other end of the tunnel under the highway, yelling.

And try not to drip on the seat. Jesus.

She pulls up and stops in front of a *NO PARKING* sign right by the front door, where the ambulances go, then runs around the hood of the car and pulls his door open. She guides him by his elbow up onto the curb as if he's a blind man or something. The waiting room is empty and museum quiet. They walk together up to the desk, and Holden feels the tightness of his mother's grip on his arm. Her vibration.

My son cut his hand quite badly, it's really bleeding a lot, what should we do?

This voice has a texture he doesn't recognize as hers. Is it anger or confusion? The intake nurse takes a look at the blood-soaked towel and glances back down to her clipboard. She asks for his medical card, and his mom fishes it out of her wallet.

Have a seat. The nurse dismisses them with a flick of her fingers toward the line of beige plastic chairs against the wall. Holden lowers himself with a thud into one of the bucket seats, and finally his mother lets go of his bicep.

How many people have died sitting in these chairs? How many people have puked and worried and writhed in pain and prayed and made deals with god or the devil right here in this chair, the third from the end?

They sit side by side, staring at the exit doors, saying nothing. Holden cradles his arm in his lap, closes his eyes, leans his head back to rest against the wall.

Don't you dare go to sleep.

The words come shooting like spit directly into his ear. Now that he can hear it clearly, he recognizes the unfamiliar texture in her voice. It's fear. She is afraid. She is terrified.

Wait, should I be afraid?

∞

Holden was still wearing his wet jeans and sweatshirt from the party. And the fight. He shivered but didn't say anything about being cold. A different nurse came out through the swinging doors, this one smiling and dressed entirely in purple. Her plastic name tag said *Jennifer*, with strawberry stickers on the corners that were almost completely rubbed off. Jennifer's tired face suggested she'd rather not be working the night shift, but maybe it gave her more days off to be with her kids.

This way, you two. She led us along the red line on the floor, down a shining hallway and into an alcove. She helped Holden up onto the bed and stood directly in front of him with her hands on his thighs. His injured hand a cherry-red mummy suspended in the air between them.

William, can you tell me what happened?

Holden laughed in spite of the situation, because this always happened when he went anywhere new.

It's Holden, he corrected her. I go by my middle name.

The William was after his father, and his father's father, and on down the line, but nobody ever used the name. It was more of an heirloom—sticking out in front like a hood ornament.

Okay then, Holden, what happened?

I don't know, exactly.

Give it a try. Jennifer cocked a hip. She was losing her patience.

I guess I tried to stab the knife into the wall. I think maybe I had it upside down, and my hand slipped down the blade or something. Could I have some water, please?

Not until after the doctor sees you. In case you need surgery.

His eyes bulged. Surgery?

Just lie down and relax. He'll be in to see you in a minute.

She pulled the curtain around us, a flimsy blue cocoon. Her footsteps faded down the hall.

How many drinks did you have?

Just a few beers. Maybe four?

That means at least eight, doesn't it? Just tell me the truth, Holden. It's important that they know exactly how much alcohol you've had. In case they need to operate.

I don't need surgery, what I need is a couple of Band-Aids, a glass of water, and a Tylenol. My head is killing me.

You're not exactly the expert here.

We waited. From somewhere down the hall came a robotic pinging. Rhythmic, like a steady heartbeat. I realized that the sound *was* someone's heartbeat. Holden's lips took on a bluish tinge, just like when he was a kid and would refuse to come out of the ocean. His teeth jittered against each other.

I'll be right back, I said, and went to find him a blanket.

Here, honey. Careful not to disturb the juicy red swaddle resting on his stomach, I covered him in layers of soft, warm blankets and tucked the edges tight around his legs and feet. I took in his sticky-sour breath. That's better, I said. You were shivering. Your jeans are wet.

As if the warmth loosened something inside him, plump tears filled his eyes and flowed down the sides of his face.

Mom, he said softly, I'm sorry. I'm such an idiot. He turned toward the wall and whispered, Will I ever be able to paint again?

I pressed my fingers across the centre of his chest and smiled as much as my fatigue would let me.

I'm sure you will. Your hand may look a bit nasty for a while, but you'll be fine.

I had no idea whether I was telling the truth.

A zing of metal rings against the track overhead, and a man in pond-green scrubs with a thick unibrow and a stethoscope around his neck stepped in, carrying the smell of coffee and soap with him. His tight demeanour suggested he wasn't in the best mood.

Hey Doc, 'sup? Holden said.

The doctor sighed. Let's take a look at your hand, William.

It's Holden, I said this time, he goes by his middle name.

He unwrapped Holden's hand, and we all got a good look at the damage for the first time. The bleeding had stopped. His fingers were pale and wrinkled, as though they'd been submerged in water for hours. One line slashed a deep, gaping gash across the bases of three of his fingers and his thumb.

The doctor laid Holden's hand palm up on a metal side table.

Make a fist.

The muscles of Holden's arm tensed, but the only finger that moved at all was the smallest one. The rest of his hand just lay there, a cold dead fish on a plate.

Hmm, was all the doctor said.

What does that mean? I asked.

The doctor met my gaze with a grim yet dispassionate expression.

Hard to tell at this point—probably ligament and nerve damage. It's beyond what I can do here. You'll have to contact the plastic surgeon on call, he said, as if we were inconveniencing him. I can't say what use you'll have, but I'll stitch you up for now, William. The doctor sidestepped through the gap in the curtain and disappeared.

It's Holden, we both said in unison to the squeak of his running shoes retreating down the hall.

Well, he's a treat. I looked to Holden, trying to reassure him.

What an asswipe.

Careful, he's in charge of the freezing.

He doesn't have to be such a prick about it.

By the time we pulled into our driveway under the big Douglas firs, daylight was leaking in. All Holden could say was, Finally, I can drink some water.

In the kitchen, he used his left hand to awkwardly fill a glass, downed it while the water ran colder, then filled it again. He turned to see me watching him, set the glass down on the pale-yellow counter, and wrapped his left arm around me, pulling me close and holding his bandaged right hand up high.

The hug said, *I'm sorry, I don't know what I'm doing. I don't know how this happened. I'm embarrassed, I'm confused, I don't know how to say what I don't know how to say.*

I rubbed his back. Then I held him at arm's length and looked directly into his eyes. Exhausted eyes that pleaded for forgiveness.

I doubt you'll ever do that again. And we laughed. I love you.

∞

There's a lot of blood on the stairs, the walls, and especially the carpet in his bedroom. He's actually alarmed by how much blood. A crime scene amount. Who died? Only the use of his right hand and any shot he ever had at being an artist. Not to mention tying his shoes, eating with a fork, playing guitar, jerking off.

The dickwad who beat him up has probably been snoring for at least six hours.

He somehow gets out of his jeans, slips into bed, and pulls the quilt up over his chest. The freezing is starting to wear off. Blood pumps through his fingers, throbbing, and behind that a burning sensation. He looks at his bandaged hand and, just like that prince of a doctor did earlier, asks it to make a fist. Once again, all that moves is the thumb—a little bit—and the pinky finger. The other three fingers couldn't give a shit.

On the border of sleep and awake, he's already dreaming. Dreaming about painting. He's standing in front of a big cinderblock wall wearing a respirator, holding a can. But his grip is weird. His hand feels strange, twisted at an awkward angle. He's pressing the cap down with his thumb instead of his finger, and flames are igniting the wall.

∞

A doctor friend of mine did some digging and found out that one of the best hand surgeons in town was on call that day at St. Paul's Hospital downtown. I woke Holden midmorning, made him a bagel with peanut butter, and helped him brush his teeth. We walked together out to the car. He didn't say much.

We drove across the Lions Gate Bridge to our second hospital in twenty-four hours, where we sat again in plastic chairs lined against beige walls under stark lighting, staring at coloured stripes on the floor. We were told Dr. Martin, the plastic surgeon, was there, but he would be in surgery for a few hours, possibly more.

We'll wait, I said.

Holden slumped. Can't we just come back later?

Your right hand is very important to the quality of your life. This guy is apparently the best. We are going to wait for however long it takes.

At least fifteen plastic shopping bags surrounded the woman sitting across from us, not counting the ones socking both her feet. Her smell was a powerful mix of urine and perfume. She searched through one of the bags, talking under her breath—something about legislation.

Two paramedics rushed past pushing a gurney with an unconscious patient and burst through the swinging doors into the inner sanctum of the ER.

Many fast-moving stretchers and many life-or-death situations later, a tall, thin man emerged from the doors and called across the waiting room.

William?

Right here! He goes by Holden, I said, before Holden, asleep on my shoulder, could even fire up a thought.

Dr. Martin's running shoes looked like they had just come out of the box, and his skin was almost as white as his shoes. Someone hadn't spent much time outside this summer. He walked toward us and sat down beside Holden. I'd never seen the hands of a concert pianist, but I imagined they would look exactly like the doctor's hands. Delicate, yet capable. Intelligent, refined hands.

Hi, Holden, I'm Dr. Martin. How are you feeling? Already so much more humane than the ER doctor at our local hospital.

Holden shrugged. All right, I guess. His voice frayed and deep. I knew that "all right" was what Holden said when he was absolutely not all right, but didn't want to get into it.

I hear you had a bit of a tangle with a sharp object. There was no blame in Dr. Martin's voice, no judgment. He spoke directly to Holden. I trusted his face.

Holden nodded. You could say that.

Come on in. Let's have a look.

The doctor led us through the double doors into an examining room. He washed his hands, and the now familiar smell of antiseptic soap filled the air. He pulled on white gloves, sat on a low rolling stool, and pushed himself close to Holden.

Strips of bandage soon piled up on the table, crusted with blood the colour of eggplant and wet clay. Under the spotlight, Holden's skin was whiter than the doctor's—puckered and zigzagged with crude stitching reminiscent of Halloween costumes. Deep-purple patches mottled his shrivelled fingers, reminding me of the bruised slugs in the garden we'd poison with salt so they wouldn't eat the hostas.

Three of Holden's fingers were cut through to the bone, the thumb not as badly. The doctor put on a pair of thick futuristic glasses and asked Holden to move each finger by pointing at it with a thin metal prod. Only the smallest finger did what it was told. The doctor pricked Holden's palm in different places with the metal stick, which made him flinch, but still no movement in his fingers.

When did this happen, exactly?

Last night, Holden said.

About 1:30 a.m., I added. How long do we have for reattachment?

At the word reattachment, Holden's eyebrows lifted and his eyes glistened.

As long as we get you put back together within forty-eight hours, things should be okay. The doctor looked directly into my eyes, his face impassive. Let's get him booked in for first thing tomorrow morning.

Thank you very much, Doctor.

Are you right-handed, son?

Yup.

And how old are you?

Seventeen.

I'd say your right hand is going to be pretty important to you, so we'll do the very best we can. They'll give you instructions at the front.

He smiled, swivelled on his stool, peeled off his gloves with a snap, and left the room.

∞

Before the surgery, Holden stays at his dad's, because his mom has to work in the morning. It's "fall ratings" at the radio station and she *has* to be there or apparently an asteroid will strike the earth. When Dad arrives to pick Holden up, Mom makes him promise to text her with any and all updates. On the front lawn, she hugs Holden way too tight for a long time.

I love you. Everything's going to be just fine. I'll be there when you wake up.

Holden and his dad spend the evening watching movies, drinking iced tea, and eating KFC.

It's one-handed food, Dad says. A burger is definitely two-handed food. Pizza is debatable.

Jeez, you thought of everything, Paps.

Why yes I did, boyo, yes I did. His dad hits play on the remote, and the opening credits of Mel Brooks's *Young Frankenstein* flash up on the screen. Soon his dad starts laughing—big and rumbling. Holden joins in. They both giggle so much that they have to pause the movie. They've stacked up a tower of pillows, and if Holden props himself up just high enough, he can see the ocean over the rooftops of other apartment buildings. His dad calls this the Crow's Nest.

In the morning Dad gently shakes him awake and helps him dress. The sky is a soft sunflower yellow as they drive up Davie Street. At the hospital, Holden is given a flimsy gown to wear. Dad has to help him tie the strings in the back.

I see London, I see France, but I don't see any underpants. Dad pokes a cold finger between Holden's butt cheeks.

Jeebus, Dad! Holden jumps, and they both laugh until there are tears in their eyes. Holden gets into the bed, and his dad takes a picture of him smiling with one cheek, giving a thumbs-up with his functioning left hand. Dad sends the photo to his mom just as a nurse comes into the room carrying a clipboard. She confirms his name and birthdate, then takes his temperature and blood pressure.

You're here for his tonsils, right? Always the jokes with Dad.

Exactly, she says, and looks to Holden. Ready to roll?

I love you, boy. Dad clamps one strong hand on Holden's shoulder and gives him a soft shake. Sweet dreams, laddy, he says in his fake Scottish accent.

Catch ya on the flip side, Holden says as the nurse rolls the bed out the door. Fluorescent lights flash above him like a string of lightsabers as they travel down the hall. He can hear his father's deep baritone receding—Bye Holden, bye Holden, bye Holden, bye Holden—until he and the nurse turn the corner at the end of the hallway and get swallowed by the elevator.

When Holden wakes up, both his parents are staring at him from either side of his hospital bed. He sees them through a soupy trance that he understands is his alone. A personal purple haze.

So I've got your appendix in a jar. That's what you wanted, right? That's Dad.

We're really glad they got it before it ruptured. And Mom.

Holden feels himself laughing, and then hears himself laughing. He watches himself laugh. He looks down at his right arm. It's bandaged completely, from the tips of his fingers right up to his armpit. The act of lifting his head brings a wave of nausea, so he lowers it back to the pillow and closes his eyes.

The doctor said it all went well. That's Mom, getting right to the point. He thinks he was able to reattach most of your tendons and even your nerves. They found one curled up inside your palm. Amazing.

Steve Austin, a man barely alive. We *can* rebuild him. Dad, of course.

Apparently they used a microscope, and the thread is thinner than a hair. You were under for five hours. Mom again, always practical.

Holden heaves. Iced-tea-coloured bile spills out onto the pillow beside his face.

Easy, fella. His Dad's warm hand is rubbing his back.

I'll go grab you another pillowcase, his mother's voice refracts.

Holden is high and low at the same time. He's not in his body, but not outside of it, either. He understands he's inside himself, but he's also separated. His skin is a rental.

I'm in a hospital bed hooked up to an IV, he tells himself. I just got my Franken-hand sewn back together. He's floating in a lake of warm flannel. He senses his parents talking more than he hears them. They're going on about something …

He has no measure for the boundary of himself. He fills the room and he is nowhere. He's aware of everything—all things, all the light and the dark, the heat and the cold—except pain. He feels no pain in his hand where pain probably should be. The sensation is pure contentment and peace. Something in Holden wonders if this is a miracle.

15

Neither grief nor memory walked a straight line. A bad day, a better day, a terrible day. More and more, they created their own weather. How could I write chronologically when my thoughts carved the path of a lightning bolt? I tried to make notes on my phone, but mostly I stayed in bed and looked out the window, chopping branches off the Spanish chestnut with my eyes until only a stump was left.

People who knew Holden told me stories about his actions over his last few months, but none of them could tell me what he'd been thinking. I needed to find a way to get closer to his mind.

I called the psychologist we had hired two years before to help Holden with his depression and anxiety. A pale man with a comforting British accent and more than thirty years' experience working with adolescents. After the pleasantries, I asked the shrink what he could tell me about Holden's mental state, but he stonewalled on his end of the line. Perhaps rewinding, perhaps scrambling for cover. Either he couldn't place Holden exactly, or he was protecting himself. He bristled.

You and I spoke after some of Holden's sessions, I reminded him. I paid you in advance.

What are you asking me, precisely?

Do. You. Remember. Him? I insisted.

What's this about? His tone irritated now.

His refusal to answer hooked an anger down low in me and fished it to the surface. Its heat needed a place to detonate, so I unsheathed the only weapon I had.

He's dead.

It's interesting how silence can originate from a certain location.

Dear god, he sputtered, what happened?

Overdose.

I've just had a cancellation, tomorrow at 3:00, the shrink said. We sit on pillows, drink tea. Two hundred dollars, cash or cheque.

I don't need therapy. Well, maybe I do. But I just want you to tell me what you think might have happened.

It's how I make my living. And he repeated, two hundred, cash or cheque. Do you want the appointment or not?

Of course, the shrink knew his power. A grieving mother will never agree that "it is what it is." She will never believe her child is "in a better place," because a better place would be in my kitchen eating curried chicken and listening with sincere appreciation to Mariah Carey.

Momz, she's legendary, just check out that range!

Holden is sitting at the table in the old yellow house. He's wearing boxer shorts and eating cereal with his left hand. His curled fingers, still bandaged and swollen from the surgery, are tapping on the keys of his laptop. Now he's dancing on the terrible carpet, and his arms are stirring the air above his head as he sings along with Mariah's cascading voice.

Do you want the appointment or not?

I could only manage a whisper. Yes.

I didn't care about the money. Clues were expensive. I was angry at his insensitivity. He of all people should know how this might feel. At least academically.

The line went dead. Another death. Small deaths all around. Dead in the water, dead centre, sorry I couldn't call you, my phone died.

The shrink didn't seem to remember that Cam and I had already sat on his convoluted pillows two years before, drinking his Lapsang souchong.

That afternoon, the shrink had asked me, What, exactly, are you afraid of?

When my eyes landed on the fat wooden Buddha over by the big window casting a shadow across the floor, I took a deep breath, held it for a moment, then let it go. Cam reached for my hand.

I guess I'm afraid my son is going to die of a drug overdose in some seedy downtown hotel.

A condescending squint, a shake of his head. The shrink's office-job fingers fiddled with a string of beads.

Not gonna happen, he said. I don't remember whether or not he added, *Trust me.* That only happens when there's been a history of sexual or emotional abuse, or abandonment. From what we've talked about, despite your divorce from his father and some tension with step-dad, your kid is loved and well supported. And hey, this is Vancouver, everybody smokes pot. This darkness he's exhibiting is a developmental phase. He's just figuring things out. He'll come through it.

Then why am I so scared?

Cam had squeezed my fingers.

Look, what's happening with your son is very common teen angst stuff. He'll work through it—I'll help him. He's a very intelligent guy. The smart ones always take life too seriously. He's going to be okay.

Really? I think I asked.

Really. I'm almost certain he'd said, while stacking empty teacups.

The relief had spread through me faster and more thoroughly than I'd thought possible. Red wine on a white linen tablecloth.

As I got closer to the shrink's office, I became an observer. I watched a woman with a tangle of dark hair and a hesitant stride walk along the sidewalk on a street named for a tree. I watched her pull her sweater tight against the winter afternoon. I watch her pause a moment and dip her chin before she approached a flight of stairs.

The shrink, a middle-aged white man with wiry grey eyebrows and a wide nose, slumped on a low wooden bench the size of a shoebox facing away from the door, away from me, toward the high windows and the dull grey sky beyond. His pale arm circling in the air ushered me to the jumble of coloured pillows on the slightly raised platform across from him.

I didn't want to sit cross-legged because it might signal compliance, but there was no other option. I dropped onto a blue square and looked around his office, surveying the objects likely curated to make him appear learned, well travelled, and enlightened in ancient Eastern traditions: the framed qualifications, the brass gong on a stone pedestal, the beaded curtain segregating his desk and chair. The shrink didn't always sit on the floor.

His feet were bare, and I smelled his bitter patchouli. He rearranged cups and an ornate cast-iron teapot as though performing an ancient ritual. The routine that two years ago had comforted me now seemed like a hoax. Rising steam fogged his wire-frame glasses, which, I noted, could have used a cleaning. He poured a stream of tea and extended a cup without a word.

I held it between my hands, but would not consume what he offered. I fixed my gaze on him.

I saw your son six times. He ran his finger along a page in a dog-eared notebook. We made a connection, we made some progress, and then he left for Montreal. Apparently we got close enough that I'm welling up with tears right now.

I didn't see any tears.

The kid was incredibly intelligent and creative. He was also full of self-loathing.

Had a kind of remorse just gathered around the puffy cushions below his eyes?

He was an artist, so I had him do some drawings for me—very dark. He had so much anger. Not uncommon.

His British accent, formerly a salve, now seemed somehow abrasive.

Can I see them?

What?

The drawings.

I don't have them. Look, we never got to figure out where that darkness came from, and I don't know what could have happened. I see no culpability here.

The shrink had yet to say hello, to use Holden's name, or to ask me a single question. Any hope I'd had for answers from this man evaporated. I had reached another dead end.

Now the faded PhD on his dingy wall felt like a deception. A carnival game I had gambled on with Holden's precious, complicated psyche. I had given more currency to a piece of paper in a frame than I had to Holden's knowing. The shrink was a quack, not to mention rudely insensitive, and I had invited him in. I had insisted Holden follow his advice. When Holden had told me the shrink didn't know what he was talking about, was "full of standard psychobabble," I had overruled him and insisted he continue with the sessions. I had even paid for them.

There was culpability here, but it did not lie with the tired man across from me, who had probably navigated his own obstacle course of despair. More than I despised the shrink in that moment, I hated myself. If I was looking for someone to blame this on, I had found her.

I reached into my bag, pulled out a rectangle of paper, and folded it in half. As I rose from the blue pillow and stood to go, I placed the cheque for two hundred dollars on the floor and set my full cup of cold tea on top of it.

16

I found a multitude of ways to punish myself. Photographs were especially effective weapons. I scrolled through hundreds of family pictures on my laptop. But rather than reflect on all the warm memories of the time we'd spent together, I could only focus on the occasions when Holden wasn't with us. The alternating Christmas mornings, the family dinners when his chair sat empty, the trips without him. Why wasn't Holden in the frame, smiling back at me from that beach five years ago, or that mountaintop in the snow? Where was he? I knew, of course, that at those times he'd been with his father, living the other half of his life, but I worried that by dividing his time, we may have cleaved his heart. Does divorce cut children in half?

I thought about the different sections of Holden's life—two homes in two distinct parts of the city, two sets of parents, two modes of living, two different homes each with their own customs, rituals, and languages, connected only by Holden. Though we did our best to make the transitions smooth for him, he was the one who'd had to span the chasm. He'd constantly traversed the gap between the distinct pods of his family, moving fluidly, adapting all the time.

Can a person be a bridge? Had he felt enhanced by the two distinct zones of his life, or dissected? I wondered how this compartmentalization affected his view of the world and its societal and cultural imbalances, which he'd undoubtedly been becoming more aware of.

∞

The two friends walk single file from Esper's house to the bus stop, their big shoes making prints in the powdered brown dirt along the edge of the part of Capilano road that cuts through the Squamish First Nation. There's no sidewalk, only weeds, gravel, and burrito wrappers from the gas station up on the corner. Along with the noise of the bridge traffic overhead, Holden can hear one of his favourite sounds: the faint *tink-tink* of glass balls stirring paint inside the cans in his backpack.

The day after Holden first saw Esper at the rail yard doing a quick throw up on a grain car, he looked up the word. "Esper" means somebody with paranormal abilities, like telepathy. Maybe Esper can read his thoughts, and that's why he doesn't need to talk too much.

Holden settled on his own tag, Sefer, when he found out it means writer or book in Hebrew. He's read that when the root letters are used without *niqqud*, or vowels, the consonants can be heard in different ways to produce different meanings, all to do with books, story, writing, or counting. He loves the potential of those letters, S-F-R, the ability to shake up the word like a Magic 8-ball, the idea that he can dismember his name and reshuffle it—be the writer and the writing at the same time. Is it possible to *be* his graffiti? To finesse those letters and rewrite himself all over the city?

They ride the bus across the Lions Gate in silence, looking out at English Bay. Holden likes to walk over the bridge sometimes. Just to see the ocean from up there. And the light. Last time he walked it, the rain had just stopped. The sea and the sky were washed out with different intensities of grey: white grey, purple grey, glossy silver grey, gunmetal, charcoal. Sunlight snuck into that gap between the low clouds and the horizon and lit the water on fire. A metallic glow oozed all over the surface of the water, swirling and drifting like liquid mercury. He could see all the way to Vancouver Island.

Holden had placed his hands flat on the green metal railing, absorbing the vibrations of rush hour right behind his back. No matter how still he stood, the bridge deck kept bucking and moaning like it was alive. He needed sea legs. He had counted the silhouettes in the bay: seven freighters, twelve small white sailboat triangles over by Jericho Beach, and five fishing boats below him, just past the sand bar at the mouth of the Capilano River. When the tide comes in, the river flows upstream, past the rail bridge he paints under sometimes. Once when he was down there, he saw seals eating spawning salmon.

At the highest point of the Lions Gate, there's a neon-yellow phone box with a sticker on it that says, *There Is Help.* Holden wonders who sits at a desk waiting for those phone calls.

Hello?

Hi, I am about to jump.

Don't do it, you have so much to live for.

Really? Name three things.

It'd be easy to get over the railing. A quick hop like jumping over the tennis net at the end of a game. One, two, see ya later. He would never do it. It's the same thing as closing his eyes and imagining a blow job from a Victoria's Secret supermodel, though. Never going to happen, but that doesn't stop him from thinking about it.

The other bridge over the inlet is the Second Narrows. It's higher and not as aesthetically pleasing; you might call it blue collar. The sidewalk over there is covered with broken glass, gravel, hunks of metal, and cigarette butts. The structure is orange, but the railings are no colour at all. Holden read a plaque up there when his crew was looking for a place to paint one time. It's called the Iron Workers Memorial Bridge, because while it was under construction, the whole thing collapsed with a crew roped to it. Seventy-nine welders hit the water. Eighteen of them got dragged to the bottom, drowned by their tool belts. Murdered by their jobs.

Both bridges cross Coal Harbour, but they couldn't be more different. The Second Narrows goes to East Van, where the houses are small and close together, and some people barely get by. The Lions Gate starts in West Van, where millionaires live in huge mansions with lawns they never mow themselves. They have people for that.

The Lions Gate is British racing green and has bike lanes and viewing platforms for tourists to take pictures of the sunset. Cruise ships pass underneath while their passengers sip champagne and wave bon voyage on their way to Alaska to see the icebergs before they're gone. It has tall towers and thick swooping cables, like the Brooklyn Bridge. From far away, it looks like bird's wings. At night the cables are lit up with big glowing lanterns that throw a kind of bat signal against the mountains.

The night before, Esper showed Holden some of his first cedar carvings of eagles, salmon and bears. Dude, Holden said, hidden talents! Espo just smiled at the floor.

He wonders if it bothers Espy that even the bay is named for Britain—that and the park, and most of the streets, rivers, and islands are all named for white guys—but he doesn't ask. Even the mountain peaks that the bridge they're crossing was named after. He learned in school that the Lions were originally called the Sisters, because twin daughters of the chief apparently helped broker some kind of peace deal between the Squamish and Haida, so the Creator immortalized them by turning them into mountains so they could be a symbol of peace forever. Then some dude changed the name because the peaks reminded him of the cats in Trafalgar Square. Should be the Sisters Bridge they're crossing.

He turns to Esper. Did you know that at night you can see the Lions Gate from the Second Narrows, but not the other way around?

Makes sense.

The bus rolls through Stanley Park and onto Georgia Street, and Holden thinks about painting the big wall. His head fills with colours, pulsing shapes, movements, and the chemical smell of tiny floating particles so microscopic that you can breathe the colour into your lungs. A low-grade adrenalin buzz simmers under his skin. He curls and uncurls his fingers, his scarred, weak, fucked-up digits. Months of therapy at the hand clinic, dipping his fingers in hot wax and having them stretched by Som the Torture King, and still when he squeezes the gizmo that measures his hand strength, his right is only about 40 percent as strong as his left. It's actually not that big of a deal; he's figured out how to do most things. He's written entire essays with his left hand, but for painting he likes to use his right. Good thing his thumb still works. The joke is, at least he can still hitchhike.

The bus snakes between the office towers downtown. Holden cranes his neck up to look at a tall sharp rectangle against the peacock-blue sky and imagines how it was built. All the work, the sweat. Every day for eight hours, Esper wears a hard hat and a green reflective vest and loads rebar. Holden's seen the bruises on his shoulders.

What's the point of working like a dog? Holden asked. What do you get for it?

Arthritis.

When Holden and Esper get off the bus on Point Grey Road, they stand looking across the bay to the North Shore, which they left less than an hour ago.

They walk down the smooth sidewalk beside a row of small trees with burgundy leaves spaced evenly along the lush boulevard. They pass one gated home, then another, and another. Quick glimpses of ocean between each one.

Just like your place on the rez, hey Espo?

Exactly, he chuckles.

Seth Rogen went to school around here you know, his company is even called Point Grey. Do you think if he really applies himself, maybe one day Seth could afford one of these shacks?

House after house of concrete, glass, topiary trees, security alarms, and closed-circuit cameras. Expensive cars rest quietly in every driveway. They're all spotless.

Holden almost has to jog to keep up with Esper.

Hey, you know how you can tell if a lady has a six-figure income?

Nope.

Her tits are bigger than her dog.

Esper stops. This is it, he says, pushing a wet branch aside. He disappears down a narrow stairway between two houses. If you didn't know it was there, you might not notice. Holden follows, paint cans rattling as his pack slaps against his back.

As soon as he steps onto the rocky beach, he smells saltwater, wet seaweed, something mildly fishy, like barnacles or mussels below the tideline, and the summers of his childhood. Camping, swimming, hiking. Roasting marshmallows on the fire. Sand under his bare feet all day long.

Since he's been at art school, Holden sees the world through different glasses. He scans the view, and what registers first are all the colours, like a palette: grey rocks, dark-blue ocean, silver buildings, green mountains, white peaks, whiter clouds, blue sky. Then form: he notices that the city skyline is not all that different from the contour of the mountains behind it. Both remind him of heartbeats on a monitor.

And there he is: the Sleeping Man. Formed by the North Shore mountains, the shape of a giant figure kicking back with his hands folded across his chest. He always looks peaceful. Holden doesn't know where the story came from but his mom first showed him the outline of the big stone grandfather when he was a little kid and they lived over here on this side. Just after his parents split up.

Today, deep wrinkles line the sleeping man's face, because there's still snow in the gullies of Dog Mountain. It's kind of like looking at the night sky and spotting Orion's belt. Only the sleeping man's belt is the strait cut through the forest for the Grouse Mountain Skyride.

He and his Mom would go down to the beach, close their eyes, and ask the Sleeping Man for a wish. Holden used to wish for his parents to get back together, but he'd tell his mom that he'd wished for Hubba Bubba.

Hey old man, how's it going? Holden says. Have you met my friend, Esper?

It's the first time Esper's smiled all day.

They take off their packs and sit on a log. Holden pulls out a joint and sparks it up. He looks out over the water, takes a deep pull, and passes the joint to Esper.

I wonder how much shit I'm gonna catch for not going to work today, Esper says in his slow, clipped monotone.

Not as much as I'm gonna catch for getting kicked out of school.

You got kicked out?

Asked not to return.

Sef, it's *art* school. How is that even possible?

Technically speaking it's a university, Holden says, and I have been placed on academic probation.

Does that mean you gotta go see your academic probation officer?

Dude, probably.

They eyeball the wall, a never-ending canvas holding up multimillion-dollar waterfront cribs.

Best sheet in town by far, Esper says. Just look at it.

I'll have to stand on your shoulders to finish the top part, Holden says. They'd tried that move once before. That was how Holden got his most recent concussion. How many was that now, six? How about a proddy that goes deep. Start wide and I'll meet you in the middle. It'll be sick.

Solid plan, Esper says.

Holden can already see the purple, blue, and yellow lines of his *SEFER*. He'll do silver flares and echoes around a sharp black outline. His letters big and bouncy like they're pumped up with air. He usually likes to make sure their colours are going to either match or contrast, but today they'll just figure that out once they join their pieces.

ESPer-seFER.

Holden pulls his respirator over his nose and mouth. What did his mom say? "At least wear your mask. You need to protect your most valuable asset." If she only knew what he breathes in. But Holden wears the respirator anyway; he feels like a freakin' warrior every time he puts it on.

He presses the cap with his thumb and starts outlining in big strokes, his arm arcing smoothly, easily, like one blade of a propeller. His body knows how to do this. The sound of the paint leaving the can is like a pressure release valve for him, too. Never fails.

They work in silence, stepping back every ten minutes or so to check on the piece as it grows.

Excuse me, boys. Excuse me! A distant voice comes at Holden from down the beach. Hello!

A lady with super-long blond hair weaves her way toward them. Slippery rocks and driftwood shift and roll under her feet, but she never loses her balance. Holden can't help but notice the long beaded necklace bouncing against her boobs as she gets closer. He likes the curve of her leg muscles under her tight white pants. She's waving. She's definitely talking to them. Her smile is huge. She could easily be on the cover of a magazine.

He stops painting and takes stock of his shit in case has to grab and go. He's been busted twice. The last time, the judge made it pretty clear: a third strike and you're out. Which meant in.

How's it going? Holden says from under his mask, wondering if she's already called the cops.

Amazing! Hey, I'm looking for some artists to paint a mural on the wall below my house. It's just down there. She turns and points behind her. Would you guys be interested?

Holden and Esper look at each other and push their masks up onto their foreheads.

You can paint whatever you want as long as it's really big and you use a lot of bright colours.

The two look at her, then their eyes shift back to each other, trying to appear chill, as if this sort of thing happens all the time. Holden is mesmerized by the extreme whiteness of her teeth. The sunlight behind her hair is causing a halo effect.

I'll pay for all the paint you need. And for your time. How about twelve hundred? she says.

A galloping kicks up in Holden's chest. Esper never says much of anything, but at this statement, Holden is speechless, too. Twelve hundred fricken' dollars? She's talking about a piece that would take them two hours at most. And it's what they were already doing, anyway. A surreal sensation surges through his bloodstream, reminding him of his first hit of molly. He realizes he's holding his breath and tries to let the air leak out of his mouth as inconspicuously as possible. The lady seems to take their confusion as some kind of bargaining tactic. She breaks the silence.

Each.

Holden leans against the wall in an attempt to look casual. It would take him a month of pressure washing to clear twelve hundred.

He looks at Esper. A shadow so quick he almost misses it passes across his friend's face. Esper's lips are pressed together in a straight, flat line, and his eyes are dark. The sleeping man over Esper's shoulder nods his approval, and the decision is made. Their faces swing in unison back to the glowing woman in white, standing with her fingers interlocked in front of her chest like she's making a wish.

No thanks, Holden says.

The woman's head jerks up slightly as if someone just popped her under the chin with a closed fist.

Are you sure? You can do it anytime you want. We're not in a hurry.

Yup, we're sure. Thanks, anyway, Holden says.

Esper dips his chin once, definitively, and turns back to the wall. He resumes filling in a section with short, sharp bursts of orange. His mask sits crooked on the top of his head, his neck torques at a weird angle, and his shoulders make him resemble a vulture sitting on a branch. His movements are faster than usual.

The woman turns away, slipping and stumbling across the rocks as she retreats back down the beach. Holden pulls his mask down and continues painting. Mid-stroke, the can slips out of his hand, clatters off a rock, and wedges under a log.

Jesus fuck! Holden yells through his mask.

Esper sits down heavily on the log and looks out to sea. Holden notices holes in the toes of both of his shoes.

Who does she think she is? Esper says, arms dangling between his legs.

Bro. Some things you can't buy.

Holden pulls off his mask and gathers up his cans, shoving everything into his backpack. He starts walking back toward the stairway. Esper follows.

From the bus stop they can see across the water, past the city to the deep-green expanse of the mountains. Clouds gather and billow over the peaks. The gentle old man is still asleep. To the left of his head, bald, square patches score the slope where the trees have been bulldozed so new houses can be built. Houses with three-car garages, swimming pools, and unobstructed views of the ocean.

No one was safe.

Just before Holden died, a young man who lived seven houses away was hit by a car and killed as he ran across the highway near our home late one night. Another boy, who lived on the corner, died of cancer shortly afterward. Three vital young men from one city block gone in the span of one year. Their parents would each be rocked in distinctly devastating ways.

If the phone rang while Cam was out and I didn't recognize the number, I refused to answer, because I wanted a bit more time before I received the news of his death. Every day when Lyla left for school or to play with friends, I whispered I love you in her ear, because it was the last true thing I wanted her to know before she died. If another officer ever approached the house, eyes black as boots, this time I'd know better. I would lock the front door and run out the back. And if, by some sadistic fluke, my daughter's name were ever to be uttered in the same cold fashion, I knew I would have no choice but to end my own life, to go to them both.

I confided this to a friend while we walked our dogs along the muddy bank of a creek one morning. And I would help you, she said, without a moment's hesitation. She had two children of her own.

One night I awoke with a too-big pain behind my sternum. A stretching beyond the capacity of my chest wall to expand. I couldn't pull half a breath without pain. In the dark, I reached for my phone and searched "heart attack symptoms women": *Women who die of heart attacks are largely those who ignore the signs and don't seek medical care.*

Hey. I nudged Cam. I'm going to the hospital.

Mmm?

I might be having a heart attack.

What? Wait, I'll take you.

No. You have to stay here. In case Lyla wakes up. When I die she can't be alone.

Death seemed easy.

The cardiologist was kind. She assured me, with wires and printouts, that my heart was cracked, but not faulty.

My five siblings and I had all worn tartan Catholic school uniforms, had all sung "Let There Be Peace on Earth" each Sunday morning, could all recite the Act of Contrition, but when we became adults, none of us stayed. Even my parents, who had slipped envelopes into the collection basket for decades to secure their spots in heaven, walked away from the white steeple after their own divorce.

Religion—formal religion, at least—held no value for me. I loved exploring old cathedrals for their architecture and history, but the shame, violence, and patriarchy of the Catholic Church repulsed me. I didn't have to look far to see the hypocrisy; the priest who had driven our school bus and led our youth group and looked like Alan Alda was a convicted pedophile who, after years of sexually assaulting a quiet, devout family friend my age, spent only ten months in jail. The same patriarchal unfairness that had made me a spitting-mad nine-year-old when I was forbidden to help during mass—"They're not called altar girls"—had probably saved me from his evil hands.

Non-conventional, non-Western forms of spirituality like yoga and meditation enticed me. I read books about Buddhism and metaphysics. I felt connected to a universal energy when I hiked, watched the snow fall, or swam in the ocean. I booked retreats. In the year before I stopped working, I would wake up thirty minutes earlier than usual to sit on a pillow in our closet and meditate. I was interested in the idea of the soul. I believed that our true essence inhabited the empty space between our cells.

But something about Holden's death brought me fiercely back to prayer. Apparently I hadn't lapsed enough. Whenever I heard the frequent sirens from up on the highway near our house, my marrow would fizz and my breasts would tingle with a mother's milk reflex. I would stop whatever I was doing and pray. I prayed no phone would ring, no red spinning lights would splash over our bricks. I prayed the noise belonged to someone else.

I saw the possibility of death, the close proximity of death, the inevitability of death everywhere. The last leaves fluttered from the Spanish chestnut, committing suicide one by one.

One winter afternoon, a bird struck our bedroom window with a sick thud.

What is it? Are you okay? Cam rushed in through the bedroom door, forehead creased.

I stared at him, blinking. Why was he here asking me these questions?

You made a weird sound, he said. You screamed.

A bird hit the widow, I said. It's dead. Could you please bury it?

He crossed the floor and looked out at the untended garden below. There's nothing there, babe, he's gone. He sat down on the edge of the bed and gathered me in his arms. He's okay, he's alive. Come here.

It could have been a girl.

Who?

The bird. It could have been a girl bird.

As the months passed, Holden's death became an obsession. The thing I wanted most every moment of every day, the one solitary object of my desire, that most necessary part of me, proved unreachable. I would be eternally incomplete. True suffering is one you know will never end.

I prayed to Holden, too. Those whispered words were all I had to talk to him with. I asked him questions, because it occurred to me that I didn't really know my son. I didn't know what he was afraid of, what he cared about, what he wanted. It is an extraordinarily painful thing to lose someone you love before you've had the chance to see them clearly. That kind of knowing takes longer than the time I had. Than we had.

But the dreams. I dreamed the solid weight of his body in my arms, the certainty of his flesh up against mine, warm and breathing. We existed together in the soft coral of early morning before anything moved or made a sound, and I'd fight not to wake, but the fighting made it so.

I tried exhaling so I could sink back down to the bottom, to sleep, where he was waiting. But no—aimless and exhausted, I'd float to the surface. I'd rise against my will into sorrow. I dreamed of him, with him, often, and in the morning after one of those exquisite dreams, I'd have to face his death all over again. Sleep was the only place where we could meet. Each night I longed for this cruelty. Please come to me tonight, Holden, I would pray as I closed my eyes. Please come back. I prayed to god and to Holden, because to me they were the same thing.

If I could be with Holden in a dream, would it be possible to somehow find him while I was awake? Could I slice the scrim that separated us and step through?

The psychic's hair was well styled with good-quality highlights. One could easily assume that she worked in a bank. Her cornflower-blue eyes accented a prudent layer of mascara. She wore small silver hoop earrings, and when I walked in, she was sitting with her bare feet planted flat on the floor. Nothing else about her looked remarkable. She was ordinary.

Welcome, I'm Rebecca. Please sit down.

Rebecca was gazing at a large painting of flowers on the other side of the room. Begonias, peonies, and roses in a vase, their distorted stems fractured bones below the waterline. I sat opposite her in a matching high-backed chair. There was enough room between us for a small, low table. Three small crystals lined the arm of her chair.

She inhaled deeply a few times, exhaling with force. She picked up the crystals and rolled them, clacking, between her palms.

Okay, I'm just going to tell you what I see.

My throat throbbed. Thank you, I tried to say, but no sound came.

She nodded and began. On the one hand you seem very strong, like, wash your face with cold water and get on with it. And then on the other hand, you're so delicate, like a Fabergé egg. I have to be very careful. You have a fragile self, but also this incredibly strong and angry self. I don't think anger is a bad thing. It's a motivator. It can be better sometimes to be angry than depressed.

When you came in here I felt like there was someone with you. Someone extra. Someone who has evolved. Is it your son who passed? Did you lose your son?

I was stunned. I hadn't told her why I was here. A friend had made the appointment for me without providing any information. Although I had come to hate the term *lost*, like my child was a set of keys or a wallet.

Yes.

I feel like he's in a healing place. And not like he's up in the clouds or something like that, he's right here. She swung her arm like a pendulum into the space between her chair and the table. He's right here. He's looking strong to me, and clear. It doesn't take away the grief or the loss or the pain, but I feel like it's important for you to know that.

It's important for him that you know that. He's with you. That's really strong, I've never seen that before, actually. He's picked himself up off the floor.

How did she know he was on the floor? Or was that just an expression, like bootstraps?

He's upright now. She tilted her head. I just feel like this world—she paused—it was hard for him to be here. I mean, he signed up for it, he came here with all the good intentions, he had some things he wanted to do here, he wanted to learn and expand. As a soul he picked a tough assignment; this world is coarse, and his energy is refined and so sensitive. It was hard for him to function.

I could only nod, because though I'd been in this woman's presence for only five minutes, she already seemed to know Holden better than I did. This world *had* been a hard place for him. He had walked uphill. If there was an easy way to do something and a difficult way, it seemed like he turned his back on easy almost every time.

Plump tears spilled down my cheeks, and she continued.

Kind of like trying to plant orchids on the windswept coast of Ireland. I mean, they're just not going to grow. The psychic's eyes were clouded over, milky. It was difficult for him, and he tried, he really tried.

She rubbed her hands together quickly, making a rasping sound against the quiet. When someone leaves in this way, so suddenly, it always opens that door to the other side. It's kind of like the people left here get a whiff of it, so it can also trigger a kind of homesickness in you.

This concept made complete sense to me. I could smell him. He was just beyond my fingertips. But for Lyla, I would have stepped through that crack to him in an instant, if it were possible. Gone home to him.

You are stronger than you think, Rebecca said, even if you don't want to be strong or don't feel strong or don't care about being strong. Something is coming that crosses your path, and it kind of catches you.

You don't have to go in search of it or force yourself—it's not work, actually. It's more like a thread that you just pull, and it's going to lead you. You can't see it right now. I see you doing something that you feel passionate about, and I'm making it sound grand, but it might not be grand, it might be kind of regular. And I think he is part of that, he's trying to help you.

She tilted her face upward. I just see him lying on the floor.

I hated going back there to that room, seeing him so cold and alone, so empty.

I just keep seeing him. Was he lying on the floor or something?

I reminded myself to breathe. Yes.

But what I'm hearing is, I'm up off the floor. That image is not going away.

She rested her palms on the arms of her chair. Is there something that can be done with what happened? Is there something that he was really interested in?

Well … I choked on words with sharp edges. He's an artist. He loves graffiti, I said. Present tense. Holden could not be in the past.

I think there's something about that. I don't know, like you start a fund for graffiti artists in his name, do you know what I mean? To take the thing he loved and celebrate it, and have other people celebrate it. I don't know if there's a lot of support for graffiti artists. Most people think that's something you scrub off your walls, but of course it's not, it's a form of expression. I think he liked it because it wasn't part of something mainstream; it's individual, there's lots of different layers to it.

She stared into the middle distance, unfocused. She ran one hand up her other arm. I keep getting goosebumps—there's something about that. I'm not sure what that's about. Maybe having a day where there's a celebration and people come and do their artwork, or something. It's really strong. He wants that to be.

Rebecca shifted forward in her chair. I watched her, as she watched an invisible scene unfold through her smoky eyes. She gestured to a grand unseen wall.

You may not want to do anything about that right now, but holy Toledo! She took several deep breaths like she had just crossed a finish line and needed to quickly suck in air. Did he leave some pieces behind? She turned from her personal fog to face me.

Pieces? I hadn't told her that a big complex graffiti painting on a wall is called a piece. But then any kind of art could be a piece, too. I risked a question. Where is this coming from?

I think it's coming from him. A whole group of people need to have a voice. I think he felt like he didn't have a voice. He did, but the voice that he had—I don't even want to use that word, "had," because he's so present—it's what gave him strength. I feel like when he's doing that work, there's such a sense of freedom and accomplishment and satisfaction, and also all the struggles of this world in general, and kind of the unfairness of people and the injustices of the world. When he was painting, a lot was coming out of him.

I wanted to climb inside her eyes and see what she was seeing. It was intoxicating to believe she might actually be with Holden. I wanted that so badly. Her energy pulled me closer.

You know how when you shake spray paint, you can hear that ball that's in the can? That's what I'm hearing. It feels like there's something big there. She peered into the air in front of her again, squinting. I'm looking at blown-up pieces of art. They're really big, and people are taking pictures.

She leaned back, and the light filtering in through the blind spilled onto her shoulder in stripes. We had been sitting for nearly an hour, but far from tiring, Rebecca seemed to be gaining momentum. He came straight here from the angelic world, because that's where he was hanging out, that realm of art and literature and science and—this may sound odd—but those dimensions of unbelievable glory, and then he came here. He had his life here. Part of him knew he was walking into a life and into a body that would have—I don't even want to use the word "struggles," because that doesn't do it justice. He kind of hand-picked all of this for himself, as a soul.

A flare of skepticism. I was glad for the heat of it. It told me there may eventually be more than just sadness.

But why would someone choose that?

It's really hard to grasp from this perspective, from this side. But we come here because we are growing our souls, and we learn from our disappointments. We have these experiences in a world full of difficulties and problems. Then we take all of those lessons, and we go back home. Then we come down again because we *want* to be able to experience it. That's what this world offers; it's a university, an incredible opportunity to learn every time we're here.

I had never thought about reincarnation as a form of education. I had never considered that perhaps Holden had asked for his life. Does everyone who suffers request their own suffering?

When you see somebody going through that, you think, why would you do that to yourself? You don't want someone to be in pain, but the truth is we don't really know what the soul is doing. This is somebody who took it on because he wanted to grow. That's why I think it's really important for you not to torture yourself about whether you could have prevented anything, or whether you could have helped, because you gave him a life, and you gave him love. You gave him every single tool he needed to fulfill his purpose. His destiny was not to be on the floor—that's not what I'm talking about. His destiny was to incorporate all these things so that he could be where he is now, and then use that to become even more of who he already is. This was not his first rodeo, this was not his tenth rodeo. This was not a job for a novice. He came because he had things to do, things to say.

My shoulders shuddered with a surge of sobs. I had always felt that Holden was wise, which made no sense, considering how recklessly he lived. His choices had made many of his days painful. These thoughts were too big to understand.

Do you have any questions? Rebecca adjusted her arms as if she'd just remembered that she had them. She folded her legs up under herself on the chair, tucked her hair behind her ears, and turned to me. I noticed a small chain of white daisies along the collar of her blouse. The same tiny flowers that form constellations on the grass in springtime.

And we are lying on our backs, heads resting on each other's shoulders, arms extended upward, pointing. That one's a race car, that one's a shark eating a hot dog. Look at that freaky clown! Do you see the map of Australia?

I noticed a ball of wet tissue in my curled fingers.

I must have had questions, but I couldn't remember any of them.

Um ... Is there anything else he wants to say to me?

Rebecca angled her head as though she were listening to a faint, far-off sound. She closed her eyes, cleared her throat.

To blame this on yourself is to take away my power. I had choices, too. I'm hearing him say, Don't worry about me, Mom. I'm fine. You can stop worrying about me now.

18

As he got older, Holden moved fluidly between his two homes based on school, work, friends, or whatever else was going on in his life. It was a casual arrangement whereby Holden could come and go as he pleased, as long as he let us know where he was. One morning when I thought he was at his dad's apartment, a friend called to tell me that Holden was sleeping on the lawn of the neighbourhood church. She was being kind—he was unconscious. He'd stepped off the bus and collapsed there. When I went to collect him, he was incoherent and combative. He told me he'd been at a party all night and had been doing shots for breakfast, but wouldn't confess to anything else. I probably should have taken him to the hospital, but instead, I watched over him while he retched and slept it off.

The last straw for Cam had been the night we were out and our babysitter's parents called, because Holden and his friends had terrified their daughter when they came into the house drunk and told her to leave. Cam and I rushed home to find Holden in the shower with a girl he'd just met on the SkyTrain, while Amin played Xbox in the basement. As the girl stood wrapped in a towel, mascara dripping down her face, Holden blurted something at Cam like, Lyla's sleeping, so what's the big deal? You're not my dad anyway, so back off.

Cam replied with something like, I'm not allowed to hit you, but I don't have to care about you anymore.

It was around this time that my hair began falling out in clumps, hives crawled up my skin, and I gained a lot of weight.

The year Holden went to art school, Cam and I finally began building our new home, a project which came with its own stresses. Holden lived with his father full time, and I was ashamed to admit that his extended absence felt like a respite. There had been so much anguish in our triangular relationship that I didn't know which axis was closest to rupturing. At the same time, inside my own parenting philosophy, I fishtailed between what John Steinbeck called the "stunning hammer blows of conditioning" and a more intuitive desire to nurture my children with tender patience.

By Christmas, Holden was placed on academic probation, and at the end of the year he was asked not to return. His behaviour became more erratic—he was apathetic, which was normal, and belligerent, which was not. We argued a lot. His dad and I talked it over, and after months of frustration and increasing tension from all sides, we decided it was time for an innovative approach, something forward-thinking and unconventional that had been recommended by a friend. Maybe this idea would help Holden see that we had faith in him, that we believed he could find his own momentum, given the opportunity. We would encourage him to go out on his own and support him while he launched by paying his first month's rent, half of the second month, and a quarter of the third.

We scheduled a family meeting. I called Holden and asked him to come over.

What's up, Momz, why the formal invite? he asked.

I just miss you and I'd love to see you, I said. There's something I'd like to talk to you about.

Holden's dad arrived first and took a seat at our dining table. Cam held back, leaning against the kitchen counter. When Holden walked in, I was pouring tea for everyone.

∞

It was probably some kind of antioxidant–green tea–ginseng thing. Holden had been surprised to see his dad sitting at the table and not surprised to see Cam across the room, leaning against the cupboards with his hands braced on his belt.

His first instinct was to laugh. *What's this, an intervention or something?*

No, honey. Why would you say that? his mom had asked.

He regretted the spliff he'd smoked on the way over.

We'd like to run an idea by you, boy, his dad said. We all think it's time for you to try living on your own.

Wha?

Don't you? His mom jumped in, not waiting for him to answer. You're twenty and you're working, so why not?

He'd nodded, not knowing what else to do. He was only working at Hysteria part-time, minimum wage, not exactly killing it. Mostly to get a deal on tats.

It'll be best for all of us, Mom said.

Dad agreed. A little space, you know?

Holden's mouth opened and closed again. A cartoon halibut.

There was a lot of overly cheerful discussion about things like creating a budget, how to make a decent omelette, and a buddy of his dad's with an extra sofa he could have. Phrases floated above his head as if pulled along by a banner-towing airplane: "moving forward as an adult" … "plans for the future" … "upgrading your skills" … "independence" …

Holden had gripped his teacup with both hands so they wouldn't see the shaking and smiled. Thanks, guys. Sounds like a pretty good idea. *No it doesn't.* I can totally pull it off. *No I can't.*

His dad had rested a hand on his shoulder. Any idea where you want to start looking for a place?

His mom held a pen and a little notepad and looked across at him with such naive optimism that he felt a little poke in his chest. She trusted him more than he deserved.

And that's why he just woke up in a legitimately skanky room in Zack's shithole of a basement suite, with Devon beside him and an slippery albino freak show for a pet.

The amphibian in the cracked glass aquarium is an inheritance from the last resident of this room, along with about an inch of dust, a broken dresser, a Black Sabbath concert poster, and probably bedbugs. The thought of which makes him scratch the hair on his belly and shiver.

Holden decided to keep the little dude after looking it up online. Axolotls are salamanders from Mexico," a website told him. "Their most unique trait is their ability to heal and regenerate. In some cases, a damaged limb might heal, while the axolotl also generates an additional one, resulting in an extra limb. They can even repair parts of the brain."

Holden could use some brain cell regeneration himself, and an extra limb wouldn't hurt, either. His hand is still messed up from when he nearly sliced his fingers off in high school.

Snorlax moves slowly along the outer edge of the mildew-streaked aquarium.

The chunk of tortilla he threw in there last night lies untouched, reminding him of the rain-soaked burrito run he and Devon did at some point.

Hola, what kind of hombre you are? Would you like some crickets, por favor? Holden thinks about walking up to the pet shop on Commercial. They sell bugs, worms, and frozen mice. Maybe in a bit.

Devon steps back into the room with dripping hair. She's wearing tie-dyed leggings and a baggy tank with basically no sides that definitely does not hide the bra under it. Holden wonders if that's the intention. It's working for him.

Why is there a pair of girl's underwear in the shower?

I have no clue.

Really.

Must be Zack's or Stepho's.

Zack and Steph are a couple. Do you think I'm an idiot?

Holden leans his bare back against the bare wall and tries his signature playful grin, using only one side of his face.

Devon's shoulders slump. She presses a hand to her forehead. What the fuck are we doing, Holden? She stares at him.

He keels over like a chopped tree onto the bed. At times like this, he has learned, it's best not to say too much. Ughhh, just when we were having such a great time.

Yeah, what could possibly be better than all this? She sweeps an arm through the air. His clothes are piled in the corner, books and CDs spill all over the dirty carpet. Old food, beer cans, garbage. His skateboard. His guitar. His amp.

Devon grabs her bag from the floor and walks out of the room. He hears the kitchen door click shut, and all that's left is her smell on his sheets hinting at some kind of perfume. It takes him back to flowers— the yellow roses and purple lilacs that used to grow along the edge of their big backyard when he was a kid. A badminton net, a trampoline. The hammock.

The pressure in the room has lowered. It feels like Devo took some of the oxygen with her when she left. A well-read paperback copy of *Shōgun* lies face down on the brown—or is it grey?—carpet. One of the series of books Cam introduced him to, along with *The Lord of the Rings*. Japanese generals would sometimes wait years to act against a foe. This strategy took remarkable restraint. One wise tactical move in its proper sequence is more powerful and effective than charging in too soon, guns blazing. Is he trying to embrace a time-honoured ancient tactical philosophy, or is he just being a lazy fuck?

His phone dangles from its charger cord, a kite with no wind against the black dresser. The cracked spiderweb of the screen lights up with a text message.

> I still love you, you prick. Come
> by the bar later? ♡☺♡

The green rectangle disappears, revealing a photo of him and Devon on a warm sunny day at the beach a couple of weeks ago, just a little drunk, smiling big. The time is stamped in white numbers across their foreheads: 4:06. Not quite 4:20, but close enough.

He reaches for the roach left in the ashtray on the floor. Inhaling deeply, he holds the skunky-sweet smoke inside his lungs for a moment, then lets it go in a wide plume. The pungent haze hangs in the glow from Snorlax's tank. Holden wonders if it's still raining. He really should go get some food. He closes his eyes, rolls onto his side, and goes back to sleep.

∞

I had stepped around a tall stack of beer cans on the sticky kitchen floor and stood in the doorway of Holden's soon-to-be bedroom with a laundry basket full of food, toilet paper, and cleaning supplies propped on my hip. Cleaning supplies I hoped he would use, but knew in all likelihood he would not. The room was small and had no window. It had probably originally been a storage closet.

This is really dangerous, not to mention completely illegal. Can you try to trade bedrooms with somebody? At least then you'd have a window you could get out of in case there's a fire.

A window would cost another hundred a month, Mom. Don't worry, it'll be okay.

Why don't we just quickly vacuum that gross carpet before you set up your bed?

I'll do it later, Momz. Thanks for your help.

Oh, really? I thought we could have lunch. There are so many cool places near here.

I just want to unpack. Maybe another day.

Okay, why don't we have lunch on the weekend?

Sure, thanks again.

I passed him the basket, and he set it down on the floor.

We did have lunch a few times, and at first things went well. Holden tried to make it work. He got a full-time job working in a warehouse, which meant getting up at 6:00 a.m. to catch the Skytrain, taking a connecting bus, and walking twenty mintutes. But he continued to go out every night, slept very little, and ate sporadically. The plan backfired.

When I arrived at the second place he'd been evicted from, to help him clean up so he could recoup some of the damage deposit his dad had put down, I found him asleep, with only a few things thrown into in a garbage bag, and mould growing in a thick layer across the water in the kitchen sink. His roommates had left behind furniture, clothes, and filth. Holden told me one of them had an eating disorder and had been vomiting out the bathroom window, leaving a streak of what looked like cheap red wine down the outside of the white apartment building.

Each time he got kicked out, Holden blamed shady landlords or roommates who were louder, more destructive, and less dependable than he was. Someone's computer got smashed. Someone spent the rent money. Someone shot holes in the living room wall with a crossbow. I was concerned about Holden and equally frustrated with him. I could see he was struggling, and I could also see that he was creating much of that struggle himself. We talked about it, but he reacted with ambivalence. I wanted to help him, and I also wanted him to take responsibility for his own life. I took Holden's few belongings to store in our basement, and he again moved in with his dad.

One job after another didn't work out; he would do well for a while, then it would fizzle out. They weren't offering him any shifts, he couldn't handle it, his boss sucked, he quit. He had stretches of unemployment, but that didn't stop him from going out most nights. I saw him sporadically for dinners or lunches, and we talked on the phone when I called him every few days, but I always had to chase him down.

Holden must have been frustrated, too, and maybe he saw that his lifestyle wasn't sustainable, because in early May he decided to leave for Montreal with a few of his graffiti friends. He told me he had a place to stay and a job lined up working construction for somebody's uncle. And I, always a fan of travel, encouraged him to go.

The change of scenery will do you good!

We texted and talked every few days, and he led me to believe he was having a great time. He told me about a new girlfriend and how he loved exploring the city with her, how he admired the architecture, especially in the older parts of town. During one phone call, I walked him through roasting a chicken. He sounded so good I booked a trip to Montreal to visit him for his twenty-first birthday in July.

19

One of Holden's friends, another graffiti artist named Julian, made a video of their time in Montreal called "Charming Bastards," or something like that. When I watched the film after his death I was nauseated by the glorification of raw destruction. The ruining of property and of themselves. The grainy footage of the "crew" trashing the city scared and nauseated me. This wasn't just some YouTuber—this was my child. I worried about Holden getting hurt, even though it was far too late to be worried.

I watched Julian, Holden, and three or four other hooded figures move like a platoon of soldiers through the purple summer shadows, making their mark on Montreal. They scrawled their secret names on metro trains, inside and out, on facades and fences, on darkened shop windows, or on lit ones when the owners had their backs turned. In one clip, a young man in a balaclava crouched low and sprayed his tag on a police car while the officers sat inside drinking coffee. I imagined Holden moving closer and closer to some kind of edge. I imagined he prickled with the thrill and the danger. Later, Julian would tell me it had been "the most fun they'd ever had." That they were "on cloud nine."

Quick edits of painting and partying set to heavy rap music. Shots of a bathtub full of paint cans and a refrigerator full of beer and Hennessy. Alcohol erased inhibitions. Bright-red cough syrup as a chaser calmed the nerves. Weed for laughs. Strippers with graffiti painted on their naked bodies, mounds of pot, lines of cocaine.

I watched from the future as recklessness rolled them under chain-link fences, bravado hoisted them over barbed wire, camaraderie urged them up rusted fire escapes onto forbidden rooftops. I imagined testosterone tempting them to steal, adrenalin turning up the music in their heads and forcing the paint from their cans. I heard laughter. They were unconcerned with the damage.

I wanted to protect Holden from something that had already happened.

One day I got a message of condolence from Audrey, the girl he had met in Montreal. She said she had taken some photographs of Holden that she thought I might like to have. The pictures were of Holden painting graffiti onto the brick and beams of a shell of a building—it looked like an old warehouse that had been bombed. He wore a blue button-up dress shirt, and he was smiling, but there were purple crescents under his eyes and always a can of beer in his hand.

Audrey agreed to speak to me on the phone. She told me, through her tears, what she could remember of Holden's two months in Montreal.

∞

The first time Holden sees Audrey in person, she's waiting for him outside the Vendômoe metro station. It's a crystal-clear afternoon, and he spots her leaning against the wall, banging the heel of her Doc Martens against the brick. She's wearing a flowered dress and sunglasses just like his. Round, reflective, John Lennon–style.

He walks up to her and says, Hi, I like hugs. She recognizes him immediately. They had met through Instagram, then moved over to Facebook to talk. Obviously they'd trolled each other.

She pushes away from the wall, and he wraps both arms loosely around her. Her face fills the space under his chin, her cheek presses his chest.

Nice to meet your face, Audrey.

The plastic bag of cold beer in his hand knocks against her back. She breaks the hug first.

Nice to see you in the fleshy flesh, she says.

They step back from each other, but he keeps a loose grip on her wrist.

You William Holden? she says.

Wait, how do you know my name?

What do you mean?

William. How did you know that my first name is William? We never talked about that.

It's an expression. It means "do you have" or "are you carrying," as in "Are you William Holden any green?"

It does? Holden's head jerks back. Is that like give me a call on the dog and bone? he says with an English accent.

I don't know. It's just a thing.

It's not a thing.

It is most definitely a thing.

Okay, it's a thing.

So, are you William Holden or not?

Yes, I am Willian Holden. And also, I've got some doobage.

They walk down the sidewalk holding hands.

I can't believe your name is actually William Holden. You must have the coolest parents.

A few weeks later, Audrey takes Holden to the Plateau, a cool section of town crowded with many low brick buildings. The air is warm for a spring morning in Montreal, and they stop for a six-pack at a depanneur. Holden opens a beer and offers it to Audrey. She shakes her head.

I have a strict policy about day drinking, she says.

What's that?

I wait until at least 2:00 p.m.

Respect.

They walk a few more blocks, then around to the back of a warehouse that looks pretty much abandoned. Audrey leads him three flights up a rusty fire escape, then yanks on the corner of a sheet of plywood covering a broken window.

Après toi. She gestures with a tilt of her head.

Holden shrugs and squeezes through, then he holds the gap open for Audrey to slip through, too.

The room is as big as a basketball court. Most of the interior walls and part of the roof have been removed, leaving just the framing; the place appears skeletal. Other than one grey metal chair, some empties, and a pile of newspapers, the space is empty. Large open holes in the rafters throw columns of daylight onto the floor in creamy rectangles.

They walk across the rough wooden planks, hand in hand, not speaking, as though they are checking out an art gallery. A snowstorm of dust specks waltz in the shafts of light.

Holden remembers a cathedral in France. The cool stillness, the musty smell of the past, incense spilling smoke for the stained-glass glow to land on.

Whoa Odds, this place is goddamn Shangri-La.

Thought you'd like it. She carefully sets her big shoulder bag on the dirty floor, and both long, pale arms disappear inside. Close your eyes, she says.

Holden listens for the muffled sound. His skin knows before he does, raising tiny bumps on his arms. He freezes and listens more closely to be certain. Marbles inside paint cans clanking against the sides—the noise that makes him feel like a kid on Christmas morning. Every time. He slowly opens his eyes and sees Audrey smiling, holding a thick, balled-up sweaterswaddling several cans of spray paint.

Voilà!

Hot damn.

I wrapped them in this so you wouldn't hear.

Grinning, Holden sets his beer on the floor. He wraps his arms around Audrey and holds her tightly for a long time. Her laughter is close to his ear.

Holden opens a playlist on his phone and chooses a metal cover of Rick Astley's "Never Gonna Give You Up." Furious tinny music fills the open room, and he swallows gulps of beer while sizing up the wall and deciding what to paint. Audrey lines up a bunch of cans at his feet.

Nice colours, he says, trying to remember any of the French he learned in school. Formidable.

Merci.

He cracks the lid off the first can with a suctiony pop—his second-favourite sound. First, he paints the outline of a big green and white throw up. His tag, and hers, too. Next, he works with shading, blending and weaving both of their tags together so it appears the letters are bouncing off the wall and each other. It's a luxury to work slowly. Lately it's all been run-and-gun.

Audrey pulls her camera from her bag and takes pictures from different angles while Holden works. She captures his body swaying, rising, and falling, smooth and rhythmic—a form of contemporary dance. Particles of dust and paint blaze in the air and swirl around him long after he's stopped moving. The chemical smell lingers even longer.

SEFER & VOID pulses from the wall. Beer and paint cans scatter across the floor.

∞

Audrey's voice, tender and brittle on the phone, whispered that she had loved Holden, that he was kind and charming and funny. During his two months in Montreal, they had spent many days together exploring different parts of the city. She also told me that as time went on, his condition deteriorated. He couldn't find a job; she'd seen a resume he'd forgotten in her room after he left and realized he hadn't included his contact information. He ran out of money, didn't eat much, drank constantly, did drugs, hardly slept because the bed he'd been given was a cot shoved in the corner of the kitchen, and he couldn't sleep anyway because he had scabies that kept him scratching all night.

She told me she had been really worried about his mental health. On one of their expeditions, he'd somehow peed on a pigeon, and afterward had insisted on standing guard over the bird, waiting for it to recover. She said he'd wept when it wouldn't fly away before they had to leave. She told me that one morning, distraught over the suicide by hanging of a friend, he had awakened on the roof of his apartment building with his arm hanging over the edge, not knowing how he'd ended up there. She'd been terrified. She told me he said if he didn't leave Montreal, he was going to do something really bad.

At the same time, Cam and I had been planning our own year-long trip. I didn't want to leave without seeing Holden, so I had arranged a three-day weekend in Montreal to spend a few days with him for his twenty-first birthday in July. I wanted to meet his friends, see where he'd been living and working, have some fun together. We never got that far.

I could always tell when Holden was impaired, because his spelling would deteriorate. As if his care about language was equal to his care for himself. I was shocked and very worried when he texted me one evening a few days before I was due to leave for Montreal.

> Hey momz just letting you know
> i might not stay here much lger
> i know you bought a ticket to

come to mont. for my b-day
but i might have to come home.
sorry.

That's okay honey, what's up in
Mtl? It's a beautiful sunset here
in Van.

i am not doing well physicall,
mentally or siritutally. I have to
come home to figure it out.

What do you mean? I thought
things were going well?

i have been battling bugs for
months mom. i'm going crazy.

What kind of bugs? Do you
mean bedbugs? Yuck!

Scabies. and i can't find a job
just everything

Do you need help? Can you call
me?

k imma walk down to the corner
and call you. too noisy here

My phone rang.
Holden, are you all right? Why didn't you tell me what was going on?
I did. His voice sounded vacant.

You said you had a rash—I was picturing something minor. You said you had a job. Do you have any money at all?

Nope.

Oh my god. When's the last time you ate something?

I don't know Mom, I just want to come home. I'm not okay.

All right, hold on, let me just check … I opened my computer. There's a flight at … 6:00 a.m. I'll email the ticket to you. And I'm sending you some money right now for food.

Thanks, Mom. I want. I just. I don't know what's happening.

I could hear him swallowing sobs. He sounded scared.

That's all right, love. You just come home. It's 9:00 here, which means it's midnight for you. Go get some food, then go to sleep for a bit. Set an alarm on your phone right now for 4:00 a.m. so you don't miss the plane. I'll send enough money for a taxi to the airport.

Okay, got it Momz, love you. Alarm at four.

Holden. That money is only for food and a taxi. Not for booze.

Thank you, Momz. See you tomorrow. Luz you.

∞

He's leaving. He's going home. Holden starts walking back toward the apartment to tell the crew. Dizziness and a swooping nausea roll over him. He raises one hand to the wall to steady himself, then continues to walk. The rough bricks slide by under his fingers. The wall feels solid, so he stops and rests his whole back against it, then slowly inches down until he's sitting on the sidewalk. Surges of relief and failure come and go, trains through a station. Hot tears soak his hot face.

Hey bruddah, what got you down?

It's Damien with the dreads and the loud girlfriend who lives in the apartment above them. Damien came down one day when he heard Holden blasting Peter Tosh, asking to borrow scissors as a way to take a break from the yelling girlfriend. He and Holden had talked, smoked, and become friends.

I'm going home, Dames.

And why that make you cry?

I don't know. Holden wipes his nose on his arm. I have to tell Audrey.

Here mon, take my pony.

Damien offers Holden his ten-speed bike with the leather seat and the wooden box strapped to the back. Holden stands, steadies himself against the wall, takes hold of the handlebars with one hand, and shakes Damien's hand with the other.

Thanks, D. He looks down at the *One Love* sticker on the bike's crossbar.

Ain't no shame in going home, my friend. Ain't no shame at all.

Damien pulls Holden toward him and, with the bike between them, wraps his long, muscular arms around Holden's pale, angular torso. Damien holds on until Holden's crying slows.

Ain't no shame, bruddah. Goina be all right.

Twenty minutes later Holden's outside the restaurant in Little Burgundy, waving at Audrey through the large front window. She stands behind the counter in a plaid skirt and a white shirt, looking like a schoolgirl. *Wait, is she a schoolgirl?* She waves at him, then points at her watch and holds up her hand like a five-fingered flower.

Holden props Damien's bike against the glass and sits once again on the ground. He leans his head back and closes his eyes.

A hand shakes his shoulder. Audrey's squatting beside him.

Hi there, what a nice surprise, she says.

Not really. You know how I told you I'm thinking of going back to Van?

Yup.

I'm going tomorrow morning.

Oh. She rocks back on her heels and lands sitting on the ground beside him. Fuck.

He can see her white underwear. I know. I just called my mom, and that's the ticket she got for me. I'm really sorry, Audrey, I just have to go. I'll come back though, as soon as I feel better, I promise.

That's okay, Skittle, I know you will. She glances down at her hands and says slowly, I think it's for the best, actually.

You do? Aren't you even going to miss me?

I'm going to miss you every minute of every day, Holden. I love you. But I've been really worried about you lately. I think maybe you need some help.

He's silent for a moment, his chin dips, then the pressure of the steam inside him increases.

Well, fuck you, then. He jumps up and yanks Damien's bike from the window, rattling the glass. The front wheel grazes her shoulder. He swings one leg over the crossbar, pushes down hard on the pedal, and wobbles away.

Back at the apartment, the boys take the news in a different way. They pool their money and buy three more flats of beer. They spray *Bon Voyage Sef* on the kitchen wall and start calling friends. Busta Rhymes gets loud.

Holden's propped in the corner of the packed, smoke-filled kitchen. He sees Audrey coming toward him, squeezing through the crowd.

There's my gummy bear, he says. His hot-sore eyes try to focus on hers. Welcome to my going away party. I am going away. His words trip and spill, a bottle of Wild Turkey dangles from his hand. When do I have to go to the airport?

Hello, and I don't know, Holden, I just got off work. I've been texting you all night, she shouts over the music. Why didn't you answer? What time is your flight?

I don't know. He reaches into his pocket for his phone and nearly topples over.

Yup, six o'clock in the morning.

Then you should be at the airport by 5:00 at the latest. You'll need to get a taxi in, like, an hour. The Metro won't be running yet.

He stands, moving like seaweed—swaying from the roots of his feet on the floor to the top of his head and the branches of his arms. He slowly lifts his face to meet her gaze, his eyelids thick and uncooperative.

His mouth is next to her ear. Will you come with me? To the airport?

Oh Skittle, I can't, I'm sorry, she yells into his ear over the music. My parents are probably freaking right now. She wraps her arms around his waist and rests her cheek on his chest the same way she did the first time they met. She staggers under his weight, and they stumble sideways together.

Some water might be a good idea, she says. She coerces the bottle from his hand and sets it on the counter, takes a dirty teacup from the sink, quickly rinses it, fills it from the tap, and hands it to him.

Thanks for showing me Montreal, Odds. I don't want to go, but I need to go. You know? Maybe you can come to Vangroovy?

I will. Absolutely. I have to go now, my parents are probably calling the FBI.

He feels her cold mouth against his hot cheek. He watches her snake her way out through the press of bodies and sound.

When Holden gets to the airport, he calls his mom.

You have a collect call from … *cough cough* … bonjour!

Yes, I'll accept the call, thank you, operator. Holden, it's 2:00 in the morning here. Are you at the airport?

I'm here Momz, I'm coming. It's all good. Très bien.

You sound very strange. Are you on something?

I am on a plane. I'm going on a plane. I'm flying across the land.

That money was for food, Holden. Only food. You said you were not well, and now you're plastered?

I'm coming. It's parfait. Chocolate parfayyyyy. I luz you, Momz.

For fuck's sake, he hears her say before the line goes dead.

∞

I was so furious with Holden for begging me to pull him out of a hole and then jumping right back into it that I asked his father to pick him up at the airport.

When Holden landed back in Vancouver, he didn't call me, and I didn't reach out to him.

If he wants to party himself into the ground, I am not about to enable it, I spouted to Cam. He needs to take responsibility for his own health and his own life.

Cam nodded. He'd been saying a version of this for the last few years. But concern showed on his face, too. He loved Holden and felt as helpless as I did. By the time Holden did come over, I had calmed down. He looked healthier than I expected. His dad had taken him to the doctor, and they'd gone for walks and swims and played golf. He looked rested and fed.

A few weeks later, nearly ready for our own departure, I asked Holden to come to the house and pack up his stuff so we could store it away with everything else while we travelled. He and I worked together in the cool of the basement, putting his extra clothes, books, CDs, and old artwork into boxes. I handed him a Sharpie—he always loved having a marker in his hand—and he labelled the boxes with his name and little drawings with captions.

He didn't say much, and neither did I.

Can I make you some lunch? It always felt better to feed him.

That's okay Momness, I gotta go.

Really? I thought we could talk, I said. *About Montreal,* I didn't say.

I'm meeting some people in Lynn Canyon.

Promise me you're not going to jump off the cliffs. People die there every year. And it's always stupid young men.

I'm not a jumper, Mom. Just going to cool off.

He hugged me, then walked out the door.

He may have stopped in the driveway and turned back to me. He may have made a small heart with his fingers and thumped it toward me from under the Spanish chestnut tree. Standing on the porch, I may have made the same shape with my hands and pressed it toward him before he disappeared behind the hedge.

Neither of us knew where to go from here. A tangible tension had grown between us. Me wanting him to grow up, sober up, and find some direction. Any direction. Him wanting me to mind my own business and let him live his life the way he desired. I hoped his breakdown in Montreal had shaken something loose. I hoped it was scary enough to lead him to some kind of therapy, a new path that could open a door to a healthier adulthood.

But Holden was in deeper trouble than I knew. His mental health was fraying, and he chose to ignore what had happened in Montreal and carry on numbing himself. Now I see that he probably didn't even remember calling me from the airport that morning. I didn't understand how much he needed me to be kind and patient instead of angry and stubborn. If I'd just been a little more compassionate, if I'd just gotten over my ego and my conditioning and brought him close, would that have saved him? Would one more kindness have kept him off the floor of that room? Retrospect is a devastating vantage point.

I rationalized that perhaps some physical space between us might be best for our relationship in the long term. I decided to trust that the life skills we'd implanted in him would rise to the surface, given the chance. He was intelligent and resourceful. Polite and capable. He knew how to budget, he could do laundry and cook. Whether he *would* do those things would be his choice.

If you can save up the airfare, you can come and join us anywhere for a few weeks, I told Holden at our goodbye dinner the night before we departed.

But you're rich, he said, implying we should pay for his ticket.

All you have to do is get there, I said. We'll take care of the rest.

For sure, Momz, that would be cool. I'll try.

We may even have clinked our green beer bottles together. But something was missing behind the usual vitality in his mossy eyes. The gesture was empty, like agreeing to "have coffee" when you know you never will. We both knew his travelling to meet up with Cam, Lyla, and me was unlikely. It was difficult to afford living in Vancouver. Saving an extra thousand dollars for a flight halfway around the world would be almost impossible. But I didn't want to give him another free ticket; I wanted him to work for it. I wanted him to be responsible for his own rewards.

I was too intent on my own life transition to pay close attention to my son's. All I could aim for was my own unknown future just over the horizon. Sometimes when you're looking for yourself, you lose sight of those closest to you.

I became preoccupied with logistics. We bought life insurance, got vaccinated for rare diseases, and updated our wills. In the notary's office, Cam and I made sure that if we both perished in a plane crash, Holden wouldn't get any inheritance until he was twenty-five. By then he'd have a prefrontal cortex and would be better able to handle it, we joked. We thought the conversation was hypothetical.

We flew away.

20

Sometime that fall or winter, Holden began using heroin. This is shocking news for any parent to hear. And because of the clinging vines the drug comes associated with, even harder to accept. Heroin is shameful. Heroin is something *other* people do—dirty skeletal shadows scratching in doorways whom nobody cares about—not my child, not my bright and beautiful son, whose head had once fit perfectly in the bowl of my hand. How could someone I valued more than anything value himself so little? How does any intelligent person decide to ingest a substance they know could at worst kill them, and at best make their life a misery? The evidence was easy to see on the streets he walked regularly. Holden was reckless, but he wasn't stupid.

On a busy street corner in East Van, one of Holden's friends reiterated some of his finer qualities: humour, creativity, the way he would always curate a song to leave playing before he left.

He'd be gone, but the music would still be playing, and I'd have that freakin' song stuck in my head all day, the friend said, pressing his chewed, black-painted fingertips to his eye sockets.

Sitting across from me at a nearby cafe, the friend told me how much fun Holden was to be around—so funny, caring, and smart—but that he often seemed to reach a summit where some kind of switch would flip, sending him racing, alone, through the dark to an invisible destination.

According to the friend, taking drugs like MDMA, magic mushrooms, and cocaine was a regular part of their culture. He spoke about drug use casually, as if referring to the oatmeal cookie sitting on the table in front on him. He told me that when they'd lived together, Holden drank heavily every day, and once he was drunk, he would consume pretty much anything. Various people corroborated this with various scenarios. A sad theme I couldn't ignore.

Holden had used heroin. He started somehow. There was a first time. He was a person who did not use heroin, and then he was a person who did. The specific details of those intersecting lines aren't as important as their impact.

The friend had a theory that Holden had used heroin for the first time by accident, thinking it was something else.

∞

He likes having the place to himself. Dad is out with a buddy, maybe on the seawall or at the local pub. Stretched out on the couch, listening to the rain rolling in off the ocean and crackling against the deck doors, Holden throws up a Facebook post. A photo of a man standing in a trailer park holding a megaphone to his mouth.

> I am going to get drunk as fuck
> tonight! I repeat: Drunk. As.
> Fuck!! Who's with me?

Replies bubble up on his screen in baby-blue rounded rectangles.

MEEEEE!

come thru!

My Dude! where, im down.

The last comment is from Darius. They've painted a few times. Darius can always hook Holden up with some booger sugar, but that would definitely not chill the rattling between his ribs. Or the unsettled, restless feeling that often seems to grab him.

He's about to go yank one off in the shower when his phone vibrates in his hand and the distorted thump of A Tribe Called Quest rises from its tiny, tinny speaker. *Here we go yo, here we go yo / So what, so what, so what's the scenario?* Best dollar he ever spent was on that ring tone.

It's Claire. Holden met her last spring in Montreal, when they were both pretty messed up. She knew some of the graf crew there. He thought she was a meth head, but she seems to be better now that she's back in Van. Mostly they just go to skuzz bars, drink a shit tonne, and paint. There's not that many chicks who can paint.

Hola, Molar!

Hey, I saw your post. I've got an extra ticket to the Venom Womb show at the Rickshaw tonight. Wanna go? I think there's like five other bands.

Absolutely, but how much are the tickets? I'm not so green at the mo.

Don't worry, I got you, she says. I owe you one from last time.

You don't owe me anything.

Whatever. Why don't you come through before we go?

Solid. Just gotta shower and I'm hittin' it, Holden says. Hey, how's your face?

Not as scarred as my couch, she laughs.

Oh damn, I forgot about that.

They make new ones all the time.

Faces?

Couches, you loser. See you in a bit.

The rain kicks up as Holden steps off the bus near Granville Street and walks along Georgia Street by the Bay with its golden doors and huge windows full of weirdly tall white-plastic people in expensive clothes. He sidesteps the long line of slick raincoats waiting at the bus stop—obedient penguins beneath umbrellas—and walks under the glass awning, his breath keeping time to his stride, which is keeping time with the Wu-Tang playing in his earbuds. There's a smell of wet pavement, the smell that says his socks won't be dry anytime soon. It's oddly comforting.

Down near the corner, on the last dry section of sidewalk, a figure sits, leaning against the wall. As he gets closer, Holden can see that the man has oozing eyes and matted hair and is wearing several layers of dirty jackets, but just one shoe—his exposed foot is puffy, almost magenta, and raw. Nicotine-stained fingers hold a worn piece of cardboard that reads, *Smile If You Masterbate.*

The man flitters the sign in his direction. Holden plucks out one earbud.

You got me on that one. He grins, digs into his pocket and flips a loonie to the man, who snatches it from the air with surprisingly quick reflexes.

I thought so!

The block of darkening sky he can see between the buildings fills with a symphony of crows. Thousands of black wingbeats brush the slate canvas. They move with both freedom and intention, like fireworks, like an underwater school of fish, like a time-lapse video of a flower blooming. Every morning they leave from someplace in Burnaby, he thinks, to scatter, move, and reassemble along the musical staff of power lines down by the rail yard. He's watched the murder many times while painting trains. Like living quarter and half notes, they change the tempo of their song as they caw and fight on the wires. Then, each night, on some unheard 5-6-7-8 count in, they swirl en masse back to the lake to roost. Every morning. Every night. A beautiful charcoal wingstorm.

One means anger; two is mirth; three a wedding; four a birth; five is heaven; six is hell; seven is the devil himself. So, what does five thousand mean?

By the time Holden gets to Claire's apartment, the shoulders of his jacket are soaked, his hair and the beard he is attempting to grow, dripping. He shakes like a wet dog outside the building. Claire buzzes him in.

At the top of the stairs, Holden sees a long tattooed arm extending into the hall through a crack in the door. The hand holds a green can of beer. Holden laughs and takes the can. The door closes. He hears laughter. Claire flings open the door and pulls him into the small apartment. The mothball smell of thrift-store clothes and cigarettes.

Hello! Claire's smile is huge, and her voice sounds like a seven-year-old's. She hugs Holden tightly, hangs up his jacket, then pushes him over to the green striped couch against the wall where *DESER* is scrawled in red across the back. She drops beside him, making the cushions bounce.

Sorry about that. Holden gestures to his tag on the back of the sofa.

No big. I'm thinking about painting the whole thing. Making it an installation.

In that case, you're welcome. He cracks the beer.

Somebody say they want to get drunk as fuck tonight? she asks, opening her own beer.

As fuck, Holden says, chugging half the can.

Just how drunk is as fuck?

Somewhere between blackout and stomach pump.

Roger that. Tough week? Claire swivels her angular body to face Holden, folding her long legs. He thinks of a mantis.

You could say that, he begins. He stops.

Claire nods but stays quiet, so Holden has to fill in the silence.

I'm living with my dad. He's cool and everything, but the place is pretty small. I just don't have another option at the moment. My dad wanted me to do something called Sober October with him.

Sounds excruciating.

It actually wasn't that bad, I made it, like, two weeks.

Claire raises her hand for a high-five.

My mom wants me to go to rehab and she's not even here, she's in fucking Portugal or Thailand or something. She keeps sending me articles about Deepak fucking Chopra.

My dad sent me to rehab and it totally cured me, Claire says.

Obviously.

They both laugh and knock their cans together.

I'm just fucking sick of talking about it, Holden says.

In that case, perhaps you'd like one of these? Claire reaches for two shot glasses sitting on the coffee table, already full of light-brown liquid. When she smiles, Holden notices the shadow of rot darkening several of her teeth.

To not talking about it, Claire says.

To never fucking talking about it.

She refills their glasses. To Sober October, she says.

May she rest in peace, Holden says and swallows his second shot.

Claire hands him the bottle, then reaches for a wooden box on the table. She pulls out a joint and lights it, exhaling a blue-grey stream.

How's the new job?

She passes the joint and Holden takes a deep drag, inflating his chest, growing taller. He holds the smoke for a moment, then exhales, deflating his body and roaring, Ahhh. It's okay. The people are nice. I help old ladies buy acrylics so they can make shitty still lifes. Flowers and fruit. So much fucking ochre. And canary. I basically just wear a cardigan and sell yellow for eight hours a day. I am a yellow seller.

Do you get a discount on cans? Claire asks.

Not yet, but I will after three months. They keep that shit locked up because of vandals like us. Holden hands her back the joint.

I've got a few cans, she says. We can paint after the show if you want.

Holden takes a pull straight from the bottle. He looks again at his tag scribbled across the back of Claire's couch. *DESER*.

He's done with Sefer, has been for a while. It's Deser now. In Dutch it means the one who gets to decide. He holds up the bottle. Can I bring this?

Be my guest.

Holden takes sips from the bottle as they walk to the club. At the mouth of an alley they pass a Dumpster embroidered with tags. Holden pulls a thick white marker from his pocket and shakes it, stirring the ink inside.

They don't keep *these* bad boys locked up, he says. He bites the lid off the pen and holds the cap in the corner of his grin like he's smoking a cigar.

Claire laughs and shakes her head.

Holden scrawls *DESER* across the end of the Dumpster and hands the marker to Claire. She squats low and adds the words *Drunk as Fuck* under his tag. He laughs and hands her the bottle. She takes a swallow and gasps, shaking her head, then offers what's left back to Holden, who drains the bottle and lobs it into the Dumpster with a loud echoing clang.

The earlier showers have pushed people even deeper into doorways and under the faded and ripped awnings that line East Hastings Street. Garbage litters the sidewalk like nowhere else in the city. Paper, glass, strips of fabric, and broken pieces of plastic. A snowfall of cigarette butts. And gum, there's always so much gum. Small groups huddle under old tents and dilapidated structures made from shopping carts, bent umbrellas, and scrap metal draped with tarps and dirty, wet blankets.

Gaunt figures dart across the street and swoop around corners into alleys. The street is alive with perpetual motion. Bodies rocking, twisting, and shifting remind Holden of sand fleas on the beach scattering in panic when their sheltering seaweed is raked away. He notices pockmarked faces, angry faces, ones with bulbous comic-book noses, women with dark smears of makeup below their eyes, ones who pace and talk to themselves. The smell is piss and garbage.

This part of town has made Holden sad ever since he was a little kid driving through with his mom and she said something like, Look at these poor souls. What happened to them? At some point they were all somebody's baby. That day he'd been shocked and afraid. Now he's used to it. Most of the people he's met painting in the alleys have been pretty decent.

A man with long black hair and a beak of a nose sits hunched against a building, a collection of bike parts, sunglasses, and tools laid out on a stained towel in front of him. A dented cowboy hat with a long feather tucked in the band is pulled low over his forehead.

Hey, buddy, what's for sale? Holden says.

The man's small black eyes scan Holden.

All kinds of shit. He extends an arm above the array of objects they both know are stolen.

Claire stands back while Holden bends to look more closely at the collection of junk on the towel. Can I buy that wrench?

For five bucks you can.

Holden's fingers emerge from his pocket with a folded ten-dollar bill. He picks up the crescent wrench, turning the heavy tool over in his hand, rolling the worm screw up and down under his thumb, watching the jaws open and close. The man slowly pats his breast pockets, searching for change they both know isn't coming.

That's all right, man, you keep it, Holden says. Hey, what's your name?

Percy.

Nice to meet you, Percy, I'm Holden. He extends a hand toward Percy, who pushes his hat back on his head and slowly shakes Holden's hand. The two nod to each other. When Holden straightens up, he loses his balance. Claire grabs his arm and pulls him down the street toward the Rickshaw.

You idiot, now you're totally broke, she says.

True, but look at this, he says, and slaps the heavy metal into the palm of his left hand with a satisfying smack. Just imagine what I can open with this. He stumbles off the edge of the curb.

The neon sign of the Rickshaw comes into view, its glow diffusing across the wet street as they cross Main.

The bright white marquee lists tonight's bands: Venom Womb, Harangue, 3 Inches of Blood, Bitchsplitter, Unravelling. As they get closer to the door, a muted thudding leaks through the walls of the club, and Holden feels the reverberation in his chest cavity. *Wump, wump, wump.* Liquid excitement spreads into his legs and arms; his fingers form chords. Holden pulls open the heavy door and waves Claire in. He follows her into a sea of noise and heads perched on shoulders.

Claire pulls two tickets from a small purse strung across her tall, thin body. She hands them to a bald-headed bouncer in a teal golf shirt, the sleeves of which seem to constrict the flow of blood to his cantaloupe biceps. The bouncer stamps their wrists with a skull and crossbones in smudged black ink.

Bag check in the corner. The bouncer gestures with his shiny head to the corner of the lobby. Claire takes off her jacket, folds it, and slips it inside her pack, then hands the bag to Holden. He rolls up his jacket and shoves it into her pack as well. Claire checks the bag, then crosses her thin arms tight against her chest. She shivers.

Inside the theatre, Holden and Claire thread down the sloped aisle toward the mosh pit, then veer off to the edge of it. Close enough to feel the heat emanating from the whirl of bodies, but far enough away so as not to get smoked by a stray elbow. They're assaulted by sound; the music is transparent yet solid—thick enough to surround Holden. The industrial rhythm and shrieking guitars fill all of his cracks. This music is exactly what he needs.

Beer? Claire yells, raising an invisible drink to her lips.

Are you sure? He's been scabbing off her all night.

She squeezes his arm and heads for the bar in the back corner. On stage, the band is raging. Necks torquing, long hair whipping, beards keeping time, fingers machinelike. The drummer, shirtless and completely tattooed, contorts on his stool, his arms an octopus blur. The lead singer growls just short of rupturing his vocal cords. Fury grows, sweat flies, the pit writhes like a bowl of steroid-jacked puppies.

The force of the sound erases any thoughts; there is only the pounding and the clang. If meditation removes the past and the future, this is his. He circles slowly at first, then wades in, leading with his left shoulder before stepping back out again. Second time in, he bounces off somebody's back and gets pushed into a damp shoulder. Bodies thrash around him, slamming into each other, advancing and retreating. Sweat, sound, heat.

The ache drips away, melting into a pool of noise and motion. His body doesn't matter. He recalls the lava lamp he had as a teenager, on the bookshelf in his basement bedroom. He is colour and shape, form morphing in a never-ending fluid rearrangement. It's everything, it's nothing, it's quiet.

Thank you, you've been splendid, fuck off.

The sudden lack of sound jolts Holden from wherever he was. He blinks. The band is leaving the stage. His chest swells, his hair soaked with sweat. He wipes his forehead on his sleeve and looks around for Claire. She isn't where he last saw her, so he joins the crowd ambling up the slope, lined with the club's original violet-velvet movie seats, and out into the lobby. His ears ring, his face burns. The room is packed with red-cheeked people lining up for the bar, shreds of conversation filling the air above their heads. He doesn't see Claire here either, so he heads for the exit.

Steam rises from pods of figures out on the sidewalk, their shapes backlit by the streetlights. Low gut laughter to his left, a shout to his right. A hand lands on his shoulder, and Holden spins, expecting to see Claire's doe eyes and red lips. Instead it's the tight curls and thick eyebrows of Darius.

Bruh, what's good? Darius sticks out a paint-splattered hand.

Oh hey, man, sup?

Darius pulls Holden in for a chest bump. Just painting under the viaduct. Thought I'd see what's the shit over here.

Rippin' show, says Holden. Set melted my face off.

Who's up next?

Holden turns to check the marquee over his shoulder. The sudden swivel throws him off balance, and he stumbles until the black-painted brick of the Rickshaw stops his motion; his shoulder hits the wall with a thwack. It's Unravelling, Holden says.

No shit, man. You, too? says Darius.

Holden laughs. No dude, the next band. He points to the names on the sign above them. Unravelling.

Darius turns and looks up. D'oh!

You can come in with me if you want, Holden offers. He holds up his wrist to show the ink stamp and licks it. They press their wrists together.

Okay sweet, how about a little bonk before we go in? Darius asks.

I'm down, says Holden. Hey, have you seen Claire out here? He's pretty sure Darius knows her.

Nope, says Darius. He heads down the block and ducks into the doorway of a darkened convenience store. Holden follows. In one smooth motion, Darius pulls out a small bag, takes a ring of keys from his pocket, and dips one of the keys into the bag to scoop up a small amount of white powder. He offers the key to Holden.

You first, bud, Darius says. It's good to see ya. We should go paint trains again soon.

We should, says Holden. He takes the key from Darius, raises it to his nose, and snorts the powder deep into his sinuses. Darius loads up the key again, and Holden does the same on the other side. His head jolts back, and his eyes clamp closed. The inside of his nose burns. Sizzles, like he's been branded.

Jesus Christ! What the fuck is that? Holden says.

Whaddaya mean?

What *is* that?

It's down.

Holy fuck, Holden says.

I thought …

Nope. Holden gasps, tasting the strange flavour in the back of his throat, bittersweet and warm. Nope, thought it was blow.

Holden searches up and down the street, as though if he leaves now, he can outrun it. He shuffles backward until his back meets the door of the convenience store, then slowly slides down the glass, his wet shirt leaving a slug trail of sweat as he descends. He lands on a welcome mat that says Pepsi.

Sweet Jesus.

It's like he's getting fifteen blowjobs at the same time. His body is molten, shimmering. He's cocooned, and his muscles are made of sugar. Every problem he's ever had, even the ones he can't even articulate, has just been solved. And it's not just relief from misery, it's the sensation of joy. He's held, carried, content, happy, euphoric. But none of these words is enough. Whatever cavity he had in his centre has been filled in. He's whole. It's the best he's ever felt in his life. The closest to himself he's ever been.

And he's sick.

He leans over, and a stream of acid projects from his stomach. He doesn't mind.

Darius, what the fuck did you do? That sounds like Claire. There she is, standing on the sidewalk, feet planted wide, hands on hips. All she needs is a cape.

Nothing, I just gave him a little salt, says Darius.

You're a fucking asshole. He's been drinking all night. Are you fucking stupid?

Claire steps into the dim alcove, squats down, and rests her hands on Holden's knees. Holden, look at me, he hears her say from somewhere far away.

He rights his head and works to keep his eyes open. Hello Ms. Claire, where did you go?

There was a lineup for the bathroom. Are you okay? she asks.

I'm fine, super duper, ten out of ten. His face tingles, his tongue is a foreign object. Never better. Let's go watch the show. He thinks about getting up, but his legs don't belong to him anymore.

We are not going to watch the show. Our good friend here just gave you H. You stay put and I'll go grab our stuff, she says. Darius, you fucking prick, stay with him until I get back.

Okay, shit, sorry, I thought he knew, Darius says.

Holden leans back against the door. He sees Darius out near the edge of the road, leaning into the passenger window of a car pulled up to the curb. Holden feels like he's here, but not here.

Claire's sitting beside him.

How's it going?

Great. Never better. The bones in his shoulders seem to be bending.

Let's go for a walk, she says. Gotta keep you awake, mister.

She stands, then hoists Holden to his feet. His posture is unsteady, liquid. She pulls his jacket out of her pack and helps him put it on, then pulls on her own and links her arm through his, guiding him down East Hastings in the direction of her apartment.

Rain falls. They walk in silence for half a block.

I'm in deep shit, aren't I? Holden says.

Highly possible.

He notices a hard and heavy lump knock against his ribs from inside his jacket. He reaches in to see what it is. Then he remembers.

It's okay, he says, I have this. I can fix anything.

21

We started in Paris, then headed south. In August, we stayed with extended family in the bottom-left corner of France, in a village so small it's not on the map. We laughed and ate delicious homegrown heirloom tomatoes and rillettes de canard on fresh baguettes and drank chilled white wine every evening in the pastel light while the cicadas sang.

Lyla and I jogged through fields of tall corn. We looked after our in-laws' dog while they attended a family reunion in Normandy, and they helped us buy an old blue Peugeot so we could go wherever we wanted, whenever we wanted.

In September we explored the north of Spain and the Douro Valley in Portugal. We stomped grapes and hiked. We surfed in the Algarve, I did yoga on rooftops while roosters crowed at the dawn, then we zig-zagged through Spain, soaking up sun, history, and art. In October we returned to France to study French for three hours every morning in the shadow of the enormous medieval fortress in Carcassonne. We ate crepes and cassoulet and lived in the tiny village of Villegailhenc. The house was a former flour mill, and Lyla's bed rested on top of an ancient granite millstone. We would send her down to the boulangerie each morning for fresh croissants. Every Friday we filled our glass jug with local wine for one euro per litre. We made friends.

In November we marked my fiftieth birthday by spending a few weeks exploring the narrow winding roads of Corsica. When the temperature dropped, I did an online search: "Where do French people go in winter?" We booked a flight to Seychelles.

Though our noses tracked the sun, my mind always returned to Holden. The entire time we travelled, I worried. I worried and I prayed and I sent beams of golden protective light to him across the universe, and when that didn't seem enough, I made offerings. I knelt in mosques. In Notre-Dame, I lit a candle for him. Another in Sacré-Coeur. I lit candles to illuminate the void where Holden should have been. As if a small flame on the other side of the world would do some good. In magnificent cathedrals, I struck matches. I sparked flames in tiny blue-domed shrines and rustic chapels that smelled of goats. I ignited thin tapers and smoking incense sticks on little islands polka-dotting the Indian Ocean. In caves filled with batshit and stalagmites and mould, wax dripped for Holden.

I said prayers for him every morning and every night, just as I had done his whole life.

Please god, protect Holden, keep him safe in the palm of your hand. He is a good person with a good heart, and he will make an exceptional adult. He's being reckless right now because he's confused. Have you ever been confused? He doesn't know what's good for him because he's very interested in what's bad for him. Have you ever been attracted to the darkness? Under the anger, he has so much to offer the world. Please protect him from harm until he can figure himself out. He will be one of your finer citizens. I promise.

I lit candles to scare away my own unthinkable thoughts. I wished upon star after star after star. Through a tropical winter, I pleaded with the Southern Cross to carry my message to any deity who had the authority to make these kinds of decisions. I dipped my fingers in tarnished bowls of last month's holy water, lobbed coins over my shoulder into fountains, and left smooth sacrificial stones on the doorstep of a woman who was said to have mystical powers. She worshiped doves.

I snapped wishbones. A flock of bird skeletons cracked in Holden's name. They broke easily, like hearts. The long, winning bones I stashed in my backpack. The unlucky stubs I threw away, choosing not to believe in them. I rationalized that if I could wish on a star, I could probably wish on anything beautiful, so I began sending my silent desires to rivers and waterfalls, sunsets, and snow-capped mountains. I stared at famous paintings in galleries and castles and implored the ghosts of the dead masters to turn my son away from destruction.

But what specific destruction was I afraid of? I didn't even know its name. I remember wondering if this was unusual behaviour. Questioning whether other people, other parents, made intimate deals with gods to spare their loved ones?

Why did I light candles and utter prayers, fracture bones and cast desperate wishes into the universe instead of flying home and taking him by the hand? Why didn't I simply say, Holden, I don't know what you're up to, but I have a terrible feeling, and I'm very worried about you? Can you tell me what is truly going on?

I have no answer. There is no answer. Because I never asked the question.

I knew Holden was a heavy drinker, as I had been in my early twenties. And as every one of my friends had been. I knew he used the occasional party drug, as I had in my early twenties. I knew he climbed to dangerous places to paint his graffiti. I can't count the number of cliffs I jumped from, landing safely in deep water.

Maybe a reckless streak was as hereditary as hazel eyes or freckles, so how could I gauge what was manageable? How could I tell the difference between typical early adult narcissism and authentic peril? Hadn't my own mother lain awake many nights, waiting for the comforting sound of the wooden gate scraping the cement walk at the side of the house and the back door closing with a click before letting herself sink fully into sleep?

Cam, Lyla, and I followed the sun to the many breathtaking islands and coastlines of Seychelles, then Mauritius. We drifted with currents along reefs, explored sunken ships, dove with small sharks, sea turtles, and a kaleidoscope of fish, and our skin tanned to milk chocolate.

I tried to reach Holden on Skype every Sunday, as we'd planned, but he rarely accepted the calls. I sent regular emails with updates on where we were, what we were doing, and photos of street art I thought he'd appreciate. He rarely returned my messages, and when he did, he wrote just a line or two.

nothing to tell you, everything's fine, just working
and painting and hanging with friends.

I begged him to tell me more. What are you thinking about? What interests you? Tell me what you're reading, which movies you've been watching. Relationships are better when we know all of each other's boring stuff! I felt like a desperate teenage girl begging for attention. In one email, I grovelled.

I'm asking you to tell me about your life!?!

It's all good, Momz, nothing to tell. Just skateboarding, watching hockey, and working.

I'd like to say the faraway time zones and sketchy Wi-Fi in the low-budget places we stayed during the three-month African part of our trip made reaching him tough, but the truth is that I was tired of propping up our relationship. Holden never made an effort to reach me. That stung. You don't necessarily have to leave home to create distance, but it helps.

At Christmas, we used dental floss to hang painted seashells on the branches of a palm. We spoke with Holden on the phone fifteen thousand kilometres away. He sounded happy, eating turkey and opening gifts. He was watching *A Christmas Story.* He sent a picture of himself wearing the jacket he'd bought with the Christmas money we sent him. I liked the idea that he was at least protected from the weather.

Later I found out he'd never bought a jacket. He'd just borrowed one, taken a picture of himself wearing it, and kept the money. We also didn't know that while we bathed in tropical breezes and Takamaka Rum, Holden was wading into the darkest, most dangerous phase of his life.

By the end of January, Holden wasn't responding to any type of contact. It was as if he had vanished. I look back over our emails of that time, and all I see is my own anger. After being ignored for so long, I lashed out.

Why the fuck aren't you replying to any of my emails?

Have you been emailing me? Haven't notice haven't been checking
I suppose. Left my job I dont know what I want to do now.
Probably going back to Montreal but all flights are rally expensive.

How can you go to Montreal with no money? How will you
survive?

I'm applying for a credit card but i will almost certainly be denied
because I bullshitted all my info. Give me a time to skype and
ill try my best to acquiesce. Its hard because I'm pretty much
couch surfng

Holden, It's quite obvious I've been trying to reach you. By email
and Skype, so don't give me that BS. How can you go to Montreal

with no money? It didn't work last time for that very reason,
remember? You were in a very bad situation. Remember!!
Holden, I want to talk to you. When can we talk? Please don't
keep ignoring me.

You can afford to be horrible to someone when you think you have
forever to apologize. No wonder he wouldn't tell me what was really
going on. I had become that clichéd nagging mother.

In mid January, Cam, Lyla, and I weathered the near-miss of Cyclone
Bansi in Mauritius. The storm carried winds of over 240 kilometres per
hour. We stocked up on water and food and made emergency plans, but
we didn't leave. When I sent Holden NASA photographs of the size of
the storm in relation to the tiny island we were stuck on—a lone crou-
ton floating in a bowl of soup—he finally replied. He was genuinely
concerned.

Holy crap Momz. Are you guys
okay? Are you in a safe place?
Jeez!

It had seemed like we were in more danger than he was.

I began having night terrors. Though I didn't outwardly acknowledge the extent of Holden's drug use, perhaps my subconscious knew
what I was not willing to face. In a semi dream state I was smothered by
a dark beast that was trying to suffocate me. My throat clamped shut.
I gasped for breath. Night after night, I would be awakened by Cam's
warm hand gently shaking my arm.

Babe, it's okay, we're fine. Lyla is in her bed, and Holden's with his
dad in Vancouver.

Why are you saying that?

Because you keep asking where the kids are and trying to climb up the wall.

Late February, back in Europe, with a friendlier time zone and reliable internet, making contact with Holden was easier. From a drafty artist's loft overlooking the Rue de Rivoli in Paris, we finally connected.

I'm so glad to see your face, how are you?

He had shaved his head close and kept his scraggly red beard. His voice was a slow, low rumble. Good, Mom, everything's all right.

Really? You look kind of different.

It's all good, I just woke up and I'm hungry, that's all.

Oh right, it's morning there. I was thinking about when we were here together. And you found out you'd been accepted to Emily Carr. Wasn't that so exciting?

I wasted that, too, he said, shaking his head, looking down at the table between his hands.

That's okay, honey, you can always go back. If you want to.

I could see a little bit of the apartment over his shoulder. Bare floor, bare walls, an unmade bed. I was elated to finally get a visual measure of how he was doing. Witnessing his physicality reassured me. He could hide behind cryptic emails, but couldn't hide from the camera. I sensed him avoiding eye contact. His elbows propped up on the table, his head pendulumming from side to side. He kept pinching the skin of his arm as if he were picking lint off of a sweater. I could see the *us and them* tattoo on his chest and the one on his arm, *courage.*

So, who is this lady friend you mentioned in your email? Are you guys getting serious? I mean, you're living together?

Her name's Jenna and no, we're not serious, she's more of a friend. We're just sharing the rent.

What's she like?

She's older. She's a barista. She makes me eat vegetables.

Then I like her already.

We both laughed at that. We talked about his job working at the art supply store.

I'm thinking of quitting. The customers give me too much anxiety.

What do you mean?

It's just a bunch of old ladies painting landscapes, Mom. I can't handle it.

I assumed he was just bored. I didn't ask him what his anxiety felt like. If it scared him. If it made his heart pound, his stomach roil, his vision blur. I didn't ask him if he had the same rattle in his chest that I did.

Well, retail is not for everyone, I said.

His physical movements were different, sort of listless and apologetic. I assumed he was in the well of another depression. We spoke for half an hour, and though he didn't ask much about what we were seeing and doing, I'm sure he asked about his little sister. He always did.

I love you, Holden. And remember, if you can scrape together your own airfare, you can still come join us anywhere over here. It would be so great to have you with us.

Sounds good, Mom. I love you, too.

When I ended the call, I felt relieved. Seeing him had reassured me. But there was something scratching at the door.

How's he doing? Cam asked. He was sitting on a wicker chair in the corner by the big floor-to-ceiling windows with Juliet balconies.

He says he's fine, but I don't know, he seems wiggly, like he's on something.

Cam looked up from his book. He could be.

And even then, I didn't get it. I didn't really put it together. Nothing in my mind even remotely suspected that he had moved on to harder drugs and was at that moment likely addicted to heroin. I didn't even hear myself talking. Or didn't care to listen closely enough.

Denial comes at many intersections along the road. It always comes after the loss, and sometimes it comes before.

22

Hi, I'm Rose, and I'm an alcoholic. Total alcoholic. As per the definition of the word.

Hi Rose! everyone chimed together, as if we were a class of schoolchildren greeting our teacher. I jolted at the sound. The low-ceilinged room appeared to double as a preschool in daylight. I smelled Play-Doh and chicken noodle soup.

Rose stood behind a folding table and called the meeting to order. She welcomed new and returning members with a warm smile and a voice so rough it could sand floors. She quickly covered housekeeping matters with the confidence of a corporate CEO. Several of Rose's teeth were missing.

The famous Twelve Steps were listed on a paper banner hanging behind her. I had never actually read the words before.

When a friend had confided in me about his daughter Jessie's heroin addiction and how she wasn't taking his calls, I offered to try and reach her, do whatever I could to help. Because now I understood how easy it was for a smart, sensitive person to find herself wearing a leghold trap, wondering, How the hell did I get here? *Hi, I'm Tara, and my son is dead.*

If I couldn't have my own child back, perhaps my friend could have his.

We were deep in a church basement in what could only be called an unfortunate part of town. Holden's friend Claire had led Jessie and me down the dark steps. When we bowed under the narrow doorway, I felt like I was entering a biker gang clubhouse—not that I'd ever been to a biker gang clubhouse. The entrance was crowded with dark leather, deep voices, and styrofoam cups.

Holden's first apartment had been near here. We'd had a family dinner together just around the corner after he moved in. The four of us around a red-checkered tablecloth, eating iceberg salad, spaghetti, and garlic bread.

Beside me, Jessie nodded, the full weight of her head falling, rising, falling, jerking back up. I put my arm around the sharp corner of her shoulder so she wouldn't tip over. She awoke with a spasm, and our faces were so close together I could smell her breath. Cigarettes, gum, and something else. Her scratched glasses, one arm taped together with a Band-Aid, had slipped down her nose. She did not, or could not, lift her hand to push them back up. She was staring at me, wide-eyed and slack. Her thick layers of clothing not doing a very good job of hiding how thin she had become.

Before heroin, Jessie had been curvy, with porcelain skin and magazine-cover makeup. She'd cared a lot about how she looked—she drank smoothies, manicured her eyebrows, and jogged. A workplace back injury in her mid-thirties resulted in pain prescriptions, then when her doctor cut her off, Jessie's addiction led her to the street.

Now her head was the largest part of her body. Her brassy blond hair, shaved close on one side, rested heavily against my neck. A small navy-blue heart was tattooed on her temple.

How are you doing? I asked.

I feel sick. It's like I'm dreaming.

A flash of chipped orange polish on her blackened nails caught Jessie's attention, and her fingers disappeared into the balled-up scarf in her lap. I noticed a black streak of ash on her swanlike neck. A sign that she had been smoking heroin. Horse, brown, skag, China white, beast. These were words I knew now.

I had learned a lot in long the months since Holden died. I had learned that a mistake can get you started, and twenty dollars can get you killed.

Jessie fidgeted and rocked beside me. It's a lot to take in, she said, her tongue sluggish, sticky.

How are *you* doing? she asked me. Her kindness had not left when addiction launched its hostile takeover. It was a reasonable question. Jessie knew better than most how I'd been gasping for breath since Holden died.

Same as you, I said.

Claire sat on my left. Upright and fresh-faced, her pixie cut and fawn eyes at odds with the jumble of homemade tattoos scribbled on her legs, arms, and fingers. It was Claire who had suggested I bring Jessie to this meeting. Claire had been in recovery since the night she came to our door and would occasionally update me on her progress.

When I had asked her what I could do to help support Jessie and her family, Claire had replied, Well, heroin wasn't my DOC. I liked the other bad one, but the program works for all kinds of addictions. I go to meetings almost every day. Why don't you come with me and see? She wanted to help. Helping was step twelve.

I'm Ray, alcoholic.

Hi, Ray!

The group's enthusiasm for sobriety offended me in a way I couldn't quite understand.

Seven years ago I got tricked into rehab. Ray scanned the crowd and smirked. I'm not kidding.

Easy laughter bubbled all around us. Metal chairs squeaked. Ray was healthy-handsome, with flecks of grey dappling his thick black hair. I suspected that he didn't live in this postal code. He had likely crossed a bridge or two to be here. His clothing appeared intentionally distressed, as if he had grabbed the grubbiest T-shirt he could find at the bottom of his laundry basket. And Ray was not the only pretender in the room—before leaving home, I had taken off my earrings and put on the jacket I wore to walk the dog.

Behind us, a man coughed over and over, phlegm rattling in his throat, very close to the back of my head. I hadn't hung my purse on the back of my chair; I cradled it in my lap.

Ray continued. My partner at the time showed me a brochure with a dog and a palm tree on it and I thought, that looks like a nice holiday. Laughter. He shrugged. When I got off the plane in the desert, there was a guy standing there holding a sign with my name on it. Ray, he said, holding up an invisible sign. I pulled down my baseball hat and walked right past him into the airport bar. Two hours later, when the bartender cut me off, the man with the sign was still standing there. Thank god.

Ray was shaking his head and toeing the podium with one expensive shoe. Addiction doesn't care about your tax bracket.

There was such a big fight going on inside of me, he said.

I watched him search the ceiling and heard his breath catch. I was running a very successful business. Nobody knew. Well, they probably knew some of it. Tears bloomed in many reddening eyes around the room. Ray's jaw muscles danced. When I woke up in the treatment centre, I was so sick. I was detoxing, you know? From more than booze. It was horrible. He stopped to pinch the bridge of his nose. It's been seven years, and I keep coming here every week, because without you guys, I would probably be dead.

All around the room heads bobbed in silent allegiance.

Probably be dead.

Ray hurried to finish. So congratulations on your clean time, and if you're starting over, congratulations to you, too, because we are never done with this. It's never over.

Low murmurs of "You got that right," and "Amen."

I covered Jessie's ice-cold hands with mine and felt her rough skin, prominent knuckles, aftershocks.

You're doing great, Jess, I'm so proud of you for being here, I whispered, and her gentle eyes overflowed. Our fingers wove together and stayed that way, a basket of hope at the end of a row of folding chairs.

One by one, they stood. Intelligent, articulate people, brave-faced and resolute. One by one they described how they'd hated themselves so intensely they couldn't stand being in their own skins. Their stories were vastly different, and all the same.

For a long time, life was terrible, said Frank, a wiry, grey-haired man in a plaid work shirt and trucker hat. He was dressed just like the bearded hipsters who rode cruiser bikes and drank boutique coffee here in gentrifying East Vancouver. After I got out of residential school, I started drinking and didn't stop for fifteen years. Now I've been sober forty-five. I found out that when I drink, I get drunk. And when I get drunk, I lose everything.

Beside me, Jessie nodded as though she understood Frank on a fundamental level.

Some experts say that when it comes to addiction, the trauma comes first, and the self-medicating comes second. So what was Holden's excruciating pain? Had something happened to him that we didn't know about? Or could the separation of his mother and father have been enough to wound his tender heart? To damage it so badly that it couldn't beat without a hitch? Was dread about our burning planet enough to throttle his spirit? I'd read that the root of addiction is not the hook in the drug, it is the unwillingness to be present in the painful part of our lives. That the opioid crisis is an epidemic of despair.

I remembered asking Holden one winter evening, when he was about nineteen and had come home wet, hungry, and smelling of booze, why he drank so much. He stared at the table for a moment, then looked into my eyes and said, To deal with being me, Mom.

After the meeting, Claire bounced into the back seat of my car. She had come such a long way since that dark night on our doorstep. The ribs crossing her chest no longer looked like lines on a page. Her eyes were bright and clear, her cheeks flushed.

I can only talk for a minute, my ride's waiting. She wedged her long torso between the front seats to rest her hand on Jessie's thigh. It's so amazing you came. How are you doing?

Tears streaked Jessie's face, reflecting the street light. She shuddered. The weight of the reckoning had levelled her.

It's such a waste of a life. What I've been doing, the last few years, horrible things, all the people I've hurt.

I know exactly how you're feeling, Claire said. Two years ago I was living under a bridge. Three years ago I was an escort. But Jessie, with this program, I have learned to let it go.

She extricated herself from between the front seats and leaned back. Her face receded into shadow. Look, nothing can erase the past—all that still happened—this just lets me put it down for a while. She paused, and I heard the glisten of optimism in her voice. Now I'm going back to school. You can have a good life, if you want to.

Jessie folded at the waist, sobbing into the pile of her scarf. I placed my hand gently on her bony spine. A thick quiet hung in the car. Her words, when they finally came, were rationed, one at a time. Nervous raindrops before a storm.

I am so tired of all of this. She took a slow, deep breath and straightened. Exhaled, then pivoted to face me fully. Her blue eyes found mine. But I don't know if I can make it. I just don't know how.

There was a time that I would have reassured her, bathed her in mothering words and blind optimism. Something like *Of course you can,* or *Everything's going to be all right.* But I didn't trust that anymore—I knew that sometimes everything was not all right. So I said what I could. I said what I thought was fair.

Neither do I, Jessie, but it's worth trying.

23

At the deep end of Holden's drug use, he lost a lot—his work, his sense of self, aspects of his physical and mental health, many of his relationships. I couldn't understand why those who called themselves his friends didn't do more to help, or at least talk to him when they saw him being so self-destructive. Perhaps they did, and he pushed them away. Still, I was incredibly angry with many of those who came to mourn, knowing they could have at least notified us about what was really happening.

One close friend shared a story about the time Holden had nodded off at the bar.

What's that about, too much weed? the friend had asked.

Nope, Holden had answered, it's H. And he offered some to the friend, who refused and got mad.

I told him to just stop, the friend said, but he said he wasn't addicted so it wasn't a big deal. That was as far as any intervention had gone. After that, Holden had used heroin openly—snorting powder off the back of his hand or a key. The friend had done nothing.

Reading through Holden's messages, I saw that Luke, his childhood friend and first graffiti buddy, had tried to confront Holden about his behaviour. They'd fought about it verbally and, evidently, physically, too.

∞

It's getting light out and Holden's still in the passenger seat of Luke's car, where he was shoved late last night after some lame blow-up at the party and told to "go the fuck to sleep."

His cheek is smudged against the glass, and he's pretending to be asleep, because Luke is fucking irate.

How long have we known each other? Luke's yelling at the windshield and pounding on the steering wheel as he drives. I mean, how fucking long have we been friends? His voice shifts gears, now slow and methodical. Kindergarten, that's how long.

Holden opens his eyes a crack. The sun's rising, making the dashboard kind of pink and gold as they cross the Second Narrows. Only one other car is on the bridge, a yellow cab just ahead. Holden risks a quick glance at Luke, then looks out the passenger window into the harbour. Cranes stand along the edge of the port like huge industrial flamingoes. Luke has one hand resting on the steering wheel, thumb drumming. They crest the bridge, and the wooden rollercoaster at Playland glows pinky gold, too.

Luke's still talking. We've done everything together, man. Everything. Remember when we got caught painting the wall at the furniture store and our dads took us down there and made us apologize? Remember that?

Of course Holden remembered. The guy actually paid them to roll over it. They used the money for pizza, then went and racked more cans from Walmart and did it again. It was Luke who was there the night the cops stopped them and took their paint and masks away.

I can't just sit back and watch you do this, man. Luke reaches over and shoves Holden's shoulder. What you are doing makes no sense. You're acting like a fuckin' junkie.

The car rolls through the quiet streets of East Van. Holden is almost asleep again when the punch lands. The blow makes solid contact with the side of his head. His eyeballs vibrate with sharp, sudden pain, and he sees a quick flash of light.

What the fuck? He raises his arms to form an X in front of his face, a barricade against what might come next.

You can't just obliterate yourself.

I can do whatever I want. He rubs his head.

Not if you want to live.

My living is none of your business.

He leans away from Luke, toward the door, exhales loudly, closes his eyes again, and lets the full weight of his face press against the window.

Come on, man, heroin? Now you're scaring *me*.

You try being in here. For just one day.

We all have problems, bro.

You didn't have to hit me.

How are you going to understand?

Holden rubs the raised mound on his head where Luke's knuckles made contact. I'd rather not rack up multiple concussions, fuckwad.

Why worry about concussions when you fucking binge on whatever drugs you can find, anyway? You're a fucking garbage can. What's your deal?

Better question is who deemed you the life advice expert? Until you've done something with your own precious existence don't preach to me about how I'm wasting mine. Makes you look like an elitist prick.

At least I'm trying, man. Never said I was an expert.

Obviously.

Why'd you quit your job at the art store? I thought you liked that one?

Social anxiety. Holden unrolls the passenger window with the hand crank and sticks his head into the morning wind, trying to blow away the questions. I'm on meds for it.

You're on meds for it. That's fucking hilarious. The peak of irony.

It's not actually. The idea of having to interact with human beings makes me want to puke.

Justify it however you want, man, learning to deal with people is a huge part of living.

You can't just learn to overcome a clinical illness.

And getting messed up beyond recognition every night helps with that?

Sure the fuck does. Holden turns up the volume on the stereo.

Soon Luke noses the car to the curb in front of Holden's dad's apartment. He pulls up hard on the emergency brake so it makes a sound like small bones breaking. They both stare straight ahead through the dirty windshield at the row of flowers forming a burgundy frame around the leaf-green lawn outside the building.

Eventually, Holden pushes open the door and heaves himself up and out. He gives the door a solid slam, then pokes his head into the open window.

Thanks for the ride. You wanna paint later?

I got cans and no plans. Luke nods, still staring forward.

How about Horseshoe Bay. Want to hit that rail tunnel?

Sure, I'll get at ya later. Unless …

Unless what?

Unless you wanna go right now.

They park beside the monkey bars at Horseshoe Bay Elementary School and finish their Sausage McMuffins. Red and yellow paper tulips are taped to the darkened windows of a classroom.

Remember when you were like sixteen and wheat-pasted those huge crow posters all over the place?

Yup.

Holden remembers cooking up flour, water, and cornstarch, and pouring the mixture into a peanut butter jar. He remembers slapping the big crows he'd sketched in charcoal on tissue paper onto the tennis courts, the transformer box on the corner, and the cinder blocks of his old elementary school with one of Cam's house-painting brushes. He remembers the thrill of seeing those big, black smudgy crows flying around the hood.

Luke is laughing now. And when the principal made an announcement asking if anybody knew anything about the vandalism, your little sister went down to the office and said, My brother did it. What was she, grade one?

She thought they were cool. The little punk. Holden laughs, too.

They *were* cool. You're a really good artist.

Cold wind rising from the ocean clings to the back of his damp neck. He squints and notices that the throbbing pain behind his sinuses has downgraded from an eleven to about a six on the hangover Richter. Across the highway, a shortbread-toned rock face stands above them. He hears the distinctive high-pitched keening of a baby eagle somewhere up in the canopy, then the whoosh of powerful wingbeats scraping the air as the mother returns to the nest with a beak full of food.

They move toward the narrow unmarked path that cuts through a cluster of aspens, then drops down and away to the old railbed below the highway. The tracks are rusted and overgrown with weeds. Below them, the ferry terminal sits on the edge of the grey Pacific. Islands recede into the distance, each one less blue than the one in front of it. They walk.

After a few minutes, Luke shoves his hands in his pockets and raises his shoulders to his ears. So, what's up, are you okay?

It takes some time for Holden to answer. I don't actually know.

They both wait for the space between them to fill.

Holden speaks first. I had a blood test. I'm waiting for the results.

What kind of blood test?

He steps up onto the rail and begins to inch along it, one foot in front of the other, as though the track is a high wire, his arms extending straight out to his sides for balance. A bag of paint cans swings from his wrist. Well, he begins, then loses his balance and falls off the rail. He exhales loudly, steps back up onto the track. I've been smoking some horse. You already know that, obviously.

Luke nods, his grey eyes angled down.

I don't actually do that much. I'm trying to stop. I've stopped before. But I always end up back in it.

Luke nods again. He steps up onto his own strand of track and begins walking.

Anyway, last week I was downtown for a metal show and I got really loaded. As one does. After the show, I was just walking around the alleys looking for someplace to paint. There are a lot of cool people down there. Super interesting and genuine, you know? He looks across to Luke, who's focused on his footing. Anyway, I started talking with this guy, and he pulled out his gear and asked me if I wanted to try. I'd never used a needle before, but I was super tanked and I just didn't give a shit about myself at that moment. I just didn't care. I'm pretty sure I saw the dude take out a brand-new needle but, I don't know, it was a blackout, I could be wrong.

Holden stops walking and steps down off the rail, his eyes re-seeing that dark alley. He takes a can of spray paint out of the bag and steps back up onto the track, balancing. I could be totally fucked.

Or you could wait for the results, says Luke. You're probably fine. The two face each other, standing on separate rails.

Holden looks away, eyes following the track to where it curves out of sight. I know it's stupid. But honestly, the stuff is just so easy to get here. It's everywhere. On every corner. And it's cheaper than beer.

Luke kicks a rock.

But it's more than that. I'm just so ... I just don't know what my life is for. Other people know what their lives are for. I know what other people's lives are for. But not mine.

I sure as fuck don't, Luke says.

I'm just tired of being confused and fucking depressed all the time. I've wasted four years—Holden blasts a small fart of red paint into the air between them—being wasted. My mom paid for art school, she paid for forklift school, she offered to pay for fricken' DJ school, whatever the fuck that is. My dad keeps offering to find me jobs. He drove me all over town making me drop off resumes, and we got in another huge fucking fight because there's not one thing I can think of that I am even remotely interested in doing. I mean, I love them, but they just don't understand me. *I* don't understand me.

Another red puff from his can.

Luke lifts his gaze to make eye contact with Holden. There's a lot of places you can go that will help, you know. If you'll just admit it.

Everybody wants me to go to rehab. But if I give up booze and drugs, I'll have to give up all of my friends, my music, and this. Holden holds down the white cap on top of the can for several seconds, sending a red shaft into the air. They watch the cloud first billow, then swirl and slowly sink. Holden waves his hand through the air, stirring the red. There won't be anything left. They watch the particles settle on the bed of sharp stones between the rails.

With all due respect, I completely fucking disagree. Did you ever consider that your life might actually be better?

Did you ever consider how fucking boring it would be?

They arrive at the tunnel, stop, and peer in as far as daylight allows. The high, arching ceiling reminds Holden of the cathedrals he saw in France. They were having breakfast in a little guesthouse when he got the official news that he'd been accepted to Emily Carr University of Art

+ Design. He'd had a mouth full of croissant when he read the email. Fucked that up, too.

Inside the tunnel, darkness, moss, and years of faded throw ups merge with the water streaming down the walls and dripping from the ceiling. If he stretches the limits of his disbelief, the washed-out colours of the old graffiti pieces could be stained-glass windows. A smell of earth and mould and something like old books hangs in the air.

Hello! Holden shouts into the tunnel, his throaty voice bouncing against the walls. He kicks a rusted empty spray can along the track. Is there anybody in there? His words echo.

Just nod if you can hear me, Luke adds.

Is there anyone home?

They hear a flutter of wings somewhere beyond their vision. The cool push of air coming at them from down the tunnel almost feels like an oncoming train. But not really, because these tracks haven't been used in years.

Holden stands close to the wall and reaches as high as he can, carving an arc of red onto the weeping concrete. He works quickly, precisely, like a dancer or a thief. Bending, dipping, reaching with rhythm and grace. He exchanges red for silver, silver for black. He works first in long streaks to create an outline, then short, sharp blasts to fill in, then back-and-forth motions to inscribe the shading that gives the piece dimension. And even as he works this sacred alchemy of smell and colour and motion, the one thought that won't go away is that he just wants someone to tell him what his life is for.

24

One morning I stood in front of the bedroom closet in my underwear, wrestling with the sliding door. It wouldn't do what I wanted it to do. Nothing did what I wanted.

Behind me, Cam pulled on his paint-covered work shorts.

What do I wear to an overdose prevention site? I yanked, and the door derailed in my hands.

Rubber gloves?

Hilarious.

I struggled to rehang the door on its metal runners. It had been broken for months. We didn't have the energy. The Christmas lights were still lying in a quiet nest on the front lawn where I'd ripped them down from the leaking gutters.

When I say lawn, I mean dirt, prickling chestnut pods, and weeds.

Cam pried the door from my fingers and propped it against the wall.

I know, but you asked, and come on, this is the weirdest one of all. He was talking about the research I'd been doing. He'd come with me to the dark nightclub and the police cells.

He enveloped me. Chest, muscle, heartbeat, soap.

Is it? How else can I find out how heroin works?

His voice vibrated against my cheek. I assume you've tried the internet?

I had, of course, but it didn't feel real enough. Close enough. My arms dropped to my sides with the weight of wet towels.

Are you sure you don't want me to come with you?

You can't miss any more work. And I'm not scared I'll get hurt, I'm just scared it's going to be sad.

It will be. The whole thing is very, very sad.

Warm air threaded in through the open window, feathering the skin on the backs of my legs. My cheek scraped against the dried paint on Cam's sleeve. A chickadee sounded, and we both turned to look, but there was no bird. Instead, our eyes fell on the memorial garden we had made for Holden under the Spanish chestnut tree. The rough chunk of granite we'd hauled from a logging road near Squamish, the white Buddha statue my sister Laureen had given us, the objects friends and family placed there, mementos you might keep in a box under your bed to remember another time: crystals, smooth heart-shaped rocks, a tiny ceramic pieta, a flattened silver spoon engraved with the words I'd rocked him to.

The ferns I had stolen last summer, dug up with a small shovel from the forest nearby and carried home, mud under my nails, to transplant in the mossy shade around the slab, had uncurled. The solitary purple hyacinth, its scent ferocious, its waxy stars too heavy to bear, had fallen over.

Will you please fix the fucking closet?

He kissed the top of my head.

I parked on East Hastings beside the community garden, bountiful with lettuce, tomatoes, and tall sunflowers. Across the street, the plump neon pig above Save On Meats smiled. She always looked cheerful, no matter what devastation was going on just below her hooves.

A small girl, maybe five years old, pushed her scooter toward me on the cracked sidewalk, one little piston leg propelling her along, braids streaming like kite tails behind her. A man I guessed was her father tried to keep up.

Yoona, wait for me!

Children rarely wait for you.

I listened for two brisk beeps from my car, then shoved my keys and phone into the back pockets of my shorts. My wallet was at home. I walked, looking into faces that used to be young, wondering how much suffering had occurred in these few square blocks. Hundreds, thousands of sons and daughters had birthed their last exhales in this postal code. I'd never cared that much about it before. Before, when these people were different from me. When they were just news stories or statistics I could ignore. Someone else's problem. But I couldn't look away anymore. I couldn't pretend I was better. I was not better.

That morning I'd read that in British Columbia, more than 1,400 people had died of illicit drug overdose in 2015, making it "the most tragic year ever," a fact that was difficult to argue.

Since Holden died, I had learned that heroin users are often filled with shame. For some, their mental illnesses—their addictions—are so stigmatized that they regularly use alone and die alone without ever asking for help or confiding in anyone. For the young ones, the parents are often the last to know.

The opposite of clean is dirty.

When Holden died, just around the corner from where I was walking, he was with Devon. He'd loved and trusted her, but even she didn't know the extent of what he was doing to settle his soul. Maybe he worried about what would she think of him? Maybe he was planning to quit anyway, so why bother? All he'd said when he asked to stay at her place was that he wasn't feeling well. He was so tired, he'd said, too tired to make it home. All he could think of was sleep.

With calloused hands and arms strengthened from all the digging and planting at work, he set his alarm for early the next morning. A buttermilk-yellow sunrise he wouldn't live to see.

My phone blipped.

I'm running a little late, are you
okay to wait for me there?

It was Sarah Blyth, the activist who ran the Overdose Prevention Society. She and I had met through Twitter one night at 3:00 a.m. when I was grief-mining about heroin. I had found a link to an article about the most influential people in Vancouver that ranked Sarah at number sixteen.

In true rogue fashion, when it became clear to her that people were dying at an alarming rate, Sarah had launched her scheme, with no permission or budget, under a couple of tents in a back alley off East Hastings. She was clever about it, the article said, by naming her project the Overdose Prevention Society; there was no mention of illegal injections in the title. This technicality meant that the police could turn a blind eye to her controversial setup. Her work would save thousands of lives.

When I messaged Sarah that my son had died of an opioid overdose and I wanted to learn about heroin use, she asked his age.

I typed the number two, and then the number one, and pressed the little paper airplane icon to send.

I am so sorry. How can I help
you?

Perhaps Sarah could solve the riddles that kept me awake. Outwardly I probably looked like a fairly normal woman, but I was weeping for hours at a time and spending large portions of each day in bed, unable to move or speak, obsessed with the same question: Why did Holden turn to heroin? Especially when everyone knew the supply was being poisoned.

I wanted to know what had taken my son away. I'd been told he most often smoked it, so I wanted to see that for myself, watch the clouds throw shadows across a person's face when the heroin hit their bloodstream. But mostly, I wanted—needed—to ask someone young and alive, Why?

As I got closer to the site, the sidewalk itself seemed to squirm in the heat. There was a lot of chewing gum and garbage, many things for sale spread out on the ground—clothing, a lawn chair, half a bicycle, an electric fan. I considered buying the fan. Groups of people sat with their backs pressed against the buildings. Some lay curled and motionless. Some stood or paced. Why was there so much gum?

One man sat on a flattened cardboard box with his stained pants pulled down below his bony knees, shooting a needle into his thigh while a woman crouched beside him, watching. Watching and also, it seemed, watching out for him. Her hand rested on his.

I wondered how it was possible or fair that a man who looked at least seventy with scabs all over his face could still be alive while my young, strong, otherwise healthy child was not. A thought that was instantly followed by a nauseous torque of something like guilt low in the cradle of my pelvis. Maybe my own oily shame.

I wondered where all of their mothers were. I wondered if I should try heroin myself to truly understand. I wondered about that first mistake. I wondered if the cold brick in my chest would ever melt.

I can wait.

I replied to Sarah's text and tentatively walked through the busy open-air market toward a construction trailer and white industrial tents at the back of an empty lot between square brick buildings. The space reminded me of a missing tooth.

A tiny cheerful woman in a blue vest greeted me at the entrance, smiling with bright fuchsia lips. Hello! Need a spot?

The air was laced with the smell of disinfectant, cigarette smoke, and those round white deodorizer pucks in porta-potties.

I'm meeting Sarah here. Is it okay if I wait?

Sure. Grab a chair. I'm Cheri.

Her voice was a two-packs-a-day kind of hoarse.

I sat on a stool with my back against the trailer. Yelling, laughter, people milling around, and the grinding of shoes on gravel. If I squinted, the scene could have been a church picnic or a family reunion.

Cheri scanned one of the tables under the tent. A frail woman in a winter coat barricaded by three large suitcases had buried her face in her crossed arms. I hoped she was sleeping.

Keep your heads up, friends. If your head is down, we start to worry, Cheri yelled, still smiling brightly while she grabbed a handful of the woman's short-cropped hair, lifting her head to inspect her face.

Piss off, the woman growled, swatting a twig of an arm at Cheri.

Fran, I've gotta check and you know it, honey. Cheri looked at me and winked.

Fran was still alive.

I looked up at the slash of flawless blue sky and thought, right now other people are at the beach, other people are riding bikes around the Stanley Park seawall. Two blocks away, on Water Street, other people are taking pictures of themselves in front of the steam clock, buying carved totem poles, and eating oysters.

Would you like to see a guy fucking a donkey? A lean, twitching man waggled his phone in front of my face, grinning. Before I could look away, I saw, on his small, cracked screen, exactly what he had just described. YouTube! It's awesome! He laughed and wheezed, and specks of his spit landed on my bare thigh.

I shifted in my chair. I'm pretty sure that's not YouTube, I said.

Cliff, leave her the hell alone. A tall woman in cowboy boots and a long floral sundress that exposed a pattern of bruises on her arms hollered, Get over here and hook me up, sweetheart!

I nodded to her. She smiled, shrugged, and returned to the urgent business of manacling her extended bicep with a length of rubber hose. Cliff obediently sat down beside her.

Two men jittered under the tent, coiled and restless, stepping from foot to foot with a repressed energy that made me nervous. They vibrated on a frequency I didn't trust. Another woman over in the corner appeared to have shrunk, as if she were a child playing dress-up in her parents' clothing, her makeup applied with inexperienced fingers.

At least she was wearing makeup. I couldn't be bothered, couldn't remember the last time I'd brushed my hair.

Fuck you, fucker! a deep shout flared over in the corner.

I told you, I didn't take nothin'!

A burly security guard sauntered over to break up the argument. The guard took one of the men by the arm and escorted him out through the gate in the tall chain-link fence.

You know the rules, Tommy. You can come back tomorrow. The guard eclipsed the entrance with his large body.

Eat my ass and die. Tommy limped away down the alley.

I felt like a plus one at a very strange wedding.

Hi, sorry to keep you. Sarah brushed toward me in a long, flowing skirt. Budget meeting. She reached for my hand. A large tattoo of a delicate blue feather ran the length of her forearm Her green hair was tied up in a bandana. Are you okay? Her warm fingers squeezed mine. I was relieved to be in her presence.

I think so. I just got to watch some porn.

Oh, these are not the most charming people, Sarah said. We can talk inside. Would you like to have a look?

I didn't want to have a look. I didn't want to need this information. I wanted my son to be on his way over for dinner after working hard all day. I wanted to hand him a big glass of ice water, hold his face between my palms, and laugh at his jokes. I wanted him to tell me about his weird co-workers and fire up a reggae playlist. I wanted to insist that he eat salad.

I followed her up the wooden steps.

Inside, the trailer looked the way I'd imagined a portable triage unit in a disaster zone might, clean and bright, with rows of open shelves filled with boxes of medical supplies, and a wall of locked cabinets. A coffee machine sputtered on the counter. A couple sat at a table against the wall, huddled over their spoons and needles, a collection of plastic grocery bags around their feet. Her erect, athletic body made her look strong. His posture appeared crestfallen, as though he'd just dropped his keys down a storm drain. I smelled bleach.

So, what would you like to know? Sarah leaned against the counter casually like we'd recently been introduced at a kitchen party and there weren't two people injecting heroin six feet away.

I, um ... Well, I'd like to see how you ... I mean, how to ... smoke it. Heroin. I'd like to talk to someone while they do it ... if it's possible to... I didn't know how to form these words in my mouth.

Let me see who's here. Sarah disappeared out the door and down the stairs before I could finish. A volunteer with a name tag that said *Wallace* mopped the floor. He looked too young to be a Wallace.

If Holden's robust heart hadn't stopped beating that night, where would he be now? Would he be under the tent outside with the other "not charming" people? Or would he be at the beach playing guitar and throwing a frisbee with his friends?

And there he was—standing barefoot on the hot sand, curled finger-tips dripping small droplets of salt water, the glow of the afternoon on his bare chest. I could hear his particular laughter, see his eyes glinting with the sea's reflection. He shone.

Sarah touched my shoulder. I noticed my hand pressed flat to my chest.

You okay? She handed me a box of tissues.

This is harder than I expected.

She nodded. Calvin has agreed to speak with you, if you're still up for it.

I'd come this far.

Sarah led the way through the crowd toward a young man with blue-black hair and a carved jaw sitting at the end of one of the long tables under the tent. His checkered shirt was ironed and buttoned up to the collar. A creamy film covered the whites of his large brown eyes, and his few long, black whiskers stood like a sparse forest.

This is Tara. She'd like to stay here with you while you fix, if that's still all right.

It's all right, Calvin said, and he shifted to make room, as if I had just asked to sit beside him on the bus. Sweat leaked out from under my bra and ran down my stomach. I wished I'd brought some water.

Thanks for letting me sit with you.

You're welcome. His forehead contracted. Why do you want to?

His movements and his voice were slow and methodical. I studied his smooth face to try and determine whether there was some way I could tell that he was a heroin user. He had what I was starting to recognize as a characteristic curled posture, as if someone were pulling a string in the middle of his back.

Well—I braced my hands on my knees—my son died of an overdose, and I'd like to see how this works.

That's bad. Calvin put his lighter down on the table and turned his face to mine. His eyes swam. My sister did, too. He looked down at the gravel between his feet, shook his head.

I'm so sorry. What's her name?

Lois. He shrugged and reached for a square of aluminum foil about the size of a piece of bread. That's how it goes.

How did you get here? I mean, how did you start using? I asked, because there was no point in being subtle now.

Oh, I came down to be with my dad. I leaned closer to hear his soft, lethargic voice. When I got here, he was going to a party with my auntie, and they asked me to come. At the party, my dad asked me if I wanted to try some.

Jesus Christ, I didn't say.

That must have been really hard for you, I did say.

Calvin paused and tilted his head as though he were back there again, on that day. I had to decide if I wanted to be with my dad. So I tried it.

When was that?

About a year ago, I think. He looked up to the white canvas shrouding us, creases gathered at the corners of his eyes.

And your dad?

He's around. I don't see him too much.

Calvin fished in his pocket and pulled out a small, flat plastic bag—a miniature Ziploc. Inside was a light-brown blob about the size of a pencil eraser. It could have been gingerbread. He squeezed the little chunk between his thumb and forefinger, then divided it into two parts, putting half back into the bag and pressing the other half onto the foil. He dug a plastic tube out of his pocket and wedged it between his lips like a cigarette.

You just put the fire under here until it burns. Then you catch the smoke.

His long fingers worked without thought; this was reflex for him. He held the flame under the foil at eye level. Soon the heroin started to liquify. It bubbled and smoked, then slid diagonally along the trough he'd made in the tilted foil. I thought of a snowflake melting on a windshield. He followed the column of smoke with his tube, sucking in the plume until all of the heroin was gone. So this was chasing the dragon. A dragon impossible to catch.

What had once been a small knob of brown heroin was now a black streak of ash. Calvin moved like syrup, placing his supplies onto the table in front of us, then leaning back in his chair, holding his breath. His eyes were open and glassy; his face seemed to have lost interest. He exhaled, and I smelled something foreign—a combination of road paving and burnt sugar and gasoline and sauna steam.

Outwardly, Calvin had not transformed into anything other than a quiet young man slouching on a folding chair, perhaps daydreaming. Mouth slightly open, jawbone slack. He was still. I waited.

Where had he gone? This was the place I lost Holden to. This was the place that was so much better. I would never see this place, but I hated it anyway.

After several minutes, Calvin licked his lips and turned to me. That's about it.

How do you feel?

He blinked as if he'd just been shaken from a dream and was trying to recognize where he was.

I just feel warm and all wrapped up. Like everything's good. His expression was deadpan. I know it's not, though, he said. I know I'm tricking myself.

I wondered what would become of Calvin. He had such a natural gentleness. I wondered where his father was. I felt protective and considered taking him home with me and making him dinner, but I pictured my daughter's young face, and the thought vanished.

Do you think you'll ever quit?

I'd like to. Probably. I just don't know what else to do.

I nod. I don't, either.

I was inside something with Calvin. Something too big, too difficult to hold. I had invaded his intimate world. He was sweet and generous and thoughtful, and I realized I had no right to pour my pain onto him when he had so much of his own. I was an intruder. My ribcage tightened, and I knew I should leave. I stood and extended my hand.

Thank you, Calvin, this has been really helpful for me. Please take care of yourself.

He straightened, ruffled, as though he'd just remembered the manners his mother or grandmother had taught him. He was much taller than he'd seemed when sitting down, and I was caught off guard when he stepped toward me and pulled me into his lean arms.

I'm really sorry about your son. His voice resonated through his chest, vibrating against the side of my face. I'll see ya later.

His shirt was soft against my cheek and smelled like laundry detergent. We stood there together for a moment, a woman and a young man, and I could feel him breathing.

25

I believe Holden was an intermittent user. Friends told me as much. Others said he used daily at times. I believe he was as surprised as anyone to find himself falling into the arms, and then the grasp, and then the collar, of heroin. How easily, how imperceptibly it had happened. I believe that as the skies brightened and the weather warmed, he became more aware of his own situation, his mental health struggles and triggers. I want to believe that he attempted to move away from using, that he was working on it in his own way.

A text message from Darius warned him to be careful, that the entire supply of heroin, everything on the street, was tainted.

All the smack in the city is being
cut with fenalyn right now super
deadly so please be careful

> I'm off it. Appreciate your
> concern tho

You are!! Good man.

> Yeah its so dumb.

Well I'm glad your off it. I wasn't
looking forward to another
funeral

Maybe he figured he'd gotten himself into the situation, so he could get himself out. There were periods of time when he was able to step back from heroin—I heard stories of frolicking bike rides, friend-filled barbecues, carefree evenings when Holden seemed healthy—and times he wasn't.

That spring and summer, Holden was in a battle for his life. He just didn't know it.

I couldn't find anyone willing to admit to using heroin with him. But I had my suspicions. The few who conceded to knowing about his habit all claimed he'd used alone.

Something I saw on his phone disturbed me.

> I'm still fucked. Definitely
> overdosed. You saved me if that
> shit really happened. like if I
> stopped breathing I mean

Ah damn, No problem!

They spoke about breathing and not breathing in such a casual way, with the same cavalier tone as talking about buying someone a coffee. Next one's on me!

My dry, cracked lips reflected in the smudged glass of Holden's phone. I ran my thumbs slowly over the cracked screen, imagining his thumbs doing the same. Scraping the shards, not remembering exactly when or how he'd shattered it. I imagined him bracing himself against the SkyTrain doors with kickstand legs, light from the screen illuminating his face, sending messages, scanning replies, searching for someone to share a few beers with on an evening when the sky was finally clear and his shoes were finally dry. I want to believe he started with the best of intentions.

He had hundreds of contacts to choose from. Maybe he started with Jose, the fellow artist whose sofa he'd spent several nights on when they worked together on Jose's graphic art projects. Maybe the evening began as casually, as innocently as any other.

> sup Hoser?

nuttin.

> come guz wit meeeee!

maybe later. Aft my shift.

> kk come thru Met. vodton
> waiting for you!

Yooooo, cheap pints tonight
right??

> zactlee

I hope he felt the click of satisfaction that comes with having a plan, a destination, and a friend to meet—someone to simply sit across the table from, talking about the Sedin twins, Deflategate, or Kendrick Lamar's new album. I want him to have known the small, sweet sensation of being connected with the human race, of belonging to something bigger.

∞

Holden slips his phone into the back pocket of his jeans, then dips his nose to smell his own armpit. Not too bad. At Stadium he steps off the train, strides to the end of the platform, and launches himself up the stairs two at a time, his legs powerful springs.

Outside the station, warm air strokes his face as he walks. It feels nice after so much rain. Cherry trees punch holes up through the concrete at even intervals, their branches laden with fat blossoms. Giant pink Afros on sticks. Every third step, another skinny trunk. *One, two, tree. One two, tree. One, two, tree.* Cotton-candy snow pools under each one, swirling around his feet as he strolls past. A steady rhythm finds him, arms swinging, shoes slapping the sidewalk. He takes a deep breath and rolls his shoulders back.

Holden notices his face reflected in a shop window. He smiles and nods hello. The last sun of the day glows against the side of the Strathcona Hotel. It would be fucking awesome to paint that wall one day. He whistles, though he can't hear the sound over the ska bounce of Rancid's "Time Bomb" inside his head.

He steps into the stale beer and ammonia smell of the Met and does a quick survey of the room. Not one familiar face. He walks up to the bar, orders his first drink, and takes it over to a table against the wall.

Hozzzy, im here, where
you at?

gym

Jim's cool. but not as cool
as this cocktail. icy fresh

summer is coming bro. abs!

ya. but you're still coming right?

sorry H-dog. can't tonight. next
time.

shit mang

Holden holds up two fingers, signalling for a double. The beginning of drunk is a relief, a pressure valve releasing, the removal of shit from the bottom of his shoe, a song to which he knows all the words. At the beginning of drunk, Holden is relaxed, and his thoughts behave. The world is kind, he's got his shizzle figured out, and everything is under control.

But you can't stop a puppy from becoming a dog.

He scans the room again to see if he recognizes any of the bodies around the pool table. He doesn't. He scrolls through his phone looking for a name to attach to a face that might come hang with him. A lot of contacts for somebody who hates being around people so much of the time. He doesn't hate people. Most of them just make him feel like he should be doing something productive. Life would be so much easier if he knew what that was.

How is it possible to be both content and anxious at the same time? Maybe it's the same as putting on a T-shirt and a jacket. He wears them both, but one is closer to his skin.

Sucking the last of his drink through the lime-green striped straw, he jabs the ice jam at the bottom. Ice with sharp edges because it hasn't had a chance to melt yet.

It's been three weeks since Holden used the computer at the library on Denman Street to google his symptoms. He clicked the little boxes in the column on the left side of the screen. Each square that applied to him turned black.

- Anxiety
- Extreme sadness
- Irrational fears
- Looping, repetitive thoughts
- Decreasing personal hygiene

- Unstable relationships and jobs
- Anger
- Feelings of emptiness
- Drug use and/or abuse
- Confusion

The result was a tower of black boxes that reminded him of the nighttime windows of the office buildings downtown. Who needs an actual shrink when you've got WebMD? He hit enter. Soon a blue bar popped up across the top of the screen. Of course it was blue. Possible Borderline Personality Disorder. And then the warning, "If you believe this condition applies to you, please consult a medical health professional immediately."

Shazam, he'd said out loud in the library.

That's me, he thought. I'm borderline. He pictured a tattered immigrant crossing into Texas loaded down with bundles of dusty clothes and cooking pots. Someone just trying to survive. Someone without a set location to tell them who they were.

Holden quickly sucks his third vodka tonic through the straw, like they used to in high school. *Chug, chug, chug.* The faster the better.

The middle of drunk could go either way; the dog is growing up, but he's not planning on tapping the brakes anytime soon. He orders another double because they're cheap tonight. It's Wet Wednesday or Thirsty Thursday, and the college kids are getting their money's worth. If he'd stayed in school, he'd be nearly done fourth year by now, like most of his friends from high school.

Holden pulls his phone out of his pocket to try again. It clatters to the table. At least the spiderweb on the screen doesn't spread any further.

dude, come out and play!

sorry man, work tomorrow.

And another.

you around? come thru the Met.

hey brudduh, studying tonight,
fucking finals!! see you on the
weekend??

The bar is full now, and so is his bladder. He could handle sitting alone if he weren't being subjected to Justin fucking Bieber.

He's lost track of how many drinks he's had, but he doesn't have much cash left, and he knows his bank card won't help. The account is empty since he quit his job, and he won't get his tax refund for two weeks.

What about Lindsay? She's cool. They've hung out together a few times—a couple of shows, beers in the park type stuff. She works around here somewhere.

yo Lindx, brain freeze, pleeeez
come defrost meee.

hiya, almost done, where
you at?

Met

k. see ya in 20.

sweeet

He orders another double and tries to make it last. When Lindsay comes in the door, he waves her over, then hugs her for what might be a little bit longer than she'd like. Her skin feels cool against his.

Looks like I have some catching up to do, she says.

Nah, just a beer or two.

Holy shit, we were so busy tonight, patio season has officially started. She hops up onto the stool across from him and spreads her hands like two starfish on the sticky table. Holden can't figure out what the letters tattooed on her fingers spell because they're upside down, and his vision's not exactly 20/20 at the moment. Lindsay's face is so smooth it's like a marble sculpture. Holden wants to press his palms to her cheeks. But even he knows that would be weird.

Holden?

He realizes she's been talking to him. Um, yeah, how was work?

Crazy. I'm used to plating for sixty, and suddenly we're plating for a hundred. Beer me, dude.

Abso-fucking-lutely. He lifts his arm to wave for the server and wobbles on his stool.

The end of drunk is anybody's guess. The dog bolts out from under the hedge, sudden and vicious. Holden is used to this by now. He exists with the knowledge that his particular brand of gloom will boomerang back at him without warning, and when the dark arrives, there's nothing to do but gut it out. He has no idea how long the heaviness will last. It envelops him like a second confining skin.

He and Lindsay are the last to push out through the door, arm in arm. It's almost 3:00 a.m., and the street is quiet. Just a few parked cars, and Gastown bar workers heading home. They turn to face each other, and Holden leans against a parking meter. There's a rope connected to something deep in the centre of his chest cavity that's pulling him in another direction. He knows he should turn for home, but the rope won't let him.

Wanna get some down? he says. Just to end off the night?

I don't really do that. Lindsay looks at something over his shoulder.

Me neither. How about we just get a little something to smooth things out. Sleep tight so the beddy bugs won't bite?

She hesitates, but not for long. I haven't really done that before, but I guess, she says. We could go to my place.

They walk no more than fifteen feet down Abbot Street before an angular figure in a jean jacket steps toward them from the alley.

Hank?

Yeah man, two points, Holden slurs.

Forty bucks.

The figure doesn't bother stepping into the shadow to make the transaction. Holden digs in his front pockets and the back ones, knowing he'll find nothing. Lindsay quickly pulls two twenty-dollar bills from her bag. The man snatches the money with one hand and passes her two flaps with the other. He turns and disappears behind a Dumpster covered in a mosaic of tags. Holden sees his old Sefer tag in white against the royal blue of the Dumpster. He's been here before.

That was easy, Lindsay says, mimicking the TV commercial.

A laugh shuffles into Holden's throat. He sways in an invisible wind, anticipation tightening the muscles of his neck and shoulders. His mouth waters. He and Lindsay walk in silence toward her place. Now they have a mission, which quickens their pace and seems to sober Holden slightly. The cavern inside him will soon be filled. The fists in his pockets loosen.

Outside Lindsay's apartment, the lock confounds her key until she jiggles it just right and pushes open the door. One last hurdle. They step into a small entrance foyer and the classic lobby smell of water-stained wallpaper and cooked onions. She leads the way up two flights of stairs, then holds open the freshly painted yellow door while Holden squeezes by her.

Nice, he says. Egg yolk or bumblebee?

Pineapple. My dad helped me paint when I first moved in, she says. My parents didn't want me living in the Downtown Eastside. But it's close to work, and it's cheap.

Lindsay flicks on a floor lamp, which turns the room tarnished gold, and drops her big bag. An old couch leans against the wall. It's one of those scratchy things that's so bad it's good again. Dried flowers are arranged in a mason jar on the windowsill. Holden flops onto the couch, extending his legs under a coffee table made from cinderblocks and a piece of painted plywood.

Nice DIY skills. I like this table situation.

Thanks, my dad again. Lindsay kneels on the carpet, rummaging in her bag. She pulls out the two small packets and tosses them onto the table, where they skid to a halt between them. Her eyes meet Holden's.

Got any tin foil? he asks.

Dude, I am almost a chef, of course I have foil. She goes to the tiny kitchen and tosses a roll to Holden, who misses completely. It falls to the floor and disappears under the couch.

Nice hand-eye coordination, Lindsay says.

Yeah, I was a total all-star on the baseball team. You should see me with a yo-yo. Holden dives into the space between the table and couch and resurfaces with the roll. On his knees now, he brings the tube to his mouth like an old-timey movie director's megaphone, and his voice distorts into caricature.

Places, people, places. You over there, lights, camera, action.

He tears off a length of foil, folds it in half to make a crease, then tears it again down that line. Two silver squares of equal size sit side by side on the painted coffee table.

How about a tube?

Lindsay rummages in her bag again. She pulls out a pen, removes the ink cartridge, and passes the tube to Holden. Her arm disappears once more and returns with a red BIC lighter.

That is one magic bag, Holden says. Ladies first.

You go ahead, she says. Arms folded against her body, Lindsay seems unsure that this is what she wants.

If you insist. Holden traps the tube between his teeth like a cigarette. Next he shakes the pea-sized plug of dark-brown heroin from one of the flaps onto the centre of one of the foil squares and presses it flat. He bends a valley into the foil and holds the flame under it. Soon a pungent plume of smoky vapour begins to rise toward his face. He tilts the foil and lets the melting liquid run away from him along the trough, then leans forward and chases the smoke into the tube between his lips. In a few seconds, the rolling, bubbling bead shrinks to nothing, and the chimney of smoke has been slurped up, taking with it the part of him that hurts.

The rope has gone slack.

His mind is maple syrup—smooth, sweet, and delicious.

He sets everything onto the table and slowly leans back, holding his breath.

His eyes droop closed, and his head lolls against the cat's tongue fabric of the sofa, which bewitches his fingertips.

The beginning of drunk is back. Warm, beautiful, and uncomplicated. He's the baby in the photo, the one smiling in the small white tub on the kitchen counter. He's wrapped in a fluffy towel, protected from the world. Before problems existed. Before language or time. Before thoughts and their implications. No torment. No trouble.

Dude, wake up. Oh fuck, please wake up! Please.

His eyes flutter open.

Lindsay's hands are clamped on his biceps. She's jerking him forward and back, whiplashing his head. His neck hurts. His head hurts, his whole body hurts.

Fuck, Jesus, stop it. What the fuck!

Holden! Lindsay yells. You weren't breathing.

What?

I think you were ODing.

She sits on the coffee table directly in front of him and drops her face into her shaking hands. She's crying.

He rests his palm on the plateau between her shoulder blades and feels her body shake.

It's all good, I'm fine. It's okay, hey, it's okay. He rubs his hand up and down her back. What happened?

She lifts her face, and this time he does touch her cheek. He was right, her skin is velvet cream.

I don't know, she says. You were fine, and the next thing I know you're making this weird fucking sound like you're choking. Stuff was coming out of your mouth.

Jesus. He wipes his chin with his sleeve.

Lindsay stands, crosses to the kitchen, turns on the tap, pours a glass of water, and brings it to Holden.

That was fucking freaky, she says. How do you feel?

Good. All good in the hood. I think I'm going to go, though.

Holden needs to be outside, he desperately needs air. He stands up and stumbles, grinding his shins against the edge of the coffee table. His muscles ache and his head throbs. He makes it to the door and stops with his hand on the knob.

Hey—he turns back—thanks.

Are you sure you're all right?

Yeah, I'll text ya later.

He walks out the door and drifts down the two flights of narrow stairs to the main door. The hands in front of him are shaking as they fumble with the lock. He hears a clunk of metal and tugs the door toward him.

Out on the sidewalk, he looks up to see patches of clouds have moved in. A glazed amber is beginning to spread to his left, chasing away a chalky purple to his right, as if the sky can't make up its mind. He takes three long strides, then doubles over and pukes into the street. Hands on his knees, he upchucks again, then takes several breaths before he can straighten.

Not again.

He told himself after the last time that he'd be more careful. That had been a freak incident anyway, a bad batch or something. He'd heard about a tainted supply. Darius texted him a warning. He'd been off it a few times since then. For weeks at a time.

Holden heads toward home, to English Bay and the fresh saltwater breeze. As he walks, the sky gets lighter. The first drops of hesitant rain dipple-dop on the tattered awnings he passes under. He walks on. Rain is no reason to stop. The cold pins jabbing at his face urge him to consider the truth. They demand honesty. They alert him to the facts. He's taken this too far. He has reached some kind of precipice.

Make good choices, his mom used to call out to the back of him as he ran out the door and down the front steps toward whatever shit he could stir up.

Make good choices, he would mimic from half a block away. He would sneer at those words. They were insulting to him. He would make whatever fucking choices he felt like making. And he had, over and over, and here he was.

Rain melds with tears on his cheeks. His hair clumps on his forehead. His pace quickens.

He sidesteps under cover at the big library on Homer Street. The cinnamon bun, they call it, because it's designed in a swirl. He knows the Wi-Fi password for the library, and he knows it works even outside the thick walls of glass and concrete. He leans against one of the doors and holds his phone in both hands, thumbs scraping the broken glass. He only has 3 percent battery power. He opens Facebook and taps with his thumbs as fast as his startled mind will let him.

∞

Yuki sent me the Facebook post Holden wrote early that morning. He deleted it soon after, but she'd taken a screenshot because she felt it was important.

> I've decided to be antisocial for a while in hopes of putting an end to the substance abuse issues I've struggled with for years. I'm tired of having my reliance upon intoxicants affect my life and the lives of those I care about. Not shooting for sobriety, that would be unrealistic, but to acquire the ability to drink casually without needing to get hammered. I'll also be attempting to quell my usage of all non-alcohol drugs.

> It scares me to think about the time I've wasted prioritizing getting loaded over definite life goals. There comes a time when living in a state of constant apathy about it is no longer justifiable.

> I'm not trying to be melodramatic, merely hoping to inform those who care (or claim to care) about me that I'm going to be missing in action until I feel as though I've attained a grip of things. I'm almost 22, I've wasted enough of my life.

> PMA*

* Positive Mental Attitude

Holden's thumb likely hovered over the icon for a few seconds before he hit post. A moment later, his phone vibrated. Maybe he enjoyed the descending xylophone sound it made when the battery died, as if his phone agreed with him and was saying goodnight.

Maybe he filled his lungs with one overflowing breath, the air spotless and brand new. Maybe he stood up and started walking home.

26

During the months we travelled, I wore two silver bracelets on my left wrist. Oval-shaped and just slightly different from each other, the bracelets represented my children, who shared DNA but were separated by ten years and different fathers—similar, yet unique. I kept the bracelets together and with me always. Somehow their gentle tinkling against each other reassured me that everything would be fine. They were elemental, solid, and I could touch them anytime I wanted.

Before our trip, I'd considered getting the bracelets engraved, one with *Holden* and the other with *Lyla*, but considered that if I lost one it would be too devastating, so they remained blank. I wore those bracelets always and everywhere. On planes, trains, scooters, boats, and bicycles. With dresses, shorts, and pyjamas. I wore them while hiking high mountain trails, surfing, sleeping. After a day of scuba diving in the crystal Indian Ocean, warm as bathwater, Lyla said, I can always tell where you are when we're down, Momma. I can hear you jingling. She didn't know one of them was her. Like the oxygen pumping from my scuba tank, the bracelets were more necessary than she could understand at eleven years old.

Close family friends joined us in Italy during Easter break. Lyla was ecstatic to have her dear little pals to hang out with. You know it's not normal for a kid to be with adults all the time, she'd said.

We met in Florence for a few days of history, pasta, and gelato, then travelled together to Rome. We rented a big, damp house on the outskirts of the city, where the girls could do cartwheels and pick the milky way of small flowers on the lawn. One day, our two families were on the train together en route to explore the Sistine Chapel and St. Peter's Basilica. I took off my coat and noticed the bracelets were not on my wrist.

This was bad. Very bad. If I lost a bracelet, that meant I would lose one of my children. If I lost both bracelets …

I tried to remember if I'd left them on the bedside table, or maybe beside the sink in the bathroom. I checked all of my pockets and plunged my hand into every available place in my backpack. Nothing.

Roman commuter trains are filthy with grit, trash, and cigarette butts. They have graffiti on the inside. That didn't stop me from getting down on my knees in the aisle to reach under every seat and sweep the floor with my hands. No bracelets—just sticky, black palms.

Cam understood perfectly well just how serious this symbolic loss was to me. For months he had listened to my increasing worries about Holden, watched me battle my growing superstitions, so he helped me search the train's seats and pockets.

You must have left them back at the house. I'm sure they're around somewhere.

I couldn't stop the rising panic. Lyla was sitting right there, playing games with her friends. Something terrible must have happened to Holden. I could sense it. I pressed my forehead to the cool glass of the window. It was the middle of the night at home, 3:45 a.m. My heart hammered in my chest—I had to fight not to vomit.

Holden. Should I call his father?

When we got off the train in Rome, I slipped my coat on. And there they were—the two bracelets had come off inside the sleeve. I cried on the platform as I pulled the bracelets over my knuckles. I could breathe again. I rested my head against Cam's shoulder. He put his arms around me.

That was close, I said. A very close call.

Our friends headed for home, and we celebrated Easter twice. The first in Bracciano, just outside Rome, where bearded actors carried heavy wooden crosses through narrow chaotic streets in a procession with horses and lambs, and soldiers snapped whips through the air. A mock crucifixion took place high on the hill, in front of the castle where Tom Cruise and Katie Holmes had gotten married, while the crowd below drank Aperol Spritzes.

The second Easter was in Greece. Orthodox. Where it is customary to light bonfires in the streets outside ornate whitewashed churches, ignite fireworks, and shoot guns into the night sky. All of this to celebrate the death and the rising.

And then, in the midst of my faraway fears, a breakthrough.

Subject: Thinking of you

Hey Mom.

Nothing much new since we last spoke. Other than my phone was cut off. Was going to pay it off with my tax return but haven't received it yet. It's been two weeks since I filed, they said I'd have the money by now!

I went to go to see Dr. D. I can't live like this anymore. Gotta figure it out and make a plan. Going back next week.

Love yaz.

H

Subject: Re: Thinking of you

Hi Holden,

I'm so glad you went to see Dr. D. She is a sincerely good person and really cares about people. And by "people" I mean you. Taking responsibility for your own health is very brave. It's the most important thing you can do. Everything in your life begins with your health. Everyone is in a constant state of improving or declining health. Always changing. Everyone.

I'm sure it won't be easy or quick. In fact, expect it to be really hard. Just asking for help is a major step. I'm so happy you did. Really, Holden. It's a big deal and I'm awfully impressed. What did Dr. D say about how to approach your mental health? Maybe you can uncover some riddles and find a slice of peace. Being open, honest, and vulnerable will be painful, but may help you wade through the confusing swamp and let go of the heaviness you've been carrying.

I really think your booze (& other things) abuse stems from your depression and anxiety. If you can find your way through that maze, you won't need to self-medicate. You are a beautiful soul. I wish I could feel how you feel so I would understand you better. Could you try to explain it to me?

I love you, Holden, and am very proud of you for taking these steps in the right direction. Keep on walking toward the positive. Even when it gets tough. It's worth it. You're worth it. The beginning is the worst. It will eventually get easier and easier. Like turning around a freighter in a current.

Love,

Mom

Subject: Re: Thinking of you

Hey Momz,

Hmm interesting. I'm not going to go to rehab, that's not an option. I don't need to and I'd just leave. I've decided not to go to montreal but to stay local and work on getting mentally healthy. No point in working toward a career if I can't handle employment. Ill be all right Mom, don't worry. What have you guys been up to?

Love,

H

The days were getting longer, the sky brighter, and Holden was replying to my emails again. He told me that our family doctor had recommended he go for an assessment. I didn't think to ask him what kind of assessment. I assumed it was to work on gaining skills to help with his anxiety. I didn't ask him why he wanted to go back to Montreal, why he so badly wanted to leave Vancouver.

Subject: Crazy driving!

Hi Holden,

I miss you and am thinking about you. We arrived in Crete yesterday. The southernmost and biggest island in Greece. We hoped for warmth and sun and long hikes, but it's rainy with a cold wind. So maybe some poking around instead.

We rented a little Fiat Panda. When we left the airport the stick shift came off in Cam's hand. That's about the tone of Greek driving. Many cars coming at you head-on, in your lane. We're just rolling with it.

I love you,

Mamz

Subject: Re: Crazy driving!

Whooaa sounds sketchy. What else is going on? I've just been playing bass and skating a bunch, it has been alternating between summery weather and dismal showers so it's tricky to skate at times. Thinking of taking up meditation again. What do you think?

Love,

H.

Subject: Re: Re: Crazy Driving!

Hi babe,

Yes, meditation is a great idea. I try to do it whenever I get a private moment over here. Which isn't very often when there's three people in one room. ha ha ha. You know all about that. I've attached another article from the Chopra Centre. As you know, Deepak is my home boy. It explains the benefits of meditation and has some guided ones.

Question: if we go to Paros and Antiparos, do they cancel each other out?

P.S. I'm pretty sure we saw Liam Gallagher on a small Greek island. He was wearing a leather jacket and a bathing suit and asked me if I had any matches. I didn't. Then a few cats started circling around his feet so I asked him if he had a fish in his sock. He didn't.

Ommmm,

x Mom

I was filled with relief. Holden was communicating with me, and it seemed as though he was returning to himself. He sounded optimistic, as though he had weathered some kind of dark winter storm and was stepping out into the light after months of hibernation. I didn't know what had brought on this sudden change in his attitude, but it didn't matter. Holden was under our doctor's care, and he was getting healthy.

27

It was strange to see our doctor outside her medical clinic. Even more strange to sit across a table from her under a black umbrella on the patio of a local restaurant. Where were the out-of-date *People* magazines, where was the diagram of prenatal development, where was the blood pressure cuff? My doctor had seen more of me than anyone else. She had searched inside my ears, shone light down my throat, executed many pap tests and breast exams, and of course, there was the C-section. She'd seen my organs. I hoped the memory didn't put her off her lunch.

I'd like the grilled cheese with tomato soup and a lemonade, thanks. She smiled as if smiling was a chore and handed the menu back to the young server.

Once, I'd bumped into our dentist on a beach in Mexico. My brain couldn't make sense of that, either. Dentists don't wear bathing suits and drink piña coladas; they wear lab coats and smell of antibacterial soap. Family doctors don't eat tomato soup; they order tests, they slide a cold stethoscope up the back of your shirt, they keep you alive.

Dr. D's straight hair was pulled back with a clip, and no sign of makeup marked her tanned face. The thin wrinkles at her temples looked distinguished, attractive. This was the kind of woman who hikes the Grouse Grind before work. Her posture was impeccable, her voice gentle.

How are you making out? she asked, her lower lip shaking slightly.

Not great, I said, trying unsuccessfully not to cry. I pulled the sunglasses down off my head. There was never a right thing to say, never a good answer to this question.

She nodded and refolded her napkin.

I was no longer opposed to crying, I just tried not to do it publicly. Sometimes the surge could get too powerful for me to control, and before I could reign it in, I would be shuddering in stained sweatpants at the dog park, or crouched and weeping in the organic cereal aisle of the grocery store.

I'm not sure why, but people who displayed true empathy, the ones who were brave enough to show up and ask, triggered the most volatile reactions. Dr. D sat in her chair, patiently waiting.

Every day hurts in a different way, I said.

I'm so sorry. Her fingers stuttered on the table. He was such a great guy. I would never have—I mean ... I just never expected something like this. She bowed her head and pinched the bridge of her nose between her thumb and index finger. I can't imagine what you're going through. Her eyes seemed to expand in their sockets.

Yes, you can, I thought. You can, and that's what makes this so terrifying.

Dr. D had children of her own. I'd seen vacation pictures of them in her office. A blond boy and a blonder girl, their arms linked around each other's necks at the beach. Bright faces, sun hats, shovels and buckets.

Okay, well, I asked you to meet me because I wanted to tell you some things about Holden—informally, outside of the office. She leaned in and pressed her palms together. Her fingertips tapped against each other. This wasn't typical doctor–patient protocol.

I want you to know that he was doing the best he'd done in a long time, years, maybe.

This woman was well acquainted with birth, death, and the myriad predicaments in between. She had taken care of our family for years. I trusted her. I remembered the texture of joy in her voice when she pulled our loud, slippery daughter from my body.

It's a girl! And apparently she's got some things to tell you!

Dr. D, Donna, was one of the first people I had spoken with about Holden's early brushes with depression when he was a young teen and we didn't even know what to call it. She had given us referrals to counsellors, clinics, and adolescent psychiatrists, all of which fizzled out when Holden bluffed the questionnaires, aced the exercises, took the fish oil capsules and breathed the deep breaths for a week or two, felt a little better, then refused to continue with any treatment.

You think I'm crazy! he'd screamed at me in the parking lot of a new therapist's office. I'm not going! Leave me alone!

We had never received an official diagnosis. He was not sick enough, consistently enough, to warrant more than that.

Donna lowered her chin and continued. As you know, Holden came in quite a few times while you guys were on your trip, every six weeks or so in the new year. He never missed an appointment. And he always answered my text messages. He was really trying to get better. I was very hopeful.

I had been hopeful, too. I felt my forehead gathering like the fabric on a drawstring bag as I waited for the "but" that was sure to follow.

He was doing all the right things. She turned to focus on a blank spot on the wall as though seeing something there. Her top teeth made a divot in her lower lip.

Subject: Holden

Hi Donna,

Hope you're well. We are having a great trip, but worried as usual about Holden at home. He's still struggling. He mentioned that he may come and see you to get more meds. I think he's looking for Valium like last time. He was totally zoned out on them before because he takes way too many at once and mixes them with alcohol. He may also have an STD.

If he does come in (I know it's none of my business because he is an adult now) please don't give him Valium. When he took them before he was very delusional, and it scared me. He asked me to get him more. I don't know what he needs. He is an alcoholic, so maybe you could suggest some treatment? I'll pay for it if he will go.

Also, please don't mention that I wrote to you. I have a hard enough time maintaining his trust as it is. He's such a mess. Really unhealthy in so many ways. I don't know what to do, especially from here, although that doesn't seem to matter much to him.

Thanks so much, Donna,
Tara

Subject: Re: Holden

Hey Tara,

Totally understand and will do. If he is really struggling this badly, I hope he would be willing to get more help (i.e., counselling or even a psychiatrist), and I agree Valium is not the answer. If he is getting it from some clinics, then I may have to stop that, which I could do, but I don't want to alienate him, either. These situations can often be very delicate!

Will keep our correspondence to ourselves and will let you know what transpires.

Best,
Donna

The server brought our drinks and set them on the table between us. The lemon slices impossibly yellow. Donna seemed relieved to have something to do with her mouth other than tell me sad things. She took a sip and placed her glass back on the table exactly where it had left a dark circle.

You mentioned when we were emailing that you sent him to the HOpe Centre? I asked.

Yes, he came in saying he felt out of control and was really struggling with his anxiety and depression. He said he was couch surfing. He told me he was using alcohol and marijuana every day, but I suspected there was more. Honestly, at that point he didn't even really know where you guys were. We started him on some antidepressants, but I wanted him to have a full mental health evaluation, and I wanted him to start working with a counsellor.

Yes, I said, he called the evaluation mumbo jumbo. He didn't even seem to understand why you had referred him.

He was pre-contemplative, she said, meaning he was considering what his life would look like as a sober person. He was starting to think about a new direction.

The volume of her voice dropped even lower. I had to lean forward to hear her. I didn't know if she was afraid of people overhearing our conversation or of what she had to say. It looked like hard work for her, pushing these words up the hill toward me.

Years later, when I requested and received a copy of the report from the mental health centre, I understood why. The words typed on the photocopied page punched me low and hard in the gut. I had been completely oblivious about the depth of Holden's substance use and mental health crisis. The answers he had provided the evaluator confused me and made me nearly vomit my scrambled eggs.

Requisition: long history of severe depression/anxiety. Now feels like he is losing control. MDD with anxiety and substance abuse. ASAP, needs help immediately.

Physical description: 21-year-old single man. Homeless. Has been "couch surfing" with friends. Had to quit last job in retail because he was too anxious.

Presenting problem: referred by GP for MDD, anxiety and ++drug use. Can't work because of anxiety.

Family History: only child. Parents divorced when he was young. Doesn't recall any time they lived as a family. Doesn't "connect" with his mother. She is currently away on a year's holiday on a ship. Father lives in Vancouver. Has no room for him. Likes his dad and respects him. He has one half-sister.

Holden had told the counsellor he was using alcohol, pot, and cocaine every day. The next section of the report clogged my throat with bile.

… more intermittently he uses heroin IV, MDMA, acid, mushrooms, crystal meth, and cigarettes. Last used heroin 4 days ago, doesn't feel physical withdrawal except for sweating. Unable to keep a job. Can't stay with his mother, has a poor relationship with her, she doesn't trust him. He doesn't think father knows about the drugs. Thinks he just drinks alcohol.

Mental status: neatly groomed young man. Polite, pleasant, forthcoming. Cognitively intact. Judgement and insight okay. Memory and concentration okay. Euthymic mood, full range of affect. Reports feeling anxious most of the day. Not suicidal.

Summary: pleasant young man. Arrived at appointment not knowing why he was here. "I just do what my doctor tells me." Unemployed, homeless. Very low motivation. Using a variety of drugs daily including IV heroin. Pre-contemplative, has been thinking about not using. This counters with his concerns about how his life would have to change, friends etc. Not confident psychotherapy would help. Had some psychotherapy as a child. Not sure he is benefiting from medication (Pristiq). Agreeable to contacting local centre for addiction treatment. No further need for clinic.

The difference between substance use disorder and other diseases is that the people suffering with addiction never seem to tell you the whole story. They don't seek treatment when they initially have trouble. They don't complain about their symptoms and rarely ask for help. Perhaps they don't want to know the truth themselves. Also, sometimes they can't, because illicit drug use is not only an illness, it's a crime. Addiction seems to be the only disease where you have to wait until someone falls through the ice and nearly drowns before you can throw them a rope. Sometimes they'll reach for it. Too often they never do.

That day in the restaurant, I didn't know the contents of the report, and Donna couldn't tell me. Either because she hadn't seen it or because of her professional obligations. She and I sat at the table under the black umbrella, and she continued. They recommended he enter a treatment program, but he told me he wanted to wait and see if the antidepressant medication would help. We were seeing some positive results. He was looking better and better. Ultimately these were his choices to make.

I nodded my head. I remembered the emails Holden and I exchanged at that time. I remembered feeling like Holden was on the brink of something more positive. He certainly seemed more open to telling me what was happening in his life. The life he was living on the other side of the world.

Subject: Re: How's it hangin?

Hi mom,

the session was weird. I didn't quite know what it was going to be but I trust doc d so I went on her referral. Turned out to be standard issue psycho babble. They want me to go to a drug and alcohol rehabilitation program but I haven't been drinking or doin anything, just skateboarding and watching hockey and movies. I did get some meds tho.

Feeling pretty alright these days. Whats new with you guys?

Love,
Holden

Subject: Re: Re: How's it hangin?

Hey Holden,

I'm so glad to hear you're feeling better and are taking some medication. I know you didn't want to but whatever helps you feel better is worth trying. I've known and loved you for long enough to know that this is a cycle. Right now you are up. And that's great.

Rehab, treatment, or whatever word you want to give it, is about breaking that cycle and being able to feel well even when things get shitty in your life. Having the skills to not go back to the drinking etc. It's not about just stopping drinking. It's about finding out about yourself and what sends you back to the booze etc. inevitably. Being well enough to build a life that includes healthy, positive relationships and work you dig (ha!), peace, and independence.

Holden, it makes me totally happy just to see you sign your name at the end of an email. You haven't for 6 months. I can't imagine how you've been feeling, and that makes me so sad. Keep on going. Keep doing the hard work to create a life that you love and deserve. Because you do.

We're wrapping up nearly two months in Greece and heading for Turkey next. Greek ferries aren't known for their stellar internet connections, so not sure when you'll get this note.

They don't leave on time or have any kind of system I can figure out. Basically they just drop the rope and everybody goes for it. Cars, trucks, people, animals, all rallying for a spot on board. Funny thing is, it seems to work out!

It's getting warmer! How are you doing this fine day?

love love love xx Momz

Subject: Re: Re: Re: It's hangin.

hey mom,

I'm doing alright, feeling pretty decent everyday, with the occasional lapse. Barely drinking and applying for landscaping jobs. I've already had a few responses. Also talking to a lady with a trades employment program about getting into painting or another trade. I feel stable enough to get my life going; it's a good feeling, one of optimism.

I want to learn to cook some meals and, as I previously mentioned, get back into meditation ... although I don't feel as though I have adequate space here to do so.

Where are you guys now? Do you have tans? It has been alternating between summery warmth and dismal rain/hail recently. Thinking of you guys a bunch.

Love,

H

Subject: Getting Warmer...

Hello, my son. My dearest,

We are in Bodrum, Turkey. People here speak with an accent kind of like the Borat voice you often mimic. "Ees veddy nice-ah." You would laugh.

Tomorrow we set sail for a week on a traditional wooden sailing boat called a gulet. We will be out of Wi-Fi range so I won't be in touch unless by some miracle we find a hotspot in a goat herder village. We will be onboard for Cam's birthday on May 17th. He loooooves the sea so it seemed a propos. Will think of you when we dive into the shiny blue.

So have a great week. Would love to hear how you are.

Did you receive the little item I sent you yet?

Xoxox mom

Subject: Re: Getting Warmer...

Hey matha dearest,

I did receive the tee shirt, thankee kindly. Gandhi is my homeboy.

I haven't been up to much aside from casually looking for work, but I'm going to amp it up starting tomorrow (monday). Feeling a bit sick today, choosing to stay in bed. Think I may have acquired a slight form of heat stroke. It's super nice here and I am burned from skating around the whole weekend.

I wish I could have sent you a response sooner so you'd be able to read it before the wifi-absence occurs ... Alas, this is the best I can do.

Happy mothers day, miss and love you like crazy. Please send pictures of your boating adventure!

Happy B-day to Cam for me.

Will be awaiting a response,
H

Subject: Re: Re: Getting Warmer...

Hi Holden,

I'm always happy when I get a note from you. Had a great week cruising around with a bunch of nice French people. Who would have thought we'd be on a boat in Turkey speaking French? I think Turkey is like the Mexico of France. Short flight, warm and afford-able. The coast is quite wild and green, not what we expected.

Turkey is very developed for tourism, so we didn't feel very "Turkish" if that makes any sense. Still, it's a beautiful country.

We are going to go to Croatia for a few weeks. We've started thinking about making our way home, which may take a while because we have to drive back to France and then sell our car before we can leave. We'll see how long that takes. Probs early July. Kind of feels like the home stretch. Would sooooo love you to fly over and join us. It would make me so happy.

What kind of work are you looking for? You sound well, although you seem to have acquired some sort of (British?) accent? So perhaps you have been going to charm school? Any school would be great! ha ha ha.

I love you,
Mama

The coldness, the wetness of a glass in my hand. I took a gulp of iced tea. I had trouble swallowing. Ice cubes wind-chiming in a glass used to be such a delightful sound.

Why didn't you tell me he was using heroin? I asked.

Because he was an adult. I couldn't tell you private things about an adult patient. But yes, he said he had tried it. A lot of kids do. Just to experiment. That's why I recommended he get assessed.

You know, I said, he wasn't always telling you the truth. I've read his messages. He went and got high with a friend right after one of his last appointments with you.

He did? Her face slackened, her mouth hung open.

I slowly nodded.

Shit. Her hands dropped to her lap. He told me he wasn't taking anything. I guess I just, I just, I missed it.

We all did, I said. He fooled all of us. Even you.

These were the kinds of sentences that snuck up on me. The ones that should possibly, probably, have remained thoughts. I didn't realize I was saying the words out loud until they were already floating in the air between us. Her tanned face turned pale, as if the light inside had been flicked off. There was food on the table, but I wasn't sure how it had gotten here.

I have a lot of patients who use street drugs and still function really well, it's pretty common. Unfortunately.

This sounded like the same kind of bargaining I had been doing. We were all rationalizing our own behaviours to mitigate our guilt.

I could see now that he was addicted, but at the time I'd had no idea either. Still, I was angry at her for not catching Holden's deceptions when he'd been sitting right in front of her. Health care was her responsibility. Protection was mine. I was angry at myself for being on the other side of the world when he needed me to call his bluff. I was angry at everything, so I inflicted a little more pain on her.

Remember the blood test he asked you to do for that STD? I raised my eyebrows. It was actually because he had used a needle for the first time with some stranger he met in an alley, and he was so out of it he wasn't sure if it was a brand-new needle or not. He was terrified he had AIDS.

Her hand rose to her mouth. She spoke through her fingers, What? Well, the test was negative.

Yes, but that doesn't really matter now. The point is he was lying to all of us.

She began to say something, but the words collapsed on her tongue before they could gain any traction. She tried again. But he looked so good. Really strong.

I agree, working outside agreed with him. I think he did want to quit, he wanted to feel better, but it had to be on his terms and in his own time. Nobody was going to tell Holden what to do, or when to do it.

She nodded and her eyes met mine. Well, I don't think he was lying about what he told me the last time he was in. Her voice wavered.

What was that?

It was a few weeks before … before he passed. He came in for a checkup, and there was something lighter about him. He seemed more peaceful and steady. He had colour in his face, and his speech was clear. He was always very polite, but I remember him joking around. The antidepressants were starting to have a cumulative effect on his mood. And he was really looking forward to you guys coming home.

He said he'd been meditating. He said he missed you, that he knew he'd hurt you and was going to do his best to repair your relationship. He said he wanted to get close to you all again. He wanted to try living with you and Cam and Lyla again. Her eyes were red and filling with tears. He wanted to be with you guys.

I could see Holden leaning back on the armchair in her examining room in a pair of baggy shorts. I could see the tongue depressors, the cotton balls, and the examination table with its paper cover. I could see Dr. D perched on her spinning stool with her perfect posture, her kind manner of non-judgmental acceptance. The way she tilted her head while she listened.

She took another sip of her drink and set the glass down.

I may have missed a few clues, but I know he wanted his life.

28

Something had pulled Holden back in. I learned, after taking a ferry to a small island for a weekend support retreat at a treatment centre with Jessie and her mother, that recovery is never a straight line. Relapse is often a normal part of the process. What force had pulled Holden off course? What was the flame to his moth?

In my own form of rudimentary forensic audit, I analyzed the few photographs Holden had sent me while we were away. In one he flashed a lopsided grin while cuddling a small cat in the crook of his arm. Another showed him and a young woman reflected in a mirror. He slouched, bare-chested, wearing large sunglasses and a jacket of some kind that was far too small. She wore a bikini over her clothes. They grinned stupidly, as if they were little kids dressing up for Halloween. They both looked high.

I printed off our email conversations and arranged them like stepping stones across the carpet. I read carefully through each one to see what I'd missed.

One month before he died:

Subject: How's u?

i'm alright. hanging out with kittens a lot. they belong to my good friend victoria.

nothing really going on other than that. friend may have found a job for me. i don't know how i feel about it.

where are you guys now?

love,

H

What should I have discerned from Holden's typed language? And not just the words, but the form they took. How did the way the text was arranged on the page relate to Holden's sense of self? What was the correlation between the font he chose, the ambivalence and white space, and his emotional and mental state? What was he not saying? Did his lack of capital letters relate to a devaluation of another kind? His sentence fragments felt as relevant to me as his blood sample may have been to the coroner.

∞

Holden doesn't realize he's fallen asleep until he wakes up. Again, and again. These pills make him so fucking tired his head could roll off his neck onto the floor, and he wouldn't bend over to pick it up.

On the bright side, when he looks in the mirror, he no longer wants to punch himself in the face. Progress. So he stays on the couch with Victoria while the medical potions strap his arms to his body and fill his legs with sand. He doubled down on the meds after his appointment with Doc D last week.

Some of my patients have a better general mood and more consistent energy at this dosage, she said. But it takes time to adjust. It's cumulative. Just keep me posted, you have my cell number. She rested her hand on his knee for a moment and squeezed it before she left the exam room.

He smoked a joint on the way home, then messaged Amin to see if he still had that blow.

He'd gone to see Dr. D after his second OD. He didn't tell her what had happened. He didn't understand it himself. He'd thought he was being careful. He didn't tell her how shook he was. He told her things were a little out of control, no specifics.

She sent him for some kind of appointment at the HOpe Centre, where they asked him a bunch of random questions and told him he needed to go to rehab. He doesn't need rehab. He just needs to knock 'er back a little. Weeks without it now, and he's fine. A little sweaty, but fine.

Victoria curls up against him on the couch like one of the five kittens in the stinking cardboard box beside the fridge. She said she found them under her porch, and "everyone deserves love." Her yoga ass and long black fingernails are nice, but there's something very needy about her.

Hey. Victoria's jabbing his ribs with her sharp elbow. The movie's over.

What time is it? he asks.

Time to die of boredom. She tumbles off the couch, crawls away from him, and kneels on the floor, reaching into the box of cats. Her sweatpants slip down over her pointed hips, revealing a string of bruises along her backbone, a blue-brown smudge on the hill of each vertebra. She pulls three kittens from the box and brings them to the couch.

These would make great earrings, Holden says, holding one kitten up against each side of his jaw.

You've always been such a sicko. She nuzzles a dappled, rusty handful of fur. Her pupils reflect the candle on the table

Always? Holden wonders how long they've actually known each other. He doesn't remember how they met, exactly, but they've been friends on Facebook for a while now. It's weird how he felt so close to her while they were messaging about getting sober.

You can come and abstain with
me, I've got cats!

But now that he's physically with her IRL, something's out of synch.
The gears don't quite line up the way they did online. He's not sure if
it's the meds or Victoria that's making him feel like he's squeezed inside
a cell that's getting smaller.

Holden doesn't know what to say to her, so he talks to the grey kitten.
Hey little fella, your box is about the same size as my last apartment. To
the black one he says, Smells about the same, too.

So, if you don't mind me asking, she says, what specifically are you
staying away *from*?

Everything, he laughs. *Why is it so much easier to be completely honest
with people you don't really know?* Actually, down. I've OD'd twice. I need
to stop.

I thought so. She nods, scratching her shins.

You? he asks.

Totally opposite. Jib. Victoria chews at the corner of a fingernail. I
love it. She spits a fleck of dead skin into the air. It's the worst.

Holden tries to get the two kittens to wrestle with each other on the
floor.

I've got the love-hate thing going on too, he says.

He notices the shaking of her hands, the darting of her eyes.

Wanna watch another movie? I hacked my ex's iTunes password.

Stolen movies are my favourite genre, Holden says.

The sound of keys wakes him up. He's under a blanket. The ceiling
seems to shimmer, like water in a swimming pool. He's not sure if it's
morning or evening. Victoria breezes by him.

Well, hello there, Mr. Snoozer. It's almost six o'clock. I got tired of waiting for your ass to wake up, so I went to the store. He watches her set a bag of cat food on the table. By the way, you snore like a flippin' bulldozer.

Sorry, these meds knock me out.

She's wearing his baseball hat.

What are they? she asks.

Antidepressants. They def take the edge off, but they make me want to sleep for like a thousand hours at a time.

Tough to be depressed when you're asleep, Victoria says, reaching up into a cupboard for a bowl.

That's probably their whole strategy.

Also tough to do anything wrong when you're sleeping. Maybe I should try them?

Go right ahead. They make the whole world dull and tasteless, it's awesome.

Holden always regrets sleeping in his clothes. His shirt is bunched up under his armpits and damp. His mouth is so dry it feels like his tongue is glued down.

Victoria puts some cat food into the bowl, then pulls a brand-new deck of cards from her back pocket and waves it in the air.

Wanna play?

The cards have totem poles on them.

Okay, just give me a sec. Holden digs in his pack for his pills and goes to the bathroom. His hair is growing in darker since he shaved it. Not too bad. He likes what's going on with the beard, too. He strokes the thick, coarse tuft of hair with his fingers like some kind of old Harry Potter professor, then pisses a long, powerful stream, churning up bubbles in the toilet. After washing his hands and face, he pops two square, pink tablets from their plastic bubbles and swallows them with a mouthful of water from the tap. His body feels like he should be doing something. He's not sure what. Going out, probably. Painting would be best, but then he'd have to go rack some cans. Maybe just walking somewhere. Something. How can he still be so tired?

In the low-ceilinged kitchen, Victoria has arranged cheese, crackers, salami, and some grapes on a plate. They play Crazy Eights, Twenty-One, and something called Egyptian Ratscrew, which involves stealing cards from each other and slapping the table. Victoria pretty much convulses with laughter the whole time. She bounces on her chair. Holden doesn't find the game all that funny. Kittens weave between his feet, tearing up the newspaper they're supposed to shit on. They paw at his legs. One kitten's tail slithers like a wet snake around his ankle. Holden eats most of the food. Victoria nibbles on a grape.

How about reverse strip poker? Victoria says.

Which is?

Every time you lose, you put on more clothes.

He lifts his eyebrows. Do we *start* naked?

No.

Unconventional, I like it.

And I get to decide which clothes, Victoria says, grinning.

Soon Holden's wearing a pair of big orange sunglasses, a small floral jacket that restricts the movement of his arms, and socks on his hands, making it tough to hold the cards. Victoria has on a red bikini top over her black hoodie, an apron around her waist, and oven mitts on her feet.

Full house, sucker, she says, fanning her cards on the table.

Holden holds up a sock-covered hand like a puppet. Dammit, the sock says.

Victoria's loud laughter rebounds off the walls.

Oh. My. God. We need a selfie!

Vic seems way more excited than she should be about this, but maybe that's just the meds slowing him down. They pose together in front of the big mirror, leaning up against the living room wall. Holden's fingers graze a metal box in the pocket of the jacket.

Treasures? he asks, holding up an old tin cigarette case.

Victoria snatches the case and opens it quickly. Inside, three joints.

Halle-freakin-lujah! she shrieks. I forgot about these! She pinches one joint between her fingers, pulling it out slowly as if she's extracting a sliver.

Shall we? She raises an eyebrow.

Hellz yeah.

They sit on the couch passing the joint back and forth. Victoria props her feet on the coffee table. The oven mitts seem to be waving at him.

I don't consider this a wagon tip, do you, Vic? I mean, I never said complete sobriety.

Weed is basically legal.

Her words clip through her closed throat. As long as it's not the hard stuff, we're good.

They lie with their heads propped on opposite ends of the couch. Victoria piles kittens onto the weave of their legs. Holden scrolls Facebook. Victoria lights the second joint.

We are a cat bridge, he says.

We should charge cat tolls.

That would be mice.

Victoria snorts and yanks behind her neck at the strings of her bikini top, flinging it onto the floor with a loud sigh.

So much better, Holden says.

Yup. Not being high sucks. Sometimes … I just can't breathe, you know? I get so scared.

Holden is about to say he knows that feeling very well, when Victoria jumps up and runs to the bathroom, leaving a pile of kittens on the couch. Holden checks his email—one from each of his parents. They're pretty much the only people on the planet who use still send emails. When Victoria comes back, she reaches for the last joint in the case and lights it. She's talking fast and pitchforking her fingers through her dirty hair.

Maybe we should go for a walk, Holden says, because Victoria seems to be freaking out. He scans the room for his shoes. Let's get some fresh air, he says. Where are his shoes?

No! And then, a little softer: I don't want to go outside right now. She joins him on the couch and pins his legs under hers with a surprising amount of strength. Maybe later, okay?

Holden's thoughts are lethargic. They arrive wrapped in soft cloth. He's not sure what's up with Victoria, but this is getting sketchy. Something is telling him he should leave.

I think I might go, Holden hears himself say. My dad wants me to play pitch and putt with him at Stanley Park.

Victoria dumps the kittens onto the floor and pulls her thin legs up to her chest.

I know what to do, she says. She hops off the couch and hurries back to the bathroom.

Holden hears the reverberation of water filling the bathtub. He takes off the floral jacket and hangs it over a kitchen chair. He puts the sunglasses on the table and pulls his own shirt on.

Victoria emerges from the bathroom wrapped in a white towel, tilting her head to the side. With her pink eyes and the way her lips are twitching, she looks a bit like a rabbit. Holden feels a wave of something rolling under his skin. He's not sure if it's a good thing or a bad thing.

Come have a bath with me. Victoria turns and drops the towel before disappearing back into the bathroom. It's nice and warm in here!

Holden doesn't really want to, but he doesn't not want to, either. He's just high enough not to care. It's not like he's never fucked and run before.

Once he was with a girl when her dad came home, and Holden had to jump off the balcony. He'd taken the bus home in his bare feet. Never did get those Vans back.

In the bathroom, Victoria's got candles burning on the windowsill. Flickering shadows swim along the walls. It's warm and damp and smells like candy. The room seems smaller than it did before. The tub is full of bubbles, and Victoria's arms are crossed over her chest. She leans forward for Holden to slip in behind her.

Taking a bath together always sounds better than it actually is. There's never enough room to really do anything. He steps into the tub, extending his legs on either side of her. The warm water does feel good. Victoria's sharp shoulder blades press against him. Her hair brushes his face.

That's better, she says.

He closes his eyes and rolls his neck back and forth against the cool rim of the tub. Holden breathes in the strawberry steam. Victoria takes his hands and guides them to her floating tits. She grinds against him. His cock is hardening, but something is telling him to override. Then she sniffs agressively through her nose, and he feels her neck and the rest of her body contract with a sudden, involuntarily jerk. She's tweaking. She's not clean at all.

I think I better get going. Holden braces his hands on the edge of the tub and tries to stand. Victoria presses her back firmly against his chest, her feet wedged against the end of the tub, holding him in place.

So that's it, you're just going to leave?

I think so. Thanks for having me. I really appreciate it.

Thanks for having me? Fuck you.

She leans forward, releasing him, the wet skin of her back shining in the candlelight. Water and bubbles splash onto the floor. He climbs out, drips across the room, and steps into the cool of the living room, scooping up the towel she dropped earlier. He fumbles into his clothes, then sits on a kitchen chair to wrestle socks onto his wet feet. Where's his backpack? Kittens mew and swirl, scratching at the newspaper on the floor that's now covered with small, dark shits. He bends to stroke an orange kitten under the table.

Okay, just leave, then.

Victoria's bare feet, wet legs, dark triangle of hair, and tapered waist are above him, her breasts shining in the light from the stove. He hears something drip on the kitchen floor. A tapping sound. A *pat-pat*, red, round. Another, *pat-pat, pat-pat.* Red, red, red, splattering now, rain. Blood.

Just go then, she says.

What did you do? Adrenalin rushes up the back of Holden's neck and along his arms into his fingers. The inside of his skull vibrates. Did you—?

It doesn't matter, Victoria says, her voice a limp-dead animal. See ya later.

Blood streams off the ends of her fingernails. The kittens sniff curiously at the growing number of splatters. They step through the patches, making tiny red footprints on the floor. Abstract patterns. Victoria doesn't move. She doesn't cry; her grey eyes are vacant, unblinking.

Just go, she says.

Holden grabs the tea towel from the oven door, uses his teeth to rip it in half, and wraps up Victoria's wrists. Kneeling in front of her, he tries to apply pressure with one hand while fumbling for the phone in his pocket until he remembers he didn't pay his bill and they fucking cut him off.

Where's your fucking phone?

Why do you even care?

He pulls her, stumbling, over to the coffee table and uses her phone to dial 911.

Doors slam. Holden sits on the top step watching the ambulance retreat slowly down the street. In the tawny glow of the porch light, he sees that his hands are streaked with rust. He sits for a long time, not knowing what to do. Even when he tries to go straight, it doesn't work. Nothing ever fucking works for him. Why even bother trying. He's a dysfunction magnet.

And somewhere in the panic of the last few minutes, the switch that had been turned off has been flipped back on.

The sky lightens, first with a muted green, then a whitewashed blue. He notices a fat splotch of thick ruby red on the toe of his shoe. When it dries, the blood will look like ordinary spilled paint, just another overspray. Like usual. Another wrong turn.

He walks back into the apartment to grab his stuff. In the bathroom, the tub is full of pink water. He blows out the candles.

In the kitchen, there's blood on the floor. So much blood. The kittens are crazy for it, meowing and tumbling over each other. He puts them in the box, pours a big bowl of food, and sets that inside the box, too. They scratch at the cardboard.

Holden sits on the couch, opens his phone, and messages Darius.

Hey, can you hook me up?

He finds his pack stashed in the bedroom closet and walks out the door.

Sometime during the longest days of the summer, the ones when you're not sure where the afternoon ends and the evening begins, we anchored our rented sailboat in a rocky cove on a tiny island off the coast of Croatia. Lyla dove off the stern, and I followed her, swimming through nearly invisible water to the head of the crevasse, where we lay on our backs on a beach of waterworn stones. Lyla squirmed to imprint herself, like she would in snow.

Sharp-winged birds circled over us, black against the indigo sky. We were the only people there, yet still she whispered. Momma, I think we should go home.

Oh really, why? My head rolled in her direction, my cheek resting on a bed of small, smooth stones. Her skin was the brownest it had ever been, her dark hair slick against her scalp, a spray of freckles across the crest of her cheeks, her turquoise bathing suit faded and loose after months of living in it. Her green eyes beamed with the purity of some-one who had never known heartbreak.

We've been away from home for so long, my brain is full. She extended her arms to the cliffs watching over us.

Mine, too. But we planned to travel for a full year. Remember?

I know, but I miss my friends a lot, and summer is super fun at home.

True and true, I said.

I just—something shifted behind her eyes—I just feel like we need to go home now. It's important. Please, Momma?

I understood what she was saying about feeling saturated; we'd experienced so much that it was becoming hard to meaningfully absorb what we were doing. Cam and I had been talking about the same feeling a few days earlier, wondering if our journey was perhaps coming to its natural conclusion. And she was right: British Columbia, with her ocean, lakes, and mountains, is spectacular in the summer.

Let's talk to Dad about it.

Really?

Really.

Lyla's full lips expanded into a slow, wide grin, and her speckled cheeks jumped. She was on her feet and knifing her way into the water before I could even sit up. Once under, she was a blaze of colour, a streaking fish propelled by her instincts. Like a spawning salmon returning to the creek where it hatched, my daughter had turned for home.

I filled my hands with stones and let them filter through my fingers. They clacked against each other as they landed. Ten months is a long time to be in motion, living out of a backpack. But it was more than that; something was pulling at me, too. It was time.

Eventually I stood, squinted up at the barren rock face and the layers of sediment that time had compressed. Beige, brown, white, taupe, gold—like a piece of layer cake. I looked at my feet, tea-stained and wide without the influence of shoes all these months, and waded into the water. Water the same temperature as my skin, so it was hard to tell where it ended and I began. I swam slowly back to the boat.

Once the homing instinct kicked in, its pull became stronger and stronger. Now I recognize it as a powerful force of nature, like a hurricane or a tsunami, but actually, it was motherhood.

We quickly drove the length of Croatia, skipped across Slovenia, and beelined across northern Italy to France, where we left our car with a clear-eyed mechanic near Toulouse who drew up a contract of sale, including his commission, and signed a promise to deposit the proceeds into our French bank account. He would later sell the car but never transfer the four thousand euros—a theft we were too bereft to care about.

Subject: Coming Home!

Hi Holden,

We're coming home! Arriving YVR about 7pm Saturday. Can't really believe it's been 10 months. If you have time on Sunday please come and see us!

Love you and can't wait to see you!!
xx Mama

Subject: Re: Coming Home!

ill come see you on sunday for sure

But he didn't. Not Sunday or Monday. And he didn't email, either. Neither of us had a functioning phone, so email on our tired laptop was the only way to communicate. Not a word. I was disappointed and angry. Didn't Holden want to see us? Hadn't he missed us?

Tuesday afternoon, Lyla and I were invited to our friends' house. The squeals of sweet reunion were still lingering when the mobile phone I had activated just an hour before chimed.

Did you know Holden is here? Cam asked.

No! When did he get there?

I don't know, he was sitting on the front porch when I got home.

Okay, we'll be right there. Please tell him to wait!

I called Lyla, who was splashing in the pool with her effervescent friends. Laughter and shouts bounced between the fence and the house and deflected out into the thick canopy of trees. Ten-story cedars and firs surrounded us in a jagged green cathedral. Trees that confirmed we were home.

Lyla, come on out and dry off, Holden's at home.

Aww, but we just got here!

Let's go!

Just then, Beth, who had travelled with her family all the way to Italy to join us that spring, emerged from the kitchen holding two glasses of chilled white wine.

Hey Lyla, I called, I guess you can swim for a few more minutes.

I took a sip, and Beth turned her body so she could keep an eye on the kids in the pool.

Holden? she asked.

I nodded. We've been home for three days now and he's finally decided to grace us with his presence. I hung around the house all day Sunday waiting for him, and yesterday, too. I think I'll just finish my wine, then go.

She held up her glass with a warm smile. Cheers! Welcome home, my friend.

Thanks, it feels good to be home.

Three minutes and half a glass of wine later, I squatted at the edge of the pool with a towel in my hands.

Okay, love, time to go.

Can't I stay for a little bit longer? I haven't seen my friends in like a whole year! Lyla bobbed in the pool with the others, her arm strangling an inflated banana. Her lower lip protruded so far a bird could have landed on it. Please?

Let's go. Your brother's waiting.

But he didn't even tell us he was coming, she grumbled.

His phone isn't working, honey, come on.

We walked the few blocks home in silence, holding hands. The closer we got to the house, the quicker my pace became. I charged up the back stairs two at a time and ran through the open back door. Holden was sprawled on a kitchen chair, legs stretched out like planks. The sight of him took my breath away. I raised a hand to my heart.

Well, hello there! I said, chest expanding under my palm.

Hey Mom, how's it going? He hoisted himself to his feet, and we held each other tight.

I'm so happy to see you, Holden, so so so happy, I said into his chest, and tears drowned my eyes. The smell of him filled my head. Grass, dirt, sweat, and something I couldn't define.

Look at you! Over my head, Holden had spotted his little sister standing in the doorway. You've grown a mile!

He released me to reach for Lyla, and my two children were touching—they clung, one encasing the other.

My children shared a visible sameness. I saw their similar moss-green eyes, their quick humour, their clever minds, their musicality, and their ease in the water. In that moment, I became whole, both of my children within arm's reach.

Lyla tried to break the embrace by looking up into her brother's face with raised eyebrows.

Not yet, kiddo, he said, don't let go. Not yet. He squeezed her more tightly in his tanned, muscular arms. He rubbed his beard on the side of her face until she laughed. I missed you, punk!

I missed you too, Holden. Nice beard, she said, inspecting his shaggy red chin hair with her curious fingertips.

Thanks, my dude. He domed her skull with the fingers of one hand, as he had done so often.

Mom, can I go back to the pool?

I guess so, but be back in an hour. We're barbecuing.

Okay. See ya soon, Holden!

Bye, twerp. See you soon! He raised his hand for a high-five. She jumped up to smack his palm.

I've missed you so much, I said. How are you? The skin of my face expanded in an uncontrollable grin.

I'm good. Work's good. Except a crow ate my lunch today, he laughed.

Nasty beasts. We don't have much food yet, but I think I can scrounge up something. We've got some chicken and salad for later. I hope you can stay?

That would be great, thanks.

I stood at the counter across from him, buttering bread, slicing cheese and tomatoes. It was the most mundane act, a mother making a sandwich for her child, yet it felt as though I had won a prize. We were home, and Holden was fine. He was sitting in our kitchen with his long torso, baggy shorts, and big feet. His dirty T-shirt was damp with sweat under the arms and around the collar. Effort showed in his look. His hair was starting to grow back from the clean shave he had given himself a few weeks before, leaving a scrub of reddish blond bristles on his head. I noticed his hairline had receded at the temples and crown.

I noticed a quietness about him.

I can't stop looking at you.

That's a little creepy.

You seem ... I don't know, robust or something.

Why thank you, Mother, I've been hearing that a lot lately. He said in a mock English accent.

The hard work must be agreeing with you.

Digging the holes is good for the souls.

He scrolled through his phone and clicked on a reggae song I didn't recognize. He propped his phone on the windowsill and bouncing music filled the kitchen.

I rummaged for a plate in the cardboard box on the counter, cut the sandwich in half, and slid the plate across the counter.

Can I take a picture with you?

Why?

Because I haven't seen your face for so long and you are very handsome.

Oh, Jeebz.

He came around the counter to stand beside me. I pulled my brand-new phone out of my shorts pocket and stretched out my arm. Holden contorted his face as I pressed the button.

Come on, I really want a nice one of us together. I deleted the first picture, and we squeezed against each other again for a second shot.

"Reunited, and it feels so good," he sang, then smiled gently at the camera as I took another picture. My forehead grazed his wiry beard, and his strong arm encircled my back. My shoulder fit snuggly under his armpit, and I felt the heat of a hard day's work radiating from him.

Thank you, I said, and I turned to face him. I was really hoping you would come and join us for a bit.

Aw Momz, that was never going to happen. He looked out the window at the apple tree in the backyard, its small green buds just starting to emerge.

Well, I wish it had, that would have been so much fun. How are things going with you?

Good, good, I really like my job. We built a retaining wall today. But my boss is a train wreck.

He's the man from down the block whose son died last year, right? What a horrible thing. How is he doing?

Not good. Yesterday he dropped us off at the job site with no tools, and it took him like four hours to come back.

So terrible. I can't imagine.

He's basically catatonic most of the time. Pretty sure he's heavily medicated.

Just for the record, you are not allowed to die.

Got it, no dying. He laughed and shook his head.

Hey, how's it going with your medication? Is it still helping you?

I guess. Doc D upped the dosage. I feel more level, I guess, but I'm thinking of stopping them.

My stomach lurched. Why?

Because they make me sleep like twenty-seven hours a day.

Isn't that to be expected at first? While you're getting used to them?

I am used to them. It's been like two months. And I can't afford them.

That's not a reason, you know we'll always pay for whatever medication you need.

And they've basically obliterated my sex drive. So there's that.

Oh. Umm … I didn't know what to say. Maybe there's a different one with fewer side effects. I know it's hard, but these things take time to figure out.

It's not hard, that's the problem. And we both laughed in a way that wasn't really laughter.

I tried to reassure him. Why don't you talk to Dr. D about it? Maybe she can adjust the dosage or something.

Maybe.

Just don't stop taking them. Please, you look so much better. You can work through this.

Holden turned away from me and picked up a dirty teacup from the counter. He filled the cup from the tap and downed the whole thing. Refilled it again, then turned to me. So, how are you guys?

Major jet lag and minor culture shock, but other than that, great. Would you like to see some pictures?

We sat on the couch, thighs touching, heat pouring from him. He clicked through photo after photo on the laptop. Beaches, hiking trails, cathedrals, food. His head nodded from time to time.

I'm really tired, do you mind if I take a nap? he said.

Of course not, let me see if I can find you some sheets. I honestly don't know where anything is yet.

I don't need sheets. I'm all dirty, and I'll just sweat all over them, anyway.

Really, when did you get so sweaty?

I guess about a year or so ago, he said.

That's weird.

But I didn't pick up what he was hinting at. Well, one of life's great pleasures is sleeping between clean sheets, so just give me a minute to find some for you. I dashed to the basement storage room where most of our possessions were still piled high.

Three hours later, I pushed open the door of the guest room to wake him for dinner. The air inside was still and dense. A warm late-day glow seeped through the white drapes. I sat on the edge of the bed and rested my hand on his arm, gave him a gentle shake.

Hey, dinner's ready.

He lifted his head from the pillow and stared at me with vacant eyes. Drool trailed along his cheek.

I'm so tired, do you mind if I skip dinner? These meds just knock me out.

Now I wonder if it really was the medication, or withdrawal. Maybe he was still using. Someone told me he'd been using at work occasionally. How he was able to do that, I couldn't imagine.

That's okay. What time do you need to get up for work?

Six.

Sounds good, I'll make you a cup of tea.

Thanks Mom, g'night. His head dropped like a sandbag back onto the pillow. I closed the door with a soft click.

The following morning, I heard Smokey Robinson singing "You've Really Got a Hold on Me" through the thin wall, and I smiled because we were home, and Holden's alarm was going off, and Motown is soulful music. I heard his heavy tread to the bathroom and a hard stream hitting the toilet bowl for what seemed a full minute at least.

That kid always did have a bladder made of steel, Cam croaked from the other side of our bed.

We're going to have tea, would you like some? I said.

I swung my legs over the side of our bed—a mattress sitting on a plywood box Cam had built. My bare feet touched our wood floor. Solid, reassuring. I padded into the bright kitchen, filled the kettle, and pulled a loaf of bread out of the cupboard. Holden walked in, shirtless, rubbing his palms over his brush of scalp.

I'm making two sandwiches, I said. One for you, and one for the crow.

He smiled and took a seat at the counter. I handed him a cup of tea.

Thanks. This is really nice. It's so good to see you guys.

Cam came into the kitchen, sat on the chair beside Holden, and leaned over to give him a one-armed hug.

Morning. How's it going, bud?

Good, thanks, just heading to work. We start at 7:00.

I always loved working outside in the summer, Cam said.

I like it, too. It smells so good first thing, said Holden.

I smiled at them both and said to Holden, Why don't you come back tonight, and we can try again on that dinner?

Got plans with somebody tonight. How about tomorrow?

Shoot, tomorrow we're driving up to get Mocha from Auntie Janet. We'll be away for a few days, but we'll be back soon.

After breakfast, Cam and I watched Holden carry his dishes to the sink, wash them, dry them, and put them away in the cupboard.

Very impressive, I said.

It's how I roll. He smiled and shrugged.

When it was time for him to leave, Holden hugged me in the doorway of the kitchen, my head hitching under his chin, the side of my face on his chest. I was aware of the density of his body, his muscular arms, and the substance of his being. He was thick with himself.

Here's your lunch. I put some beans in there. When's the last time you ate something green?

I do not know, Momz.

See you when we get back on Friday. I still owe you that dinner.

For sure, see you soon, guys.

I love you, I said. Or did I? I can't be sure.

Bye, Mom. Love you, too.

Later, once the day had warmed, I walk into the room where Holden had slept to open the window. His smell hovered, a scent that was only his. Earth and sun and leaves. He had made the bed. He had carefully folded down the white sheet and arranged the pillows just so.

30

About a month before he died, Holden met a woman named Lobo. She was five years older than him, supported herself with migrant farm work, and lived out of her vehicle. I never met Lobo in person, but when I thought of them together, I pictured her wearing a vintage dress and matte-red lipstick, gesturing with her hand while she talked. I imagined a large tattoo of a wolf capping her shoulder. I saw them sitting on a blanket near the edge of a lake on a warm evening, listening to music, smiling. Maybe Holden's head rested in her lap, maybe her fingers traced shapes in the short stubble of his hair. I want Holden to have felt a puzzle-piece click, I want him to have experienced a magical, bone-deep kind of love. I want him to have had that.

They talked about music, meditation, and the places they'd each travelled. Lobo had spent a lot of time up north, learning to live off the land. Once, she'd shot a caribou and skinned it. She knew about sled dogs. She told him dogs used to deliver the mail all over Alaska. She thought the whole Santa and reindeer thing was a sled dog rip-off. The more they talked, the more Holden was drawn to her. They connected intellectually and ideologically.

I'm NFA by choice.

NFA?

No fixed address. Paying rent to a rich landlord is a racket for suckers!

Or maybe none of that happened.

Lobo agreed to speak with me on the phone. The pages of my notebook are filled with fragments of our conversation. *Apathetic nihilism,*

mood swings, graffiti made him feel so stoked, trust him to be kind/loyal—
yes. To not use—no.

∞

The small windows on either side of the van are wide open, but the air rolling in across Holden's stomach doesn't do much to cool him. He's prickling with heat, inside and out. He heard somewhere that this summer's been the hottest and driest on record. Thanks, global warming. He can't remember the last time he woke up feeling this peaceful. He stays perfectly still, listening to the movements in the park outside. For now it's just birds and the garbage truck driver whistling as he empties the trash cans. Wet earth and freshly cut grass ride the soft breeze from the edge of the lake through the windows of the van. It's a pure, green smell.

The summer Holden was eleven, they camped at Christina Lake. He and his cousin Nicholas, who was exactly one year older and came along so Holden would have a buddy, set up the orange tent and threw their backpacks inside. For a week, that tent was their inner sanctum. They stretched out on sleeping bags reading comic books, drawing in their sketchbooks, and listening to Outkast on this cool new thing Holden had just been given for his birthday called an iPod. His was metallic blue and could hold ninety-nine songs. Ninety-nine songs! He and Nick lay close together, one earbud each. Earbuds were a new thing, too.

At night he and Nicholas would slither out of the tent on their elbows like army recruits and sneak around the campsite, messing with people's stuff. They never stole anything; they just rearranged it. He and Nick hung beach towels in trees, stacked lawn chairs on picnic tables, and clothes-pegged boxes of cereal to clotheslines. They turned bicycles upside down, and impaled paper napkins on car antennas.

When they couldn't hold in their laughter anymore, they ran through the trees down to the lake and lay side by side on the dock, gazing wide-eyed at the sparkling canopy of stars from one horizon to the other. Holden had never seen so many. It felt like they were inside a twinkling snow globe. He remembers feeling both infinite and insignificant.

Lyla was a baby then; she had just walked for the first time. She, Mom, and Cam slept inside the camper, with no idea of what the boys were up to. The parentals thought the sleeping in was due to growth spurts, not three hours of moonlight ninja capers. In the morning, Mom made what she called "floatmeal" on the camp stove, then Holden and Nick plunged into the lake, where they pretty much stayed until dinnertime.

One night, sitting around the campfire on sagging lawn chairs to roast marshmallows, Cam looked across the crackling flames and asked the boys if they'd ever heard of SDFL.

Holden and Nick looked at each other, firelight splashing their faces, and shook their heads.

You've never heard of the Skinny Dippers for Life Club? Cam said in a serious tone. Then let's go.

Holden and Nick turned to each other again, shrugged, and followed Cam down the steep, rocky trail through the sweet-smelling pines to the beach, busting with nervousness and excitement.

One, two, three, drop your laundry! Cam said.

Shirts and shorts landed in three piles on the sand, then they charged into the cool blackness until the water was deep enough to dive. The sensation of fresh mountain water streaming along Holden's prepubescent body with no fabric to intervene was one he would never forget. As they stood shivering, waist deep, with just a thumbnail of moon keeping watch overhead, Cam shook Holden's hand, then Nick's.

You are now officially card-carrying members of the Skinny Dippers for Life Club.

Cam placed one hand on each of the two boys' heads and ceremonially dunked them. A Canadian baptism.

When Holden broke through the surface and took a big gulp of air in the moonlight, he had never felt more alive. He and Nicholas splashed each other as they swam and dove, their laughter echoing across the surface of the lake.

There are shelves in the van, and curtains with palm trees. There's a mirror. A framed picture of snowy mountains with a log cabin in the foreground is glued to the ceiling above the built-in bed.

The sign beside the van they are sleeping in says, NO OVERNIGHT PARKING. Holden pointed to it the night before, when Lobo grabbed his hand and pulled him toward her.

Nobody cares, she said.

Roger that. And they climbed inside.

A small camping stove sits on the side counter beside a bag of granola and a box of peaches. There are baskets of clothes. A towel hangs on a hook.

Lobo's not homeless; this is her home. She lives in here. And for a few minutes last night, while they got it on, he was fully alive, too. He was surprised by the feeling of ice cracking inside him, breaking apart. He was even more shocked when he started to cry. He didn't let Lobo see, though; he buried his face in the pillow beside her head, faking exaltation until he could get his shit together.

Maybe there's a reason heroin and heroine sound exactly the same: he can be saved by either one. Apparently, he needs a lady. He could leave the first if he had the second. He can stop if he wants to. He wants to. He's stopping. He's already stopped.

Mmm, hello, Lobo says. Her thick breath spreads warmly across his cheek. We're having a picnic today, she whispers, lifting her arm from its resting place across his chest. She sings into the side of his neck, O Canada, our home and native land ... Her sticky thigh pins his leg in place. It's going to be so nice to spend the whole day together. I'm really glad you could get the day off. You've been working almost every day since we met.

Holden drags his fingertips across her bare hip. Eyes closed, he replays last night. After the pizza and the beer, the weed and the swim in the dark waters of the lake, after everyone had left the park, the two of them walked hand in hand to the far corner of the gravel parking lot and climbed into the back of Roscoe, her van.

For the most part, Holden has always referred to sex as fucking, but last night it was bumped to a new status. Upgraded. The experience surprised him with its simplicity and its magnitude. He was transported from his usual state of overwhelming shittiness to somewhere beautiful. What a relief to escape his cesspool of a brain for a while. He smiled up at the little log cabin.

Or maybe the momentary slice of peace has more to do with the fact that he stopped taking his antidepressants a couple of days ago. He had to—he couldn't get hard while he was on them. And if he happened to have any H on board, he couldn't finish. He could screw for hours and never cross the finish line. It had happened last weekend, parked in the dark down by Jericho Beach.

I'm sorry, he'd said, I think it's the meds I'm taking.

Don't worry about it, Lobo had said. If they're helping you feel better, I really don't care.

I fucking care.

I'd rather have your heart and your mind than your dick.

He'd rolled away from her. A few days later, he stopped taking his meds, and last night he was granite.

He hears the garbage truck pull up beside the van and release its air brakes. He rolls to face Lobo, and with just that slight movement, a knife pierces the epicentre of his brain. He groans.

What's up? Lobo covers herself with the sheet.

Nothing, just an ice pick impaling my skull. His tongue is hot, pulsating. Do you have any water in here? His arms and legs are heavy, and his back is aching. Why does he have such a huge fucking headache? He never gets headaches.

Lobo pulls a dripping wine bottle half full of water from the cooler under the bookshelf and rolls it up his arm. The cold makes him flinch but is also enough of a distraction that he appreciates it.

You're my saviour. He props himself up on one elbow, pulls the cork with his teeth, and drains it. He burps long and loud. That's better, he says. But he doesn't feel better, he feels worse. He could easily hurl all over the palm tree curtains. I need to take a whiz.

Sitting up quickly is a bad idea—a wave swerves up from his stomach into the back of his mouth. He pulls on his shorts as fast as he can, pushes the door of the van open, and jumps out just in time to spew onto the gravel. He looks left and right, relieved to see the garbage truck pulling out of the parking lot and no other people close by. He runs his hands over the whiskers on his head and looks up through the branches. Again, he smells the earthy, wet undercurrent of the lake.

You okay out there? Lobo calls from inside the van.

All good, thanks.

His forehead is dappled with sweat even though it's still early and they're parked in the shade. He feels the wind shuffling the leaves like playing cards above his head, feels the ground vibrating slightly under his feet. It's loud, and it's weird. He heaves again. Nothing left but a hollow *hulk* sound deep down in his throat.

Could you pass me a cold one, please?

You want a beer at 9:00 a.m.?

The night they first met, Lobo made it very clear that she broke up with her last boyfriend because he was using. Holden told her his habit was "in the past." How far in the past, he didn't specify. But if Holden wants to stay with her, he has to stop for good. Now.

He chased his last dragon on Tuesday and called a ceasefire on the meds at the same time. If he can make it through the next few days, he should be over the shitstorm. From what he's read online and what he's heard from Yuki about detoxing, it takes about a week. She's worth it. Fuck, he's worth it. It's about time.

You don't sound so good. Maybe this is a better idea? Lobo passes Holden another wine bottle full of water through the door of the van. He rolls the clear, cool glass back and forth across his forehead a few times. He takes a sip.

Now he's shivering. Goosebumps crawl up his arms. He pisses against a tree, crawls back into the van, and pulls the blanket up to his chin. He tips—first to the left and then to the right—so the blanket encases him.

Lobo sits on the corner of the bed in a white dress with small pink flowers on it and thin string like shoelaces holding it up.

Hey, beautiful, he says. She strokes a brush through her hair. He looks into the eyes of the wolf staring at him from her shoulder, then reaches for her elbow and pulls her toward him, kissing her arm.

For you I would cross a thousand deserts, he says.

How about you cross the parking lot and brush your teeth in the water fountain?

They both laugh.

His stomach cramps up again. He curls his knees to his chest, closes his eyes, and waits for the wave to pass. He's just reaching for his shirt, which is covered in work dirt from yesterday, when a hard banging on the side of the van makes them both jump.

Rise and shine! Wakey-bakey!

Holden recognizes Darren's voice. He paints with Darren, goes to shows with Darren, even lived with Darren for a while until they got kicked out. Darren has a solid-gold heart, but also a few loose fucking screws. You never know which Darren you're going to meet. It was Darren who thumped Holden back to life when he stopped breathing at China Creek Skatepark. CPR and the whole deal, apparently. Since that night, Darren always hugs Holden too hard, too long, but he's never said another word about it other than "I love you, man." Holden appreciates that.

Lobo slides the curtain along the wire, and Darren's angular face fills the window frame like Jack Nicholson in *The Shining*. He blows a thick stream of skunky smoke into the back of the van.

Happy Canada Day, citizens, he says, his eyes already glassy.

Lobo waves her arms, slicing the smoke. Goodbye, Darren. She closes the curtain over his face and turns to Holden. We are spending the day together. We are having a picnic. We are going to the beach, just the two of us. She sounds like a hypnotist programming her subject. We talked about this last night.

The slugs of Lobo's eyebrows inch closer together. This is the face of a woman who will not be taking any shit. Her index finger fiddles with the filigreed ring hanging from her septum.

But a little bit of grass will probably help with the nausea. By the weekend he'll be totally fine. If he can just muscle through the next few days, he'll be with Lobo as a whole and unburdened person by next week. He can't risk telling her he's detoxing now, that would blow everything.

You know, the cannabis leaf does look shockingly similar to the maple leaf, Holden says. Maybe that's what our founding fathers were thinking when they put it on the flag. He runs his hand across her lower back.

You're a dick. She shifts away from him.

Just one little toot and I'm all yours. For the entire day, I promise. Give me five minutes and I'll take you for breakfast.

Lobo squints into the mirror, and she goes back to brushing her hair, faster than before. Holden steps out the door of the van.

You are a parking goddess! Holden yells over the loud Kendrick Lamar. Lobo pulls her van up to the empty space directly in front of Bon's Off Broadway and raises her knuckles for a fist bump. A wall of frying bacon and burnt toast smells greets Holden when he opens the door. The joint he smoked with Darren has settled his stomach, and he's actually feeling hungry for the first time in a couple of days.

This place always has a lineup, he says, but it's worth it—$2.95 for a huge breakfast. He swings his backpack over one shoulder and checks the back pocket of his shorts for his wallet.

Lobo joins him on the sidewalk. He drapes one arm around her waist, and they head toward the entrance.

You smell way better than me. He pulls her close and presses his face into her hair.

That's not difficult, Lobo laughs.

So, what's up with this picnic? he asks.

I was thinking we could grab some red and white foods and hit the beach, maybe catch the fireworks later.

Red and white foods?

For Canada Day. Tomato and mozzarella salad. Strawberries and cream. Chips and salsa.

Colonial, yet tasty, he laughs. And what would Canada Day be without our national beverage?

They're ushered to a table in the corner. Holden pulls out a chair for Lobo and pushes it in behind her as she sits. She smiles at him. He forces a grin, wipes the sweat off his forehead with the shoulder of his work shirt, and takes the seat across from her. The waiter drops two menus on the table and gestures toward a counter stacked with white cups.

Self-serve coffee's over there, a buck for a bottomless cup.

How about some water? Holden asks.

It's over there, too.

I'll go, he says, but when he stands, the swirling in his stomach sends him in the opposite direction, down the hall toward the bathrooms. The smell in the men's room brings Holden close to upchucking again. Pancakes, lemon floor cleaner, and morning dumps. Holden hurries into a stall and sits. His guts release, and his insides rain out of him. Eventually, he stands at the sink, washes his hands, then turns off the hot tap and lets the pure cold gush over his hands. He splashes cold water onto his face over and over, which helps soothe the sizzle of his skin. Leaning closer to the mirror, Holden locks eyes with his dripping reflection. His hair has grown a little, and his beard is filling in along his jawline. His cheeks are red, and so are the whites of his eyes.

Hang in there, buddy, a few more days and you'll be good. You can do this. His hands grip the cool edges of the sink.

Holden arrives back at the table, and Lobo raises her shoulders in question.

Water? Coffee? she says, and pushes out her chair to stand. I'll get it. Are you okay?

Never better. He thuds onto his chair.

I ordered you the special.

Sweet, thanks. He closes his eyes and his throat to press the puke back down. The walls are covered with graffiti, and Holden imagines he's painting a big throw up over everything. Under the table, his knees bob and vibrate, matching the buzzing in his head. He manages to eat a few bites of toast before the waiter comes back and clears the plates away.

Are you sure you're all right? Lobo's plate is empty. You seem distracted.

I'm fine, all right? Stop fucking asking me.

Holden stands and grabs his pack from the back of his chair, drops a ten-dollar bill on the table, and walks out the door, not bothering to wait for Lobo.

Another hot, clear day. It's been like this for two weeks straight. Strange for Vancouver, even in the middle of summer. Lobo rests her hand on his sweaty back.

Let's walk up and grab the beer, she says. Fresh air might help you feel better.

I told you, I'm fine.

He takes her hand, and they start walking up Nanaimo. They turn onto a side street, and after a few blocks he squeezes her hand. Lobo doesn't return the squeeze. He may have lost her, but he can't tell her why, that he's already lied to her. One block more and Holden lifts her hand to his lips, kisses her knuckles. She continues looking straight ahead. Their feet strike the sidewalk in tandem.

If I guess your real name, will you tell me? Holden asks.

What makes you think Lobo isn't my real name?

Like, when your mom first saw you, she thought, what a sweet little baby, I think I'll name her after a wild dog?

Lobo looks over at him, rolls her eyes, and smiles.

Is it Zoe?

No answer.

How about Isabelle?

No answer.

I know, Shakira!

Lobo tries not to smile.

That's it. Nailed it! Damn, I'd change my name, too.

They turn right onto Commercial Drive. Soon they pass a small vegetable market, and Holden takes an orange from one of the boxes out front. He tosses the orange up into the air and catches it. They walk another block.

Why did you do that? Lobo asks.

Do what?

Take that orange. It doesn't belong to you.

Give me a fucking break.

That's stealing, and you're being a bit of a jerk. Do you want to tell me what's going on?

Nope.

Holden tosses the orange in the air over and over. Toss. Catch. Toss. Catch. Lobo drops his hand, and they walk the last few blocks at arm's length from each other. It feels like they're on opposite sides of the street. In front of the liquor store, he hands her the orange.

Peace offering. You're right, I'm feeling a little messed up today. Just working too much. I'll be okay once we get to the beach. I just need a swim. It's so fucking hot. He lifts the bottom of his T-shirt to mop his face.

Lobo waits outside, leaning against a planter full of marigolds. Inside the store, Holden chooses peach cider for her and six beers for himself. On the way to the front counter, he passes the whiskey section— Jameson bottles lined up like bowling pins grab his eye.

Hello Jimmy, my old friend. You'll help me through this, won't you? He slips a bottle into his backpack and walks up to the cash register to pay for the beer and cider.

Outside the air-conditioned shop, the heat of high noon lands hard on his bristled head. He leans against a garbage can to steady himself.

Excuse me, sir, just a moment. Holden turns to see a small woman who was shopping inside the store. Did he forget his wallet?

Yeah? he answers.

Security. I'd like to check your backpack, please. Her hand rests on his arm. Her eyes are lined in black.

Fuck you, lady. Holden takes a step back.

What's going on? Lobo says, half an orange dripping in her hand.

Nothing, let's go. He grabs her hand and pulls her in the direction they came from.

Wait! The woman from the store grabs the strap of his backpack. Holden yanks on the other strap, throwing her off balance, but she won't let go. She unzips the pack, reaches an arm inside, and pulls out the bottle of whiskey.

You are going to have to wait here. The police have been called. She grabs a handful of fabric near the shoulder of his shirt.

Let go, you can't fucking hold me. Holden dips his head and bites the woman's wrist, just hard enough to make her let go. She cries out. He drops the beer and cider and takes off running, cutting across the traffic on Commercial Drive and up the other side, toward the mountains.

Holden! Wait! It's Charlotte. Charlotte is my real name.

But he's already rounding the corner by the coffee shop.

He runs along the street, glancing back over his shoulder to see if anyone is following him. After three blocks, he cuts between two houses and slows down, his chest heaving. His throat aches. Sweat is streaming down his face and neck. His workboots are made of stone. He's almost at the end of the lane when he sees what he thinks is a police car in the distance. He takes off running again, in the opposite direction. He doesn't know how long he can keep going. His heart pounds in his ears, his face burns, his pack slaps against his back with every stride. He jogs over one block and up one block, down another back lane, and up another block, zigzagging like Pac-Man.

He has no idea where he is. His lungs have never expanded this much—they're stretched and cracking under the strain. He slows, he walks. He stops. The grass and sidewalk bulge up at him, the trees in a neat row along the boulevard bend toward and away from him. He collapses to his hands and knees on the grass.

Gradually, his vision clears enough to look up. He's kneeling in front of two white lions at the front gate of a flamingo-pink house. He sloughs off his pack, takes off his shirt, and uses it to mop his face and neck, lifting his ribcage to make room for more air. He takes a few long breaths and blinks up at the sun directly overhead. *Holy fuck, that was close.*

Then he hears the thrusting engine and aggressive pitch of a car engine accelerating. He hears hard braking and doors opening. He can't get up, he can't run anymore. His stomach heaves, but there's nothing left inside him.

31

More time passed, and I did not become less sad—I became more obsessive. I couldn't walk the dog, smell bread toasting, or hear a song without sensing the edge of Holden's shadow, his flapping shirttail slipping through my outstretched fingers.

Learning what I could about the escalation of Holden's substance use and writing it all down was the opposite of cathartic; it left me confused, scared, and anxious. I operated under the delusion that by uncovering details of Holden's last year, I could intersect time and prevent what had already happened from happening. I worried about my own mental health, which made me more empathetic to Holden's mental health. Time looped, and some days I received fresh burns that blistered. Long bouts of weeping continued, and I often went days without leaving the house or talking to anyone.

More than once, I called Cam from the edge of a road where I had pulled over, unable to speak because song lyrics or someone's innocent question at the yoga studio—what have you been doing with yourself lately?—had ripped Holden away again. Cam would leave his job site to find me and hold me in his arms until my breathing slowed, my mind found traction, and my feet gained purchase on the ground again.

Holden became a spinning magnet that both attracted and repelled me. I oscillated. Some days, the trepidation about what I might find out was offset by ravenous hunger for even the most opaque sighting of him. Some days I was tempted to throw the stacks of papers into the fire; others, I wanted the whole world to read every failing word so that they might learn—about opioids and how good people can do distasteful things to try and mask their pain, and that doesn't make them bad people. It makes them human. Some days I knew I would never feel joy again, and then the delicate song of a black-capped chickadee in the branches of the Spanish chestnut at dawn would shift something inside my heart.

Rumi's words made sense.

Your grief for what you've lost lifts a mirror
up to where you're bravely working.

Expecting the worst, you look, and instead,
here's the joyful face you've been wanting to see.

Your hand opens and closes and opens and closes.
If it were always a fist or always stretched open,
you would be paralyzed.

Your deepest presence is in every small contracting and expanding,
the two as beautifully balanced and coordinated
as bird wings.

Ethical questions troubled me. How would Holden's friends respond to my fictional amalgamations of them, to the scenes I'd orchestrated? How would my family react? And Cam and Lyla—how could I protect the living while unravelling the story of someone who was not? Obviously, I couldn't keep anyone safe, so that was a non-starter. But I worried. Worrying was all I did. What was the writer's version of the Hippocratic oath? Is it ever possible to do no harm? How could I artistically and symbolically depict the full spectrum of my son's life and his struggle? How does any writer fully illuminate the 360 degrees of any character? And the biggest conundrum: whose story was this to tell?

For one thing, I seemed to be uncovering mostly bad news. The sordid nights of drunkenness and serious mistakes. The times Holden crossed lines with himself and others. I guessed at a lot of it, at most of it. But people told me Holden walked around whistling much of the time, too. His life was not a misery; his pendulum swung wide. In my writings, he seemed pathetic. But Holden was never in any way pathetic. Why couldn't I zero in on him riding a skateboard with the wind at his back, or telling a joke over Eggs Benedict and having more than enough in his wallet to pay for it? The sunny days, when music played and colours flew and nobody cried? Why couldn't I focus on warm memories, like his nineteenth-birthday dinner at a new restaurant overlooking Coal Harbour? We ate prawns, Cam and I bought him his first legal beer, and Holden blew out a candle. Lyla presented him with a sock monkey he immediately named Steve, and we gave him a gift-wrapped case of Ichiban noodles.

I tried to remember Holden's capacity for joy. I found some in an email from his grade one teacher, a delight of a woman, an insightful educator and caring heart who, though I'm sure she was very busy with her own three children, attended Holden's birthday party when he invited her.

I have spent the last few days since I heard trying to begin to accept your loss of Holden's quirky, passionate self ... I am so sad inside ... Holden was truly the most joyful, spirited, and spontaneous young man I have ever had the special pleasure of teaching. When I recall moments of our Grade 1 year together, his creative thinking still makes me laugh out loud. I remember describing him as having a party inside ... if someone popped him, confetti and balloons would pour out!

A random note on a scrap of paper directed me to "find the happy." Holden had known happiness—people told me so, and I witnessed it myself more often than not—but I was too sad to conjure any of that. *I* didn't know what happiness was anymore, so how could I tell his?

The few people who were aware I was writing about Holden would occasionally ask if the process was helping me to mend. And they would nod, because they already believed that to be a truth.

It must be helping you heal, they'd say.

No, it's excruciating, I'd say.

And they would not ask the next question, the one they wanted to ask: *Then why are you doing it?*

I didn't know why. I didn't know what I was making. I just felt compelled to keep going, and I didn't know how to do anything else. I didn't want to do nothing. I was afraid that if I did nothing, my life would be nothing—that Holden's life would mean nothing. So I sat at my desk and asked Holden what he wanted to tell me.

What's important to you? I'd say out loud. What do you want people to know? What would you like me to know?

I wanted to keep talking to him, and in the ridiculous way that grief allows, I held the fallacy of our eternal conversation as fact. Fuck physics or the laws of thermodynamics or whatever this was. I manifested Holden in the small clicking spark germinating in the pre-moment before a thought arrived in my consciousness, the thoughts that ended up on the screen of my MacBook Air. Occasionally I'd go back and read over passages with no memory of having written them, as though I were reading someone else's words. As if Holden were writing his own story.

I started getting more daring with my questions. They felt imperative. I was on the lam with nothing to lose, and my grief was leading the way—it had become my loyal companion.

I wanted to know specifically what had happened on Holden's last day. There must have been a catastrophic series of events for this life to have ended in such a frivolous way. Something I had read about plane crashes being the result of not one big mistake, but a prolonged series of smaller, cumulative errors rang true. A first officer who doesn't want to overstep their rank by pointing out the tired captain's oversight, a minor mechanical malfunction that goes unchecked, a stripped screw or forgotten gasket that leads to a wing fuselage peeling off during flight, a few degrees of misnavigation that send the airliner off course into a foggy mountainside.

If I wanted to get specific, I needed to find details; if I wanted to get closer to the bone, I needed to be brave. I wrote a letter to the chief of the Vancouver Police Department.

Dear Chief Andrews,

I have heard you are a kind person, so I am writing to ask for your help, but first I have a story to tell you. Two summers ago, my beautiful son Holden died of an accidental drug and alcohol overdose. He was only twenty-one, and like many young men, just beginning to imagine what kind of adult he might become.

My son was a paradox. He was a talented artist who could play music by ear and had completed one year at Emily Carr University. He had a loving and supportive family. He was kind, quick to laugh, and generous. He was a warm and protective big brother. At the same time, Holden could be quite disagreeable. He struggled with his mental health and a curious self-loathing. Though we offered many other options, some he accepted, some he didn't, he chose to self-medicate.
We thought this was largely with alcohol and pot, but found out later it was with heroin, too. This is terribly upsetting for a parent to hear.

Coroner Waheed told me there was likely not enough heroin in Holden's system to kill him; it was the combination with alcohol and traces of other street drugs, likely from tainted supply, that slowed his breathing and eventually stopped his sensitive heart.

In the months before his death, Holden was trying to free himself from his substance abuse and find a healthier path. He visited our family doctor, who prescribed antidepressants. He began taking them, which helped level his anxiety and depression. He had a full-time job working as a landscaper. He seemed happy.

Holden told me later he was considering stopping his medication because it prevented him from performing sexually. Think of yourself at twenty-one—not being able to "get it up" would be a big deal, wouldn't it? So he stopped taking his meds. Cold turkey. Sudden withdrawal from these medications can send patients into black depression and an elevated state of anxiety. According to our doctor, it's pretty much the worst a person can feel.

On Canada Day, Holden went with his new girlfriend to the liquor store on Commercial Drive to get some beer for their picnic. By that time, he was two or three days into his withdrawal from the antidepressant medication and likely also detoxing from heroin. The combination of these two factors would have created an extremely high state of agitation.

Holden's default was to use alcohol to soothe this uneasiness. He stole a bottle of whiskey from the store. The security guard caught him and attempted to hold him until the police came. I'm sure Holden was verbally abusive and probably aggressive. He could be combative at times, especially when he knew he was wrong.

He was apprehended by your officers and spent the night in jail. That meant he missed work the next morning and was undoubtedly concerned about losing his job. Friends who saw him after he was released said he appeared distraught and conflicted.

I don't know much about what happened after that, but clearly, he went to the street to find something to ease his pain. Instead of going home, he stayed with a friend that night, who told me Holden said he wasn't feeling well and just needed to rest. Though he seemed okay when he went to sleep, she was unable to revive him in the morning.

On July 3, 2015, a police officer came to our front door and uttered the words that no mother wants to hear. The loss of our son and brother has been devastating for our whole family.

Holden was a complex person who made many mistakes. He was also extraordinary. His life deserves respect, and I believe his story is an important one. I hope to understand more fully what happened, why Holden chose to go down such a dangerous road. In time I would like to write about it. In telling his story, I hope that others may recognize themselves or someone they love. I hope that perhaps some people will find empathy and forgiveness. Maybe some will feel less alone.

This is where I need your help. I am asking for your assistance in my research. I know it's not customary, but I would like to see the jail area where my son spent the night so that I can accurately describe the experiences of his last day. It would be tremendously helpful in illustrating honestly what happened.

I look forward to your favourable response.

With sincere gratitude,
Tara McGuire

A few weeks later, while I was standing on the edge of a grass field watching Lyla play one of her first high school rugby games, I received a phone call from a blocked number.

A deep, calm voice said, This is highly unusual, but the chief has asked me to arrange for you to visit the VPD jail, and I am to answer any questions you might have.

32

Cam and I parked on East Cordova near Main Street, where the mini-mart on the corner had bars on the windows and graffiti draping the walls. A thin man huddled under the awning, searching through an overloaded shopping cart. He spoke to himself as we passed. Cam's hand rested on my lower back while we crossed Main Street.

A tall police sergeant in a tailored suit with slicked-back hair met us outside and informed us that this kind of access was very rare before escorting us inside. We were taken into the office of a grey-haired inspector who offered his sincere condolences and patiently read us the report on Holden's arrest. He then escorted us across the street to the VPD jail, where he showed us the cells, medical room, intake, fingerprinting, and mug shot areas. He explained the procedure for when someone is brought in and how Holden would have been processed. I could hardly speak. I couldn't shake the image of Holden sleeping in one of these small cells, shivering under a blanket. Cam's warm hand held mine. When he could tell I was holding my breath, he'd gently squeeze to remind me to breathe.

We returned to the inspector's office and sat at a round table across from his desk, which was stacked with files. He asked us if we had any further questions, then surreptitiously slid a piece of folded paper across the table. A photocopy of Holden's mug shot. I had never seen such hatred in my son's eyes.

∞

The police officer stands over Holden, legs forming a triangle, hand within easy reach of her gun.

Nice day for a jog. Her blond hair is pulled back in a tight ponytail, and her bulletproof vest flattens her chest. She looks down at Holden sitting slumped in resignation on the sidewalk. What's your name?

Go fuck yourself. His face burns. His skull throbs.

The officer walks around behind him and squats down to handcuff him, one wrist at a time. The cuffs make a ratcheting sound.

Finished your tantrum?

Holden clenches his teeth and tightens his face to fight the tears quickly rising to his eyes.

I'm going to take a look in your bag, she says, and reaches for his pack, unzipping the pocket. She retrieves his passport. William Holden. Is that you?

Holden stares straight ahead. The other officer, male and bulky, stands in the shade of a tree on the boulevard, writing in a small notepad. Want to make this easier and just tell me your name?

Fuck you. Write that in your fucking book.

William, I am arresting you for robbery. You have the right to retain and instruct counsel without delay. You also have the right to free and immediate legal advice. Do you understand?

Holden closes his eyes. How can this be happening?

Do you wish to call a lawyer?

He clears his throat and spits a wad of phlegm onto the sidewalk.

You also have the right to apply for legal assistance through the provincial legal aid program. Do you understand? He feels a thudding in his hands. He might throw up.

He nods his head once.

The back of the police van smells of rusted metal and piss. His bare shoulders stick to the tin wall, and his arms, pulled tight behind his back by the handcuffs, are aching. His fingers tingle. What's he supposed to do now? He tries counting his breaths, a new meditation he's been practicing. Inhale—one. Exhale—two. Inhale—one. Exhale—two. He leans forward to see if he can catch a sip of the light-blue air flowing in through the screen on the door. Sweat and tears drip down his face and stream off the tip of his nose and the ends of his beard onto the floor. He straightens his back, smears the wetness with his workboot, and closes his eyes.

One, two, one, two, one, two.

The clanking of an industrial door rolling up alerts him. The police van pulls into a shaded courtyard. He hears keys in the van door. It swings open, and cool air floods over him.

Step down, please.

His workboots are difficult to maneuver, his legs incredibly heavy. He stumbles, and the officer takes his arm to guide him down the walkway toward a metal door, where another officer stands waiting. This one has short, black hair, biceps trying to escape his short sleeves, and a closely shaved face. He thinks they could be the same age. The officer checks his clipboard.

Stand here for search. Am I going to find any needles?

Nope.

Good to hear. Those types aren't lasting too long these days.

The officer puts the clipboard down on a table against the wall and pulls on pair of blue surgical gloves, the same kind Holden sometimes wears when he's painting. He searches Holden thoroughly, even running his fingers around his ankles inside his socks. Holden's skin hurts and his muscles ache. His mouth is sour. He needs water. He needs to explain. He needs someone to listen.

Buttons are pushed, beeps and buzzes flash through the air. He's taken through a heavy metal door into an entryway where they wait for the first door to slowly close behind them, then proceed through the second metal door, which also latches securely before they continue. Sounds crawl up his neck. It's like he's inside a garbage can that someone is kicking.

The receiving officer is bald, with shoulders so wide they dissolve any thought of resistance. He takes Holden's elbow and guides him down a dull hallway into a small windowless room. The floor is damp, freshly mopped.

There's a concrete bench attached to the wall and a drain in the floor. The fluorescent light behind a cage on the ceiling flickers intermittently, and its vibrating hum makes him feel like he might break into pieces.

Secondary search, the large officer says.

Déjà fucking vu, Holden says.

Second time's a charm. Have you got any surprises for me?

Same answer as last time, fuckwad.

The officer notes the tattoos on Holden's upper body on his clipboard.

Upper right chest, *us and them*. Left forearm, *courage*. Left arm general, sleeve including hourglass, teeth, flower, dagger, ship. I'm going to take your cuffs off. Are we cool?

Whatever, Holden says. He won't allow them the satisfaction of being decent. He's too fucking incensed.

The officer hands him his shirt, and he slips it on—it smells like two days of digging and a night sleeping in a truck. Holden shivers in the air-conditioning. His clothes and hair are soaked with sweat.

Would you like to call a lawyer? You're entitled to legal advice free of charge.

For one bottle of booze? You've got to be fucking kidding me. You realize all I did was shoplift, right?

Theft plus assault equals robbery, William, a very serious charge. I suggest you take advantage of the legal support available to you.

I suggest you take advantage of that clipboard and shove it up your ass.

Any mental health concerns?

Apparently I have borderline personality disorder.

There's a shocker. The nurse on staff can speak to you about any medications you don't have with you. He can also give you Suboxone for withdrawal if necessary, and the doctor will be by in about an hour to check you over. Would you like to make a phone call?

How many fucking times do I have to tell you dipshits, I don't want to talk to anyone, I don't need anything, I don't want to call anyone. I shouldn't be here. Just leave me the fuck alone.

Ten-four.

The officer writes something on his clipboard and leaves the cell. One big chunk of metal drops into another, and smaller gears fall into place.

Holden sits down on the hard bench, leans against the cement wall, and stretches out his legs. The opposite wall is almost close enough to touch with his toes. He's more thirsty than he's ever been. Closing his eyes, flashbacks begin to roll in sequence—swimming in the dark, sex with Lobo, waking up in the van, being sick in the parking lot, breakfast at Bon's, walking to the liquor store, running, running, running.

The aching is back. Holden curls onto his side on the cold bench.

Twenty minutes later the same officer comes into the cell and, with a hand the size of a baseball glove, offers a bottle of water. Holden sits up, opens the bottle, drops the lid on the floor, and downs the whole thing. He drops the bottle on the floor and hears the hollow sound when it bounces. The officer seems unfazed.

Time for your close-up, sweetheart.

They go to an open area with a check-in desk like a hotel would have.

Stand on the yellow footprints and smile for the birdie.

Holden's familiar with all of these steps. He's been caught and released for spray painting before, like some kind of too-small fish, but this time is ridiculous. He should be at the beach by now, celebrating Canada Day with Lobo and a low-grade beer buzz.

He stares down the eye of the camera with all the contempt he can muster. The huge officer walks him down another hall to another room, where his fingers are rolled in black ink and pressed onto white paper.

Any questions?

Can I go now? All I did was shoplift.

This, my friend, is a statutory holiday—no court today. So you get to have a sleepover at our fine establishment. I'll be by later to put a chocolate on your pillow. Happy Canada Day.

33

The next morning, Holden stood before a judge, who separated the felony charge of robbery into two lesser offences: theft under five thousand dollars and assault. A crumpled piece of paper in his bag noted that the following week, he was to reappear in court for sentencing. His signature—illegible loops of hostile scrawl, a hybrid of his initials and his tag—was the only subversive act available to him.

I imagined the judge speaking to him in an authoritative monotone. William, you seem to be an intelligent person doing some very unintelligent things. You need to get your act together, as I suspect you can. I am going to give some thought as to what I feel is in your best interest. I suggest you do the same. Please read and agree to the conditions I have set out for you and return next week. If I see you here in the meantime, I will have no choice but to consider incarceration, and I don't think you want that, do you?

Holden must have felt he needed a certain kind of help that morning, because he didn't call either of his parents, or even Lobo, from the jail's phone. He called Yuki and left her a voicemail: Meet me at Sailor's at one.

When the grey metal door finally opened, I pictured Holden gathering all the bravado he had left to stride out of the jail with his chest puffed and his bleary, bruised-looking eyes levelled at the horizon. Maybe, once he was around the corner onto Main Street, he stopped, pressed a hand against the warm stone wall, and let his shoulders slump. Maybe he took a long, slow breath, maybe he made a decision.

To get to the SeaBus terminal from the jail, he would have first passed through several blocks of utter poverty and despair in the Downtown Eastside—thin figures sprawled on the sidewalk or huddled together in doorways, smoking, injecting, selling what they could, trying to survive. Then the abrupt transition to the affluent cobblestones of Gastown with its signature art-deco, cast-iron lampposts and hanging baskets of purple petunias. The day was another link in a long chain of hot ones. Along Water Street, tourists probably sat under colourful umbrellas on sidewalk patios, drinking craft beer and eating locally smoked salmon. Leftover flags and red balloons from yesterday's Canada Day celebrations likely lingered in shop windows.

Holden had a way of throwing his feet out in front of him with each step. A kind of a toss and flip motion. The soles of his workboots would have spanked the stones as he made his way up the gradual incline of the street, toward Waterfront station. I saw him yanking open an ornate glass door, traversing the cathedral-like entrance hall with its high arches, coffered ceiling, and marble floor, then taking a quick look left and right for security before vaulting over the turnstile.

He had a lot to think about. A lot left unresolved. Had he lost his job because he hadn't shown up that morning? Had Lobo left him because he got busted? Would Cam and I allow him to move back in if we found out about his arrest? Would he have a criminal record? His stomach may have churned with anxiety and withdrawal. Or maybe he didn't think about anything other than meeting Yuki and getting his hands on a cold beer.

A year and a half later, on an afternoon when the heavy rain made most people cancel their outdoor plans, Yuki pulled up in front of our house in a rusted car. I got in and searched her large, remorseful eyes. The long, thick braid that had used to hang like a black rope over her shoulder was gone. She'd shaved what I could see of her head, making her appear like a little boy in her winter hat and jacket.

Thank you. Thank you for trying to help, I hope I said. Thank you for being his friend.

Yuki and Holden had first become close in high school band class. They'd lost touch over the years, but had reconnected through Facebook when Holden made his sobriety post on Facebook a few months before he died. Yuki had recently extricated herself from her own four-year heroin addiction and was in the process of becoming a substance abuse counsellor. When she saw Holden's public proclamation, she'd reached out to him and told him her story. In response, he'd been completely open with her about his habits.

It's so fucking sad, she said, as she reached across the car to hug me. I'll tell you everything I can remember.

Holden had loved Wreck Beach. He would take the bus for more than an hour to get there, then descend the long flights of stairs to the wide stretch of warm grey sand intersected by sections of smooth logs. Wreck, or Wrecked, as some people call it, is a clothing-optional beach close to the university at the westernmost tip of Point Grey, below the bluffs that look out over the Pacific toward Vancouver Island. It's a sort of lawless hippie territory of margaritas, open drug use, drumming and belly dancing the day away. While he enjoyed the atmosphere, Holden preferred to keep his clothes on. Naked swimming was for nighttime, and for limited company.

The weekend before he died, Holden met up with Yuki and her partner, Lina, who in a strange twist had briefly dated Holden in high school. He was with Darren that day. They had a squirt gun full of tequila, and the magic mushrooms they had taken were just kicking in. Darren was on his own tangent. He tried for a solid hour to persuade Lina to stare directly into his eyes so they could achieve a soul connection.

Don't scare these ladies away with your creepiness, Holden said, and they all laughed together.

There, digging their toes in the hot sand, Holden told them about his new girlfriend, Lobo. They'd been on a few dates, bike riding and a picnic most recently, and he'd had a blast. He also described the previous weekend at Wreck, when he'd saved a man from drowning.

It was actually pretty intense, he said.

In the early evening, they all went to a restaurant on Broadway and sat on the patio, listening to '90s hip hop.

He knew every word, Yuki told me. I never saw Holden happier than when he was listening to music. He rapped along with Biggie Smalls, ate sushi and then a deep-fried Mars bar with ice cream for dessert.

After dinner, outside the restaurant, a man with an Irish accent noticed Yuki and Lina holding hands and screamed in their faces, Suck my dick you fucking lesbians!

Small-minded goof! Holden yelled back while Yuki and Lina grabbed his shirt to keep him from fighting. That's just not okay! He was visibly upset.

In the car with me, Yuki explained drug-user behaviour, and how she could tell Holden was using again after a period of appearing healthier. He took a hundred dollars' cash out of the bank machine, then paid for his dinner with debit. He asked her specific questions about her own addiction and withdrawal. Yuki and Lina offered to drive him home, but he refused. He was noncommittal about where he was going.

Got some stuff to do downtown, he said.

It's not an impulse, she told me. It's a need in the back of your mind that you're always trying to fulfill. It can wait for a while, and you can look really normal, but it never leaves you alone completely.

We drove to the spot where she and Lina had met with Holden eighteen months earlier, on the last day of his life, not far from where they were living with Lina's mom. Yuki stopped the car on a street with a wide grass boulevard and pointed at the top step of a flight of wooden stairs leading up to a small children's playground.

That's where he was sitting when we met him, she said. I was on my skateboard, so I got here first, then Lina came with the dog. He looked like shit, dark rings under his eyes. I don't think he'd slept. He seemed off-kilter. He already had a six-pack of Wildcat beside him.

The windshield wipers flapped back and forth, clearing thick sheets of relentless water. The stairs were there, then gone, there, then gone.

∞

Hey dude, how's it going? Yuki's round face shines up at him like a small moon from the sidewalk below. She always looks like a little kid.

Heyo!

Did you save one of those bad boys for me? Her men's basketball jersey shows off muscular, tattooed arms. A long, thick braid hangs from one side of her head.

Sure did, Cukes.

He's so tired he can't get up. He waits for Yuki to climb the stairs and sit down beside him before handing her a beer. She loops her arm around his shoulders and pulls him close, pressing a long wet kiss onto his cheek.

Don't hug me, I stink.

You're burning up, man. Whatcha been doing? Running a marathon?

Something like that. I spent last night in lock-up.

What for?

Nothing. Stupid shit.

There you guys are! Lina calls up to them, breathing hard. You're too fast for me on that thing, Yuki. Lina's bleached blond hair swirls in dreadlock snakes around her pointed face. A few long sections are wrapped in colourful ribbons, and various piercings dot her lips, nose, and eyebrows with glints of silver. The strap of her tank slips off her shoulder. Their dog, Dexter, drags Lina up the stairs.

Hi Holden, how're ya doing?

Good, good, Linus. All good. He nods, scratching Dexter's ears.

That's not what I hear, Lina says.

Actually, I've been better.

Well, it's good to see you again. I'll let you guys talk. Lina trails her long fingers along Holden's arm as she passes. She pulls Dexter up the stairs into the park.

Holden turns to Yuki. I take it you told her?

Lina's cool. She nursed me through my own withdrawal last year. I couldn't have gotten clean without her.

Now it seems ironic that he broke up with Lina when they were sixteen because *she* was too crazy, doing things that were too risky, like jumping between moving freight trains and slashing her own skin with a knife.

So, where you at? Yuki asks.

Haven't used since I think Monday, so what's that, three days? Feeling pretty fuckin' shitty.

Yuki's nodding. Let me guess, aching muscles, killer headache, wicked cramps, black depression, you basically want to die?

That's the highlights.

Should only be a few more days, and the worst will be over. Bananas help with the muscle pain. Yuki sips her beer.

Does clean include beer? Holden gestures to the green can in her hand.

Well—she peers up at him intensely—you start with the stuff that will kill you first, then work your way down. The occasional beer and hoot of weed's about all I've got left. How long have you been using again?

Honestly, I don't really know, this whole year's been pretty fucking scraped.

Okay, well, why don't we go to the river and chill? Then we can talk more about it. They stand and walk down the stairs together.

Sure, but what I really want to do is take a ride on your skate.

Be my guest.

Yuki passes her skateboard to Holden with a wide grin. He trades her his backpack, then tromps down the stairs and drops the board onto the road, placing one foot on top to steady it and himself. The workboots make for an awkward stance, and the two beers he just chugged don't help his balance. It takes him half a block to get a decent rhythm going. Pump, glide, pump, glide, pump. And he's riding, gliding smoothly, past a strip of brand-new condos, wind cooling his face. He raises his arms in the air to wave at Yuki before slicing across the traffic of Lonsdale.

∞

I got out of the car and walked up the steps to one of the last places that Holden had been. Stubs of grass grew optimistically in the cracks. At the top, I turned. I wanted to see what he'd seen that day. Rain speckled the hood of my jacket, a high hat in my ears. Between two buildings, across the grey inlet with its barges and tanker ships, I could just make out the misty silver outline of the downtown skyline. The harbour bustled with floating activity.

Next Yuki drove us to the Seymour River. The gravel parking lot beside the picnic area was empty, and low cloud obscured the opposite bank of the fast-flowing river. These kinds of days verified that we were living in a rainforest. The field was deserted. On summer days, families would crowd the picnic tables with coolers, barbecues, and inflatable plastic toys. Dust would billow as cars pulled in. Children would zigzag over the grass. The river would wander.

We cracked the windows to let in a trickle of cool air and help clear the windshield. The staticky sound of the churning, swollen river rushed in, too, its current only ever moving in one direction—away.

We were living with Lina's mom while we saved up for our own place, Yuki told me. She let us use her car, and Holden sat in the back seat with the dog. He connected his Bluetooth and insisted on playing loud music the whole way here. I remember him sticking his head out the window and screaming along with Black Sabbath's "War Pigs."

Yuki said she tried to help Holden relax that day so he would open up to her, trust her, allow her to help him. She said she could tell he was in a very vulnerable state.

We got out of the car and followed the path along the shore. The rain had let up, but the air was still saturated.

∞

When they arrive, the park is packed with people sitting on blankets. Kids are splashing in the shallows, shrieking while they fling handfuls of icy water at each other.

Let's walk upstream, says Yuki. It'll be quieter.

Dexter charges into the river, lapping up water with her long tongue.

I need to get in there, too. I'm so fucking hot.

Just a little bit farther. It's worth it, trust me.

Holden follows Yuki and Lina up the curving trail along the bank.

A few minutes later, they round a bend, and the river widens and slows. Somebody's built a shallow pool by piling up rocks to make a retaining wall. A few larger boulders in the centre of the pool make a perfect place to sit.

Holy shit, it's Fred Flintstone's living room, Holden says.

He leans forward to untie his bootlaces and almost falls over.

I gotcha. Lina hooks her fingers under the waistband of his shorts like a suitcase handle. Holden peels off his T-shirt, drops his cargo shorts in the middle of the path, and, wearing just his boxers and baseball hat, strides three steps into the river and falls forward, submerging his body. This water is melted snow from the mountains above them. The stream instantly douses the crackling fire of his skin. His lungs seize with the shock, and sections of his skull contract. He surfaces and takes an urgent breath.

Sweet Jesus! Holden's deep voice echoes off the trees on the opposite bank. He tries to stand up, but the smooth, round rocks under his bare feet are covered in slime. He can't get his footing; he falls and submerges again, but this time it's not such a shock. He reaches for the largest boulder in the pool and pulls himself up onto it, sputtering. He sits with his feet resting on two smaller rocks, as if he's on a throne. Raises the can of beer that is somehow still in his hand.

Cheers, my loyal subjects.

Over on the bank, Yuki and Lina laugh and clap. Dexter wades into the pool. Holden swivels on the rock so the sun can warm his back. He spins his hat so the brim shades the back of his neck. The mountains are a high, verdant wall. He hears a thrum in the distance—either the water rushing along, rattling through the rounded stones along the shore, or the drone of cars on the highway just above them. Hard to tell.

Yuki teeters toward him, stepping from rock to rock. She takes off her green high-tops and places them beside Holden, then stashes another six-pack in the river, weighing it down with a few rocks. Over on the bank, Lina pulls a camera with a long lens out of her bag and steps into the shallows, taking photos.

Work with me, baby. I'll send you some of these shots, Holden, you can update your lame Facebook photo.

Then I'm gonna profe pic all day for you, he says.

Currently his Facebook profile picture shows him passed out on the grass with a beer in his hand while a cat walks past, giving him some kind of elitist snub. That one might be hard to beat. Most of his Instagram posts were taken in some stage of inebriation. He tilts his chin down and away to partially obscure his face. Lina steps up on a rock, focuses on him, and presses the shutter.

So, what's the deal? Yuki asks, standing in the river.

I don't actually know. Holden takes off his hat, drops it on the rock beside him, and scoops handfuls of water over his face and head. I want to do better, I want to quit, but it's fucking rough. So many times I've thought I had it under control, and then some insane shit happens and I'm fucked again. It's so hard to avoid. I mean, it's everywhere. What if I can't get out of this?

You can. That's just the way it works, Yuki says. I know it's tough, but you can do it.

Sometimes I think I'll just keep going, it might be easier. Just keep it small and manageable, you know?

I do, actually, I did that for years and my parents didn't know, but trust me, heroin is never manageable. Especially now. But this is something you can handle. Shit, if I can do it, so can you. She uses her foot to splash water at his bare chest. Holden doesn't react to the cold; he takes a long drink and tosses the empty toward Yuki. She picks up the can before it can float downstream, crushes it against a rock, and tucks it into the pocket of her way-too-big shorts. Holden reaches into the pool to grab another beer.

What would you like to happen? Yuki asks.

I'd like to keep working—my job's great. Maybe move back in with my mom. They just got back from their big trip, but I don't know if they'll let me. I'd like to hang with my little sister, she's so cool.

If your life's anything like mine, it can take a while to build that trust back up again. But that'll happen, too. Just give it some time.

Holden looks up at the sun and squints. Dexter splashes over to them and shakes her fur, soaking them both.

Remember when we all slept out on the football field? Yuki says.

Remember that ski trip to Big White when we all tried E? Holden says.

Remember the band teacher kicking you out of class for playing Nirvana on your sax when the rest of us were playing Beethoven? You had us all convinced you were the Nirvana baby. Yuki laughs and shoves his shoulder.

I am the Nirvana baby, Holden deadpans.

Yuki grins and sits down beside Holden, both their feet in the icy river.

He looks down and shakes his head. Drinks some more of his beer.

I know you're struggling, Holden, but you have to listen to me on this—do not not not use H when you're drinking. It's super bad news. Every addict knows that.

But he's not addicted, so how would he know? He's been off for three days now and hasn't shit his pants like she said he would. He hasn't puked since yesterday. He doesn't even use every day. He tips over backward into the river.

When the last beer is empty and the air has cooled a little, he stands and negotiates his way back to shore. I should head, gotta make it to work in the morning.

Why don't we go get some sushi? Lina says. I'm starving.

Sounds nice but I'm outta green. Holden's sitting on the grass, pulling on his dirty socks and workboots.

We gotcha, says Yuki. She links her arm through his and ushers him down the shaded path back to the car. Lina follows, dragging Dexter, who does not want to leave.

With the first taste of California roll, Holden realizes how hungry he is. The last thing he ate was a peanut butter sandwich at the cop shop early this morning. He can't count how many beers he's had since then.

Whoever invented sushi should get a goddamn trophy, he says. The skin on his shoulders is tight and crisp inside his shirt. His elbow slips off the table, and he pokes himself in the cheek with a chopstick.

I know right? Orgasmic, Lina says.

He leans back against the wooden bench and looks across the table at Yuki and Lina sharing food from each other's plates, sword fighting with chopsticks. They tilt toward each other as though the tops of their heads are magnetized.

I can almost see the electrons pulling you guys together, Holden says, his eyes filling with tears.

Silence descends on the table, and their eyes flick from one to another, then laughter bursts out from all of them at once.

You big dork. Getting all sentimental on us. Yuki comes around to sit beside Holden on the bench and puts her arms around him. Hey, bud, What's going on?

Nothing, it's okay. I just need to get some sleep. Will you guys drop me off at the SeaBus?

Holden wipes his eyes with a paper napkin and tries to slide sideways out of the booth. Yuki blocks him in.

You could stay with us tonight, Lina offers.

Thanks, but I've gotta go home and change. Gotta make it to work tomorrow.

Then let's get you there, Yuki says.

She pulls some bills out of her pocket and leaves them on the table.

∞

Back in the car, the windows were completely fogged over. The striped blanket in the back seat gave off a dank wet-dog smell. Yuki and I were cocooned, holding hands, leaping back and forth across time. I could feel the persistent, panting heat of that summer's day—time counting down to zero for Holden—and I could also hear the river outside, high and heavy with rain, a torrent of brown, churning water tumbling the smooth stones of the riverbed with a low *clack clack clack*. Rain pounded the roof. I couldn't see it falling, but I trusted it was there.

I had seen the photos Lina took that day. Holden in his boxer shorts sitting on a large rock with a beer can in his hand, his feet refracted in the clear water, his back hunched cobra-like, eyes cast down and away, watching the current.

We didn't want to let him go, Yuki said. We were both really worried. He was very emotional, kind of fatalistic. He was obsessing about not going to work that day. He borrowed my phone to call his boss at least five times, but it kept going straight to voicemail. He tried Lobo, too, couldn't understand why she wasn't answering his messages, and he just seemed really despondent. I could see him struggling, the battle between the choices he was making and being accountable for his future. He didn't know who he would be without the drinking and the drugs.

Why do you think he called you that day?

I think he just wanted some stability. Maybe he wanted to know what it would be like on the other side.

Tell me what wanting heroin feels like.

Like there's a hole in you expanding and contracting, squeezing and stretching. It's a powerful force pulling you, like a rope attached to the centre of your chest, pulling you. It's very hard to resist. Nearly impossible.

34

The car creeps along the curb and stops. When Yuki turns off the ignition, the thrash metal filling his head cuts off midsong. In the front seat, Lina's shoulders rise in a subtle shrug. She and Yuki look at each other with big eyes, but don't say anything.

Holden reclines across the back seat, one hand scratching Dexter between the ears, the other arm dangling out the window as if it's the wing of a strange bird readying for takeoff.

Hey Dex, Holden says, looking into the dog's hopeful face, I bet you want to go back and lie down in that river again. Me too, pal. Me too. Another time.

He gathers his backpack and lugs himself out into the touristy smell of french fries and salt water. Somewhere on the pier, a busker plays flute through a cheap amp. A thin song threads the air. Teenagers sit in a circle on the ground outside McDonald's, pointing to their phones and laughing. He closes the door a little too hard and stumbles over the thick soles of his workboots.

Holden! Lina calls, her fragile voice straining. She reaches out a pale, slender arm. It's so good to see you again. Please take care of yourself. Her outstretched fingers seem to be trying to pull him back.

I will. He glances at the countdown clock above the entrance … 2:25, 2:24, 2:23. Passengers in shorts and fluttering sundresses stream toward the turnstiles. Holden rests his hands on the hot door of the car and pokes his head through the window.

Thanks for everything, you guys. I'll hit you back when I get paid.

No prob, bud, Yuki says from the driver's seat.

Lina presses her cool hand to his cheek. I still have the poem you wrote for me in grade eleven.

Oh snap! He laughs low in his throat. Why would you keep that melodramatic shit?

Because you are a very special person.

No, he says, I'm not. But you guys are. And he smiles. It's rad that you two freaks ended up together.

Yuki stretches across the car to grasp Holden's fingers.

Why don't we just drive you over to your dad's place right now? We're not doing anything. It's no big deal, Yuki says. Lina nods her head—it's the fastest she's moved all day.

No thanks. He turns to check the countdown clock. 1:18, 1:17, 1:16. Better hit it.

Yuki tightens her grasp on his hand. I'll sit with you, get you some ginger ale and bananas. These are the worst couple of days, it'll get easier.

Thanks, but I'm good. Really. He extricates his hand from Yuki's fingers. I got this. I'll see you lesbos later.

He hikes up his loose canvas shorts, turns, and strides across the plaza to the entrance, his legs cycling slowly, boots thudding on the pavement. Under the clock at the top of the ramp, he turns back toward them, flashes a wide grin, removes his sweat-stained ball cap, and bows low, as though he's a performer basking in an encore. Then he vaults over the arm of the turnstile and lets the momentum carry him down the ramp.

∞

Maybe he walked to the front row so he could watch the city grow larger. He would have taken a seat in a row white plastic chairs that look like egg cartons. The smooth chair might have felt alien to his body, slippery and artificial compared to the rock he'd been sitting on all afternoon at the river. He probably pulled his hat down low over his eyes and extended his legs into the aisle. That's how I see him. Boots crossed at the ankles, holding the back of his own head in the hammock of his woven fingers.

The SeaBus was usually crowded. He would have been surrounded by the noise of many people talking and children running around chattering with the small, sweet excitement of a trip across the water. Maybe the sound was a reminder. I want him to have remembered the happiness he felt as a child. I want to remember the happiness I knew watching him grow.

Through the big front windows, Vancouver's skyline was a metallic fish skin of flashing silver and glass. Boats and seaplanes crisscrossed Coal Harbour, cutting white slices through the water like a sword fighter's damage. Maybe he saw a sailboat bucking in a power cruiser's wake. My hope is that a memory flashed across his vision of the many sailing trips Cam took Holden and his friends on, that he had a recollection of salt spray in his face, and that a fondness crept over him. I want him to have considered the many beaches of our summer holidays and smiled, but I know that my nostalgic desires are unlikely. It's more probable that a hostile worm roiled in his lower belly, sending his focus elsewhere.

And this is where the cord gets yanked from the wall, and the screen goes scratchy grey, then black. I don't know what happened next. Here sits an empty chunk of time. A few blank hours of radio silence. If anyone does know what happened, they haven't been able or brave enough to tell me. I know Holden was exhausted, emotionally and physically. I know he was drunk and didn't have much money. I know he got on the SeaBus, and I know he didn't go home.

He had many friends who loved him and wanted to help him. I know he was rarely alone for long. I know he was in terrible shape when he walked into the bar at the Metropole around 11:00 p.m. with a questionable young man who didn't stay long. I know Devon was there, playing pool with some other friends, when he arrived.

In this liminal space, I want Holden to have fought hard for his life, I want him to have had chance after chance after chance. One more opportunity to save himself. To go home, where his dad would have welcomed him, fed him, made him laugh.

There are hundreds of small decisions he would have made, could have made—some of which may have sent him west to a cool shower, a meal, and a bed, to a hangover and a wake-up call for work. So many different scenarios are possible. I believe Holden struggled, I believe he truly wanted to start fresh in the morning. I believe he tried. As best he could at the time, he tried.

Naturally, I want him to have made different decisions. Just one infinitesimal shift could have changed everything. I also acknowledge that his young-adult male mindset wouldn't have known he was making survival choices that evening. In spite of what he'd been through during his last couple of days, I believe Holden would have held on to a certain optimism as he sat on that white plastic chair watching the downtown skyline approach. He may have heard a voice that said, one more time won't hurt you. Just one more time and that's it.

∞

One little bump to take away the crackle under his skin. Then he'll go home, pick a day maybe next week, get ready, call Yuki, and that'll be it. Quittin' time. For now, he only has to get through tonight. He needs to make it to work tomorrow, if he still has a job. He wants his job.

Holden likes the fresh air, and the money, and the older guy with the thick accent he works with, and having something to do all day. He likes coming home tired so he doesn't need to go out and wreck himself to sleep. He likes the way his workboots look on his feet. The way his back feels strong when he digs in the soil. He likes the calluses thickening on his palms. He even likes the flowers.

He needs a plan, a set of directions to follow, something to tell him, step by step, the right thing to do when the wrong thing presents itself, like it always does. The wrong thing always seems so much more attractive. Easier. Maybe he can drink himself into a coma, sleep through the pull, and make it to work tomorrow morning. Once he's working, he'll be fine.

He connects to the onboard Wi-Fi and opens Maps. Though he's walked to his dad's place more times than he can remember, he measures the distance from Waterfront station to the apartment. Google tells him it's 2.6 kilometres. A thirty-two-minute walk. That Google dude must be a slow walker.

He taps the Facebook app and checks for a message from Lobo. Still nothing. He types out another message to her.

> Hey there, wondering where you are? Seabus at the mo then home. Hit me up and I'll explain evting. i'm sorrrry. Working toms then I can come meet you at Trout, or anywhere.

He presses send.
He types another message.

> Or tonight? Need to seeeee you. Where are you? Are you ok? x H.

Are we okay? he wonders.

The ferry bounces up against the downtown dock, and passengers crowd the door. A man and two young children stand in line waiting for the doors to slide open. The smaller of the two, a boy with blond hair, stares at Holden. Holden does an old magic trick with his fingers, making it look like his thumb is cut in half. The boy grins and hides behind the fabric of his dad's shorts, then his two wide eyes peek out again. Holden's face finds what he hopes is a funny expression, and when the boy laughs, Holden can't stop the corners of his own mouth from lifting, too.

Almost everyone has gone before Holden pushes himself to standing. He braces himself, one hand on the back of his chair, until his head clears. In the empty holding area, he takes a long drink from the water fountain. In the stainless steel basin, somebody's spit their bubble gum, a shrunken pink brain.

He's the last passenger walking along the long glass bridge that leads to the station. Below him, the railyard is lined with hundreds of freight cars splashed with bright graffiti. Orange, purple, green. From here the trains look like toys. He'd love to paint right now—that would give him something to focus on. He scans for pieces by writers he knows. Oodles, Wesso, Molar, Mercy, Guph, Esper. He checks to see if any of his pieces are visible.

The coolest day of his life was when he saw SEFER roll past him on a grain car at a railyard in Montreal. He was nationwide! His mind conjures the smell of paint and the sound of the blast jetting from the can. The way the can jumps a little bit when he presses down on the cap with his thumb.

Maybe he could give Montreal another try. Get away from here, find a job, and just paint and paint and paint. Until it got bad, Montreal was very very good—maybe the best time of his life. He can picture the red bricks and fire escapes he climbed. He can see his work flying, large and loud, and the thought shifts something in the space behind the flat bone in the centre of his chest. Maybe something beautiful, something good, is possible.

There's a beer and wine store across from the station. Holden plunks a six-pack of Cariboo on the counter. He thinks he's got about forty bucks left in his account. Payday should be tomorrow, but money never works out right for him.

The machine makes an affirmative beep, and Holden slips the cold beer into his backpack. He moves along Cordova Street, heading for home. In five minutes he will stop for his first beer. Well, he had quite a few by the river, so technically not his first, but whatever. If he has one beer every five minutes, by the time he gets to his dad's apartment, he'll be able to pass out. He's aware this is not the best strategy, but it's the only one he can think of at the moment. It's something.

Once he's home, Dad will hug him, offer him some food, and ask him where he's been. He'll have to make something up. They'll joke and laugh, Dad will talk, Holden will listen for a while and then pretend to listen, they'll watch a movie together, and Holden will fall asleep on the couch during the movie. He'll wake up and go to work tomorrow, and that's the plan. It's the only thing he has.

The sun is starting to lean. It's lost some of its earlier intensity. A soft shade of muted peach gently coats the buildings.

He passes the Lions Pub with the two big stone cats guarding the entrance and climbs up the wide flight of stairs into a courtyard with round sections of lawn. If the buildings of the city are glass and metal trees, this is a clearing, a postmodern alpine meadow. Holden has hung out here before, skateboarding and smoking with a few buds, but never with this many people. Every red chair at every red table is occupied. Everyone seems to be drinking coffee. He can't understand drinking coffee on a warm summer night. He doesn't understand coffee at all—it gives him the jitters.

Bright-red geraniums line the courtyard. He knows they're geraniums because he planted about six thousand of them last week at a job in West Van. He likes the red. Not fire engine, not cherry.

He picks a spot in the shade under the row of trees. Three little kids are doing cartwheels. They tumble over each other into a pile and look up, laughing, in his direction. He smiles and waves. He sits cross-legged on the grass, unzips his pack, and reaches in for one of the cans. At the click and fizz, his mouth waters. He downs half the beer, extends his legs, and leans back on his elbows to look up through the leafy branches. Above the shifting canopy, silver buildings reflect each other. He finishes the beer and crushes the can against his thigh. This sound of crumpling aluminum is one of his favourite noises. He considers standing and moving on to the next location, just five minutes away, five minutes closer to bed. *Let's go, you big dumb shit, you can do this, stick to the plan.* But his body doesn't want to move. He's so tired. Is this how twenty-one is supposed to feel? Almost twenty-two—his birthday is in a couple of weeks. He pulls a second beer from the bag, drinks most of it, then stretches out on his back. The grass feels alive between his fingers, the ground solid under his spine. He can smell the dampness in the earth. Time to get going. Time to go home. He closes his eyes.

Hey, you vagrant.

The hard toe of a shoe prods Holden's ribs. He rolls onto his side, wipes an elastic string of saliva from his cheek, and squints up at a silhouette. The sky behind the person attached to the shoe has changed to a different shade—darker, deeper, closing in on cobalt. The ground under him has cooled, and the back of his shirt is wet.

Holy fuck, what time is it? he says.

Nine-thirtyish, says the barbed female voice. What the hell are you doing sleeping in a park like some kinda homeless person?

Who the fuck are you? Holden says.

It's Patty from Hysteria. She crouches to his level, and long ribbons of hair swing out from under a big hat. Piercings dot the line of one eyebrow.

He knows Patty. She's cool. Older. They went to a few shows together. Even partied with the band one night. They had a lot of decent conversations during those ten-hour shifts at the store.

There's a strange metallic taste in his mouth and a tingling in one of his arms. He reaches into his bag and fumbles for a beer. Not exactly cold. Whatever. His brain is sludge. Did he really sleep for three hours?

Patty sits down on the grass beside him.

Mind if I join you?

Looks like you already did. Beer? His voice lazy with sleep.

No thanks, I'm good.

The courtyard has emptied. Only one other person is left at the red tables on the far side of the plaza—a lady looking at her phone. The coffee shop is closed. Above them, lights are coming on in some of the apartment windows. A Rubik's Cube of yellow-white. Between the buildings, Holden can see the watery grey of the harbour, and beyond that, the last glow of the day, still warming the emerald rise of the North Shore. The mountains are a carved silhouette.

After an entire day piercing nipples, it's nice just to sit down, Patty says with a loud exhale. She's wearing a dress and Converse runners.

What are you doing here? Holden asks.

I'm meeting some friends, thought I'd go for a bit of a walk first. Standing around all day makes me grumpy. She shoves Holden's shoulder, and he tips over onto the grass. The question is, what are you doing here?

Holden pushes himself back up to sitting without spilling his beer. Do you mean that existentially, or in the practical sense?

Either. Patty wedges her dress between her tanned legs.

I actually don't have a fucking clue about either one. Holden spits out a laugh and shakes his head. He chugs his beer and tosses the can on the grass, then digs in his pack for another.

Whoa, somebody's thirsty, Patty says.

Diversionary tactic.

Classic move.

And Holden remembers how much he likes Patty. He remembers the night a few years ago that he spent at her kitchen table, talking with her for hours about her fucked-up childhood and her horrible boyfriend. She rubs her thumb back and forth over a purple poker chip in her hand. Is this a specific diversion, or just a life-in-general type of diversion? she asks. Her face looks like she actually cares.

Holden has lost his desire to contain the mass in his gut. Or maybe it's just become so big and combustible he no longer can. Maybe Patty's face looks kind, like an older sister, or maybe he's just too worn down to care anymore. It starts slowly, but once the restraints are off, the entire mess comes raging out.

Let's see, I spent last night in jail, so I have to go to court next week. Which means I may have a criminal record, which will seriously impress my boss and also my parents. I thought I had a girlfriend, I mean, I thought it was real, but she ghosted. I missed work today because of the stupid fucking jail thing, and my boss won't answer his fucking phone, so I may already have lost my job, which I really need. I haven't paid my phone bill, and they cut me off so I can't even. And … and, there's a pretty fucking crippling mental health situation happening, but I just stopped those meds, too, so I feel like ass, and best of all, I seem to have a small but significant drug problem.

By the time Holden stops talking, he is gulping air. His face is a smear of tears and snot, his chest is heaving, and his hands rest helplessly in his lap like a pair of empty gloves.

Patty looks at him, her face smooth, eyes patient. She nods for a while, then says, Is that all?

When Holden laughs, a stream of spit flies from his mouth. He wipes his face with his sleeve. Patty reaches out to offer a hug.

Don't, he says, I reek.

Dude, I pierced three dicks today, don't talk to me about stink. She shifts closer and puts an arm around him.

How can a person not care about anything? Holden looks down. I don't care about the future, or possessions, or my life. I never have. I truly do not care.

About anything?

Anything. Especially myself. I mean, other people, yes, I probably care more about you than I do about me, and I hardly even know you.

Oh, I think we know each other pretty well, Patty says.

Look, I fucked up. I always fuck up. Which means I am a fuck-up. Inescapable fact. The crawling under Holden's skin is getting stronger.

Not true. Just because you *have* fucked up doesn't mean you *are* a fuck-up. I mean, just because I baked a pie last week doesn't make me a pastry chef.

Profound. Thanks for that. He reaches into his pack, his fingers tracing two cans. He pulls one out and opens it.

I mean it, Holden. You are not your deeds.

No? Then what am I? He searches her face.

You are a person who's made some mistakes. News flash, that's basically the human condition.

No, a mistake is like, dropping your phone in the toilet. Intentionally ruining your entire life is something else. His chest is heaving. It's hard to breathe.

You do have some things to clear up, but none of them are insurmountable. I think for tonight you just need to give yourself a break. Where are you going? I mean, right now?

Home, my dad's place. I need to shower and sleep. Gotta go to work tomorrow.

That sounds like a very good idea. Patty gives his shoulder another squeeze, stands, smooths her dress, and reaches out an arm to pull Holden to his feet. Steady, big fella.

They walk together out to the street. The sign on the post above them says *West Hastings* and has a red poppy on it. Something about veterans, probably.

Wait. Patty looks directly into Holden's eyes. The truth is, I'm not meeting friends. She's holding up the poker chip.

No?

I'm actually heading to a meeting. Why don't you come with me?

What kind of meeting?

AA.

A laugh skips out from between Holden's lips. Nope. No way. He shakes his head.

It's not as creepy as it sounds. The people are actually pretty cool. They know what you're going through, they've all been there. I've been sober four months now. She moves to rest a hand on his arm. He jerks away.

Why does everyone want me to go to fucking rehab? He takes a step back as if she's holding a knife rather than a sobriety chip.

Because it seems like you might be ready to make some changes in your life. Aren't you getting tired of feeling like this?

He looks up to the night sky and sees a faint first star, nearly obscured by the glare of the city lights. Star light, star bright. I appreciate the offer and everything, but what I need right now is sleep, so I'm going home. Holden spins on his heels and walks away from her up Hornby Street. He knows Patty's standing on the corner watching him walk away—he feels her eyes on him.

See ya! he yells, and raises one arm while moving forward. He keeps walking until he rounds the corner onto Pender Street, out of her sight, then drops onto the bench at the bus stop.

Jesus fucking Christ, why don't people just mind their own fucking business?

There's a throbbing at the base of his skull and a bitter taste in his throat. He pulls off his pack and reaches inside for the final can. By now the beer is basically warm foam. He sets the can on the bench beside him, rests his elbows on his knees, and cradles his head in his hands.

If he turns right and starts walking home right now, in twenty minutes he'll be lying down on a bed. He can hop in the shower and take his meds. They always knock him out. He can sleep this off and start tomorrow. Dad will probably even get up at 6:00 a.m. with him and give him a ride to work.

Or.

Or, he could turn left and in five minutes, he'll be at Devon's place. Also a bed. And Devon won't bug him with too many questions. What day is this? Thursday? When did he last use? Monday? Tuesday? He could get a little hit on the way. Get his ass to work in the morning. He'll start clean tomorrow. Sweat it out at work.

He hears the hiss of hydraulics as a bus pulls up and the front doors yawn open. He could step on the bus, and it would take him almost all the way home. If he takes three steps, he will be on the bus. He should get on the bus. The craving in his gut pulses. Spit oozes from somewhere behind his back molars.

Ya coming? the driver yells to him.

Or.

Holden shakes his head. The driver nods, and the vertical mouth of the doors closes. The bus ambles away, taillights glowing red. There's a couple kissing in the back seat. Through the back window they look like a painting. Holden's legs are liquid metal. The low hum in his head is getting louder, interrupting any song he can hold there.

He stands, turns left, and begins walking slowly down the gradual slope, something invisible pulling him.

This is a familiar journey. He's walked in the same direction many times, following a wavering compass needle, for many different reasons, in many different kinds of weather. He's drawn to a thing he can't seem to touch or see. Something missing that he can't explain but needs very badly.

By the time he crosses Victory Square, his pace has increased, and all he can focus on is how to pick up. Where to pick up. Just enough to stop the grinding low in his belly. Just enough so he can think. He needs to take a shit. The benches around the cenotaph are active with movement, bodies, some hunched over shopping carts, some rigid and rocking, some huddled in groups laughing, some alone, staring.

There's Mikey, a skinny kid he's bought from a couple of times before, tromping down the stairs, carrying a TV in his thin arms. Holden signals to him with a lift of his chin. Mikey shuffles toward Holden, hugging the TV. There's a dark space where his front teeth should be.

You need? Mikey asks.

A point of brown, please. The skin of Holden's face is hot and tight. Pearls of sweat bloom on his forehead.

That's twenty, Mikey says.

I can get it for you at the Met. Can you come with me?

Hold on a sec. Mikey steps away and talks to a woman sitting on a bench. She nods and he sets the TV down beside her.

Let's go, Mikey says, pointing down the road with his lips.

They walk around the corner and down another block toward the neon sign of the Metropole Hotel. There's no reason to talk. This is not friendship. The Met doors are wide open—music, light, and voices spill out onto the sidewalk. Holden steps inside and sees the familiar line of Devon at the pool table, sunglasses perched on the top of her head, long pink hair framing her pale face as she leans over the shamrock-green felt to take a shot. He never knows what colour her hair will be.

Hey, Dev.

Hi there! How are you doing? She smiles and hugs him with one arm, holding the pool cue in the other. You look—whoa—and smell like shit.

Why, thank you, he says. Still can't believe you passed up a fine piece of real estate such as this.

What can I say? I'm a fool. She winks at him, and her pretty smile spreads slowly across her face. The history between them allows her to overlook his current state. He knows she still loves him, even in this crapulous condition. She accepts his wreckage, as he accepts hers. It's an unspoken agreement.

Hey, can I stay with you tonight? I'm super tired and I have to work tomorrow.

You're super DEFCON 5, and yes you can. As long as you promise not to barf.

Holden raises a flat palm as if he's about to testify in court, which makes him laugh to himself, because he basically did that this morning. I swear.

Devon looks past him to Mikey, who is hovering in the doorway with his hands in his pockets. She shakes her head. Nice friend, Holden, really nice.

I'm just gonna grab a drink to cool off, then I'll head up, if that's okay. Holden lifts his eyes to the ceiling, as though he can see through three floors of wood and plaster to Devon's apartment upstairs.

I'm going to finish my game, let me know when you want the key.

Thanks D-Train, you're the cat's PJs. He goes to the bar and holds up his bank card. Hey, Andy, can I get a double tall G and T and twenty cash back?

Holden drops his drink on Devon's table and follows Mikey out of the bar and around the corner into the alley. They step behind a green Dumpster, and Mikey digs in his pocket for a small square of folded paper. Holden hands him the twenty. Mikey presses the flap into Holden's palm and walks away without a word.

The turbulence in Holden's stomach is lurching now. His mouth gushes with saliva. He hurries half a block down to the drugstore and buys a roll of aluminum foil, then heads back into the alley. He tears off a section of foil and rips that in half. He shoves the roll into his pack and pulls out his lighter. Pressing half of the plug of H onto the foil with his thumb, he heats it from underneath and sucks up the smoke as best he can. He repeats the process with the second half.

Slowly, his knees soften and bend, his eyelids lower, thick and heavy. He leans against the wall, his backpack protecting him from the hardness of the bricks.

And now it's all gone—everything that was hanging off him has flown away, nothing hurts, nothing matters, he's a whole and perfect person and everything is going to be fine. Everything *is* fine. He can't even remember what his problems may have felt like. All he feels is his own blood flowing through his limbs, his body bright and glimmering.

For about the length of time it takes to smoke a cigarette.

Eventually Holden re-enters the real world. He braces himself against the pressure of being returned to his body, a feeling not unlike pulling on a heavy winter coat. His mind slowly refocuses, and his first clear vision is the memory of being busted the day before, the expression of disgust and sadness on Lobo's face just before he turned away from her and sprinted across Commercial Drive. Holden notes the flap of paper crumpled in his palm, flattens it, and sees that it's been ripped from a magazine; it's a picture of a lake with trees along the bank and a floating red canoe.

Back inside, Holden joins Devon and a couple of others at their table. He's met them all before, but can't remember any of their names. He is not yet ready to speak. The people whose names Holden can't remember leave the table to smoke outside, and Devon directs the beam of her gaze at him.

What's up? she says.

Whaddaya mean?

You're totally fucked up.

Cool liquid slops down his arm from the glass he just realized is in his hand. He tries to explain to Devon what's been going on. Tries to get it out clearly, but he can hear that his words are not making sense.

Missed work today, don't know where Lobo went. We were totally together yesterday, but after I got busted she took off. Messaged her like a million times, but she won't message me back. She really gets me. She accepts me for who I am. One hundred percent. I love her.

Whoever this Lobo person is, she obviously hasn't seen enough of your bullshit yet. And did you say jail? For what?

I don't know, he slurs. Robbery. Wait, theft, I guess. And then a fight. But it wasn't a fight. It was just dumb. I bit somebody. The light above the table hurts his eyes. I slept in lock-up last night, but it's not a big deal.

Seems like it might be, Devon says. She rests her chin in the cup of her palm to examine him more closely. Her eyes narrow—she's trying to make eye contact. He stares at the lime floating in his drink.

What're you on?

Nothing. Beer, that's it. Hey, can I use your phone to call my boss?

Devon continues staring at Holden. Her shiny pink lips squeeze together. Reluctantly, she digs her phone out of her back pocket and sets it on the table between them. Very slowly, she slides it in his direction with one finger. Her face looks suspicious.

Holden clumsily taps in a number with his thumbs. He leaves a muddled message. Hi, this is Holden. I'm sorry. I missed work today. I was. Um. Sick. I'll be there tomorrow. For sure. Thanks. Thank you. Bye. See you tomorrow. This is Holden. He fumbles the phone, and it clatters to the table.

Why are you here? Devon asks.

Why is anybody in here? To get a drink. His head falls—he has to pick it up with his neck. It falls again.

Seems like maybe you've had enough of those.

Truth. Could I head up now? I feel like shit. Gotta sleep. Gotta make it to work tomorrow. KK Devo? So tired, so so tired.

Holden thinks he may throw up, but he's not going to tell Devon that. He needs to lie down. Immediately. He's never been this exhausted.

I'll come up and open the door for you. Devon grabs Holden's pack from the chair and loops an arm around his back. Together they walk out the back exit of the bar and down the narrow hall toward the elevator. The door opens, and they step inside.

Thanks for taking care of me again, D.

You're welcome, again.

Holden tugs off his baseball hat and rubs his bristled head against Devon's neck. His beard scrapes the skin of her shoulder, and she groans, then laughs. She lowers the sunglasses from her head until they rest on her nose. He looks at their joined reflection in the mirror, heads touching.

Tomorrow is another chance. Tomorrow he'll start over. They smile at each other in the warped glass as the elevator announces its arrival on the third floor.

35

I bought a sky-blue dress because it seemed to be July, and weren't black dresses for winter or for cocktail parties? Under the too-bright lights at a too-loud store, I sat limp on some kind of modern sofa while my dearest friend brought me options to try on. Lyla helped choose a pair of shoes to match.

Something summery, Momma, she said, setting a pair of cream sandals on the carpet in front of me. She was wearing a pair of black women's wedges with her shorts. Lyla was only eleven, but her feet had galloped ahead of her, so she was slipping into her first grown-up shoes, for the wrong reason. I wondered if the joy of shoes would be ruined for her. When she gets dressed for her graduation or goes to her first nightclub, when she puts on those shoes with the heels and the straps, the ones that are supposed to make her feel beautiful and powerful, will a hesitation find her fingers?

We were trying to comprehend how a person we loved so much could disappear so completely. For this, apparently, we needed new shoes.

Holden's birthday was coming up, his twenty-second, so the occasion must be a party. A surprise celebration where his friends would jump out from behind the curtains. The guest of honour would walk in the door, and there would be a thunk of quiet shock, followed by an explosion of cheers and laughter.

I was having a hard time reconciling what I wanted with what I had been given.

Should I wear mascara? I asked another friend.

I don't think you'll need any. That must have been a clue that this was not, in fact, a party.

We pulled up outside a restored warehouse, once a shipbuilding factory, now used for special events, and I thought about refusing to open the door. *Let's just drive away,* I tried to silently signal to Cam at the other end of the back seat, sombre and sweating in a dark jacket. I wanted him to read the thoughts rising from the hollow cradle of my pelvis. That scooped nest where I'd first felt the flutter of Holden moving and known I would be his mother. Lyla sat between us. We probably held hands. My mother drove the car.

Figures stood waiting, solemn in the heat. People jockeyed to greet us before we could even enter the building. I felt preyed upon. Family, friends, former colleagues, all reaching out to rest a hand on my bare arms. Some whispered, some couldn't make eye contact. Some dissolved into sobs when they touched me. Some stared from a distance. What did they see when they looked at me? A person dissected? Poisonous? I didn't want any of them to be here. Acknowledging their presence meant that something terrible must have happened. Something to deliver them to this date and time like homing pigeons, not fully understanding why they had come, just that they must. It hurt my bones to see the helplessness in their faces.

Inside the building were hundreds more, forlorn and mumbling. There were photographs and flowers. Folding chairs, perfume, neckties. There was the whir and scrape of ceiling fans. Cam, Lyla, and I sat in the front row. When there are no other chairs in front of you at a funeral, it's bad. Where were my parents, my siblings, where was the person in charge, the one who would tell me there had been an error? Why wasn't someone gathering us, orchestrating, ringmastering, saying something to make sense of this? There was my sister, beside me, my mother a few rows back. Why were there so many people? Why were they all so young?

People spoke, people sang, people cried. Stories were told. Tributes fluttered in the rafters, words on the wind I would never recall. It was right not to wear mascara. Sweat poured in a single rivulet down the trough at the centre of my back while I shivered like winter. When it was time, I rose in my cream sandals and sky-blue dress.

At the podium I took one long, deep breath. And another. Then divided myself in two: the woman who could no longer speak, and the one who felt compelled to; the mother who was a lightbulb striking pavement, and the person who wanted everyone to know how extraordinary her son was. I stepped into the version on the left and began.

Thank you all for coming here today to honour Holden. I don't care for the phrase "celebration of life," because I don't feel like celebrating, and I'm sure you don't, either. Still, it's fitting that we are here today, together in this old warehouse, a space that represents Holden well with its rough edges and its charm. You can even see some of his art from here. Just outside, there are a couple of rusty old cranes. On one of them, over near the water, is a tag of Holden's graffiti. Way up high, looking down on us. It scares me to think of him climbing up there. I still worry he might get hurt.

We are also close to the SeaBus that Holden often rode to cross the inlet between the different parts of his life. He sometimes got kicked off or fined for not having a ticket. He never bought a ticket. And so it makes sense that we are all here in this location, between his art and his lawlessness. Together. To pay our respects. I thank you all for being here today, and for supporting us as we try to navigate this most difficult terrain.

I would like to tell you a little about my son, Holden. Our son, Holden. Our brother and grandson. Our nephew and cousin and friend.

When he was born on this day twenty-two years ago, he was beautiful. And I'm not just saying that because I'm his mother. He probably wouldn't like me telling you this, but he really was gorgeous. He was calm and wise-looking, and his father and I felt that somehow he already knew quite a lot. His skin was flawless, and his eyes had a way of being both dark and bright at the same time.

It wasn't an easy delivery. Holden tried to be born bottom first, a breech birth, which made his first day challenging. We didn't know it at the time, but his birth was the first of thousands of experiences Holden would approach in his own unique way, with his own personal style. He was and always would be unconventional.

As a baby, Holden was content to sit and observe. He wasn't in a rush to walk. Which is interesting, considering what a fabulous walker he became as a young man, although I suspect all that walking allowed him to spend his bus fare on other things.

When he was about a year old, I took him to the Vancouver Art Gallery. In a lofty room on the second floor, Holden lifted his arms to be taken out of his stroller. Up to that point he had only walked holding our hands or the edge of the coffee table, but when he saw, at the other end of the vast space, what I remember as an enormous and colourful Jack Shadbolt painting, he marched toward it like a little soldier. No wobbling, no faltering—he was on his own path, and nobody would stop him. I had to gather him up before he pressed his sticky little hands all over the canvas. The security guard wasn't very impressed, but Holden didn't care. It was as though he wanted to walk right inside the abstract world and spend some time there. Perhaps that was his first act of rebellion against authority.

Holden had the soul of an artist. He was naturally poetic and imaginative. As a little guy he would say such marvellous things that I started writing them down in a book called *Holden Said*. When he was three years old, he told me quite earnestly, "Mama, O is a letter, and a number, and a word." One day he informed me that he could "tell poetry with his brain tied behind his back." I would overhear him introducing himself to new kids on the playground by saying things like, "I do have a name, but you can call me Storm."

And, as you may have experienced, he was funny. Once, when he spilled his cereal, he looked up at me from under his blond curtain of hair and said, "Bran overboard."

He was very intelligent. He had an advanced vocabulary, and in grade four he was reading at grade twelve level. We would read the same books, then talk about them together. I remember discussing the dystopian world of Margaret Atwood's *Oryx and Crake* over grilled cheese sandwiches.

As most kids do, Holden made a lot of art. Piles and piles of it. Finger paintings at first, then more involved pictures with colourful planets and vivid animals and funny little hybrid creatures of his own invention. He began to create what we now think of as graphic novels. He called them comix, with an X, and they told stories of everyday objects like mushrooms, cubes, and bouncing balls that had come to life and were now best friends going on interplanetary expeditions and waging great battles over important matters, like liberating the cheese.

These books were always visually clever and sharply humorous. I found one recently, in a big box of his work, that explained how Mr. Ball, with his bulging eyes and Mickey Mouse hands, could keep bouncing back to life after being mortally wounded—it was because of a rare "systemic anomaly." He was about eight years old when he wrote that one. On the back of each these stapled-together stacks of paper, Holden would add his own trademark. These logos evolved over time, but now I see they were his first pseudonyms, or tags. Holden's alter egos would eventually become his graffiti names: Miner, RuleR, Sefer, Deser.

In about grade six or seven, Holden and his good friend, Luke, formed their first crew, called PB&J. Luke still won't tell me what the acronym stands for, but they painted their new, ingenious tag all over the neighbourhood and seemed genuinely surprised when it became clear some residents didn't think their spray painting was such a brilliant idea. Cam and Luke's dad took them around to all the fences and garages they had vandalized to apologize and sand off or paint over the PB&Js. This was embarrassing and time-consuming, but as you know, it did not throw Holden off. Quite the opposite. A big part of the thrill of making graffiti is the extremely high likelihood that you will get caught. And he did. Many times.

I don't think Holden realized how wonderfully talented he was. He didn't think it was a big deal. He just did what he did because he wanted, needed, to do it. Not for any other reason. He could play guitar and piano by ear. He was accepted to the Emily Carr School of Art + Design based on a small oil portrait of Bill Murray, a few charcoal sketches, and many photographs of his graffiti. To put together his portfolio, we had to climb over chain-link fences, skirt railway tracks, and duck under bridges to document his pieces.

In true Holden fashion, he always went to class, but rarely brought a pencil or a book. He told me he thought the professors and even some of the students were pretentious assholes. After his first year, the school requested that Holden not return.

As a teen, all of Holden's spare time and money was spent on spray painting. Under highway overpasses, on warehouse walls, in railyards, high up on rooftops, and who knows where else. When he was at home, he was constantly drawing. On scraps of paper and all over his school books, bubbly letters and all kinds of fonts, over and over and over again, slowly discovering his own style. I'm told his "writing," as the art form is called, is easily recognizable in the graffiti community because it's "dancy and alive." He was very proud that one of his pieces was still "flying" under the Westview overpass six months after he had painted it, which apparently is a major accolade.

I never understood why, but Holden was driven, urged, compelled to paint graffiti. It was his passion, and nothing would stop him. Not injuries, arguments, fights, dangerous situations, or even getting arrested. Now, I'm told, his pieces all over the city are not being touched, or rolled over, as a sign of respect.

Holden was a deeply thoughtful person. He cared about people, and he didn't think it was fair that some had so much while others had so little. He was drawn to the marginalized. Each winter during high school he stood out in the cold wearing a Santa Claus hat, ringing the bells to collect money for the Salvation Army. As a child he would often give his allowance to people on the street, even when he had very little himself, something he continued to do throughout his short life.

He thought a lot about his place in this world, his meaning, what his life was about, which, as you know, can be a very confusing topic. Sometimes I think he just didn't know where to put all of his thoughts and feelings. They were heavy for him to carry.

My son was an enigma. While he felt at home on the streets of the city, he also loved being in nature. The simple beauty of it. The peace and calm of it. The freshness. He very much enjoyed his recent work landscaping because it felt so good, he said, to have his hands in the earth.

As a little guy walking along a forest trail, he would often hum quietly to himself. Just happy to be there, in the moment, in the woods, with the breeze and the birds and the green. Once he asked me, How many greens there are? He may have thought in colours as well as words.

Holden loved being in beauty, looking at beauty, creating beauty, and expressing himself in beautiful ways. Although he often tried to cover it up with toughness, humour, and bravado, he was fragile. He felt it all. He possessed a depth of emotional understanding and creative possibility greater than most of us will ever know.

And Holden had not two, but three parents. He was loved and supported by his dad and me, and also wholeheartedly cherished by my husband Cam. I am forever grateful for his conscious decision to love Holden as his own.

Please remember our dear Holden. Remember him as a friend. As a beautiful and loving brother, son, grandson, cousin, and nephew. As a unique and amazing human being.

Happy birthday, Holden. I am so grateful to have had the privilege of being your mom. You are forever imprinted on my heart.

After the service I stood in one spot, mostly quiet, beside a white chair that would soon be folded and taken away, aching for my bed and for none of this to be happening. A line formed in front of me, a very long line. I recognized every flushed face. My head seared, my muscles felt loose and unattached, I could see hydrangeas, blue and soft, washed-out green, in mason jars on tables around the room. Music played, music must have played, Holden's father had curated each song. At the back of the hall, a friend had hung a large canvas on the wall and placed a box of paint markers below it. The children were the first to make their marks, writing their names and drawing shapes and words, like it was a school project. Over time, the whole canvas filled with colour and scrawl. I will always love you, Holden. Sefer forever. I miss you, buddy. You were my best friend. Rest in Paint.

I stood there, nodding solemnly, pressing my lips together, trying not to crack open and scream. Cam was just close enough that I could feel his presence and reach for him if I needed to. I noticed that he had polished his dress shoes. Lyla, in a black dress with lace across the shoulders and her hair pulled up in a ballet bun, held my hand, then was pulled away by a flock of her small, sweet friends to the table where the cookies and fruit were laid out.

I wasn't prepared for this part. I hadn't been warned that so many people would want to touch me, look to me with their own red-rimmed eyes, and tell me things about Holden. I wanted to pour out my pain, not receive more. People fumbled for something, anything to say—I used to babysit him, I worked with him, I taught him, I went to school with him, he was kind to me. Some wept as they embraced me with hot, heavy arms, devastated by the certainty of our loss and terrified by the possibility of their own. The tears of hundreds soaked into my pores.

The warehouse was so thick with sadness and humidity that my blue dress clung to my skin. Sweat streamed down the backs of my legs into my sandals as I listened to people with varnished eyes and slumped shoulders try to tell me what they were unable to. I was very grateful for these devout gestures, and I despised the fact of them.

In my memory, the photo loop of Holden continued cycling on a big screen at the front of the warehouse. I could stand on the concrete and turn my head away from the waiting queue of condolences and see him just over my shoulder. There he is at three years old, barefoot on Long Beach, swinging from my extended arms, there he is at twelve squeezed between his buddies, grinning and holding a hockey stick, there he is graduating from high school, beaming in a cap and gown, there he is in a baseball hat spray-painting a cement wall. There he is.

A group of Holden's graffiti friends gathered in the courtyard outside the warehouse. I imagine they were stricken and unnerved by the loss of their friend. I don't know if any of them looked up to see the rusted yellow crane towering over them, the one Holden had once climbed in the dark to paint his name. A man in a dirty jacket who appeared to be homeless lay curled on a bench off to one side. Someone pulled out a can and spray painted *Deser* across the back of the man's jacket as he slept. Someone else took a photograph. Some of them shook their heads, and some laughed at this cruelty because they didn't know what else to do.

The group decided to walk through the railway tunnel to Waterfront Park. I imagine they tagged the walls on the way. Someone took a run up to Sailor's for a dozen beers while the rest stretched out on the grass and gazed out over Burrard Inlet. The SeaBus continued its steady rhythm back and forth across the harbour, from downtown to the North Shore and back again. Someone went for another dozen. I don't know what anyone said, but I'm told one of these friends brought out some cocaine and did a few lines.

Epilogue

I dreamt that I was dreaming. That Holden walked into the house in a navy-blue work shirt and boots. He came toward me in the kitchen. He reached out his arms, pulled me close, and held me.

I'm sorry, Mom. It was a mistake. I'm here now, he said, and I held him, too. I was sure it was real because I could feel the weight of him, the density, and the breath moving through him.

It was a test, he said. It was just a test, and you passed.

∞

I have no grave to place flowers on. No headstone to polish and sweep. What I do have is a smooth maplewood box made with great care by my husband Cam that we keep in a cupboard on the same shelf as the vodka. We don't reach for the vodka very often, or the box. Inside the box are the burned bones of my son.

Sometimes we take his ashes on trips with us. His molecules are mingling with the powdered white sand on the endless beach in Tulum. He is crashing to shore on the West Coast Trail of Vancouver Island. He swims in the Pacific and the Caribbean.

After Holden's death, some of his friends got together and created a massive mural in his honour. The location of the mural is not majestic or peaceful or particularly beautiful. It's just a retaining wall in a parking lot off Main Street in East Vancouver.

But the wall—the wall is glorious. It's twenty-one metres long and more than three metres high, covered in burgundy paint and reproductions of Holden's own graffiti. There are replicas of some of his tattoos, tributes, jokes, and secret messages. From the centre of the wall, a huge portrait of Holden's face in black and white smiles out at the world. He looks truly happy. I visit this wall every season, and his expression never changes.

There is no good resting place for a child. However, this wall makes sense. If there must be a symbolic location for Holden to be recognized and remembered, this wall is perfection. When Oodles was working on the portrait, carefully spraying the cheekbones and chin, I knelt down beside him and poured a small jar of Holden's ashes into the paint tray. He looked at me in silent surprise, then nodded, stirred it up, and rolled the paint onto that wall.

What the psychic had seen behind her smoke-filled eyes had manifested. A fund in Holden's name will support street artists. From his side of the veil, Holden will continue to help graffiti writers express themselves, through generosity, through community, through colour.

On a cloudless summer morning, Holden's friends assembled, armed with cans of spray paint, sketches, masks, stories. They came with loud music, folding chairs, and beer. They cried, they sat together, and they painted. For Holden, and I hope for themselves. For the lives they have lived so far, and the lives they have yet to live. Thousands of others gathered, too, as part of the Vancouver Mural Festival, to watch the mural take shape.

Luke wore a mask and a shirt emblazoned with *Holden* across the back. Devon arrived, tearful in sunglasses, with rainbow hair. Julian, the friend who'd travelled to Montreal with Holden and made the film, brought ladders, a projector, and ideas. Amin showed up sheepish and sad, with booze on his breath. We hugged—I know I don't understand his particular suffering. Yuki came, with big brown eyes, a freshly shaved head, and a new partner, and squeezed me in a long embrace.

Lina arrived early, before the crowds, with her mom and her dog. She's training to be a nurse. Claire, tall, strong, and sober, worked all day to reproduce the roses from Holden's arms on the wall. Darren arrived late, but before he got too drunk, he held me long and hard, then painted beautiful renditions of Sefer and Deser pieces. Jenna drove all the way from Oregon. She had never been pregnant—I had imagined that, and I mourned the loss of the grandchild I was never meant to have. Lindsay preferred not to talk about it. I understand that. But I was pleased to know she really is a chef now, at a top restaurant. Esper stopped by for a few minutes. He didn't speak much—his eyes said everything.

Lobo had moved up north. We talked on the phone a few times. She said she'd waited until noon the next day for Holden to call her, and when he didn't, she turned off her phone and drove across the border into the US to pick grapes. She talked about how special he was to her, even though she knew him for only a short time. Victoria confided that she had attempted suicide in Holden's presence, though it may not have been what drove him back to using. Patty told me how, when they'd worked together, Holden had once sat at her kitchen table and talked all night with her because she'd been struggling to process a childhood trauma. Another night, they had gone to a metal show together, and when they got to party with the band after the show, Holden had been thrilled to talk music for hours with a guitarist he admired. She was never there on his last day, trying to persuade him to go home to himself— I created that, but I wish someone had been. Someone to give him one more chance. A slice of grace he could grab and hold on to. A chance that may have changed it all. Jessie went from AA to rehab. She relapsed, went to rehab again, had a good, long healthy stretch, then relapsed. Nobody knows where she is, but her family never gives up hope. I always slow down and look for her while I'm driving in the Downtown Eastside.

Sarah Blyth still runs Vancouver's Overdose Prevention Society—her work and her team have saved innumerable lives.

Many more made a point of showing up the day the mural was created: family, neighbours, friends, and co-workers. Even the parents of the boys from the Garage Hockey League were all present to paint their love for Holden onto the concrete.

I asked Julian, as he outlined the huge white letters of Holden's name, what his friend might have thought of all this. Of his name and his face big and bold on the wall.

Would he think it's weird that his mom is here?

Are you kidding? Julian said. He'd love it. He'd fucking love it. I can hear him laughing.

Watching those kids work so hard to create a physical memorial for their lost friend was a transformative experience, a modern ritual of reverence and affection, an urban tribute to a fallen comrade. They honoured Holden in a way that couldn't be done in a church, a way that was intrinsic. The gesture was a precious gift to all of us. I will forever be grateful for their beautiful work, their sincere efforts, their openness, and their friendship.

Of course, I wish Holden's life had been longer. I wish he'd had the chance to take many more long walks. I wish he'd been able to experience the other side of his trouble: vibrant good health, world travel, love and fatherhood. I wish I could call him right now to go for a beer, or to an art show. I want his life to have been rich. Instead, mine is. Holden has taught me about devotion and what it means to ache every day for something you can't have or even describe accurately. He has helped me to become a writer. And here is the greatest surprise: in surrendering his life, Holden has made mine vast, distilled, and more substantial than I ever could have imagined. And I am far from the only one.

I have been moved over and over by the stories people have told me about how much Holden affected their lives with his kindness, his understanding, his non-judgemental acceptance, and his unique charms. His life has sent ripples through many hearts. We all miss Holden, and I believe he misses us, too. He would have a lot to say about the world right now.

He would be thrilled to know how wonderful his sister is, to witness her thriving through her own life's challenges, defining herself with grace and resilience, even while quietly suffering his absence. To see how smart and beautiful she is, how very funny, and, at times, very sad. How her hands, which used to hold his, are capable. And how, though she has a different father, when the light is just right, her eyes share the exact shade of mossy green as his. And to know that she carries him in that soft, golden place that only he can occupy.

How long will it stay? someone asked me the day the mural was painted.

I really can't say.

Maybe a year, until it gets painted over. Who knows? Maybe the whole wall will be torn down for development. Retail on the bottom, condos up top. Maybe that's why the developer offered the wall in the first place. Or maybe next week some little punk will zigzag a drunken tag over Holden's beaming face. That would make me fume, and it would also be quite fitting. Impermanence is the true nature of street art. And of life.

How long will you *be*? I really can't say.

I am not ashamed of my son. I am ashamed that I didn't know what to do or how to help him. That I didn't fully see or understand him and what his struggles were really about. I am ashamed that he couldn't tell me he was in trouble with his mental health. Ashamed and devastated that we couldn't talk openly about his illness like we would have if he'd had diabetes or cancer. I am ashamed that when he needed me most, I was on the other side of the planet.

If only Holden had been as kind to himself as he was to the many people who have contacted me since his death to say, Holden was the only one who really understood me, Holden was there for me when I felt completely alone, your son stayed up all night with me, he made me laugh like nobody else, he was the smartest person I've ever known, he was my boyfriend, he was my best friend.

Later in the evening, when the crowd had thinned, the air had cooled, and the mural was almost finished, I got the chance to use a little bit of spray paint to add my mark. As I stood there in front of the wall, shaking the can, feeling the thump of the balls inside stirring the paint, I understood a little bit of how Holden may have felt when he painted.

Brave and unlimited. Alive. And free.

∞

When the one-year anniversary of Holden's death approached, a quaking restlessness grew in me. I didn't know how to mark the day, but I knew I didn't want to be at home, waiting. I didn't want to be anywhere, but I felt the day needed to be acknowledged with some kind of ritual, some kind of significant effort. So we did what we had done so many times the year we travelled: Cam, Lyla, and I loaded our backpacks and set off.

We drove north for an hour to the Squamish Valley, with its towering granite sentinel, the Stawamus Chief, then walked up a mountain until we hit snow. And we kept walking. Though it was early July and the sun warmed our shoulders, the previous winter's five-metre snowfall had yet to melt completely. Hours later, as we traversed a slippery alpine slope and descended the trail toward our campsite at Elfin Lakes, we could see the peak of Diamond Head and the Opal Cone across the steep valley shining white and sharp against an impossibly blue sky. Brooding clouds rolled along the edge of the majestic range like tumbleweeds.

The images I had Googled the day before showed green alpine meadows freckled with pink and purple wildflowers, and hikers swimming in one of the two lakes to cool off after the eleven-kilometre uphill trek. Any snow was in the distance, where it belonged.

But when we arrived late that afternoon, the lakes were almost completely frozen over, and we had to shovel snow off the wooden platform before we could set up our tent. We pulled off our sweat-soaked T-shirts and put on every piece of dry clothing we'd brought. Lyla bashed a hole in the ice to fill our pot with water, and Cam rehydrated a curry chicken dinner on our one-burner cookstove.

We found a private spot with a big memorable rock we could easily find again and spread some of Holden's ashes among the salal and curling lichen. Lyla drew a beautiful chalk mandala for her brother, the artist. We read messages from friends and family, and some passages from books and teachers who had helped us grieve during our long year of sorrow. We acknowledged the loss of Holden and all of the pain we had felt in his absence. We told him how much we treasured him, loved him, and forgave him. We asked for his love and forgiveness, too.

As it got dark, we melted snow to make hot chocolate, then ran out of fuel. Somehow, our unpreparedness seemed appropriate. Nobody complained. Over the last year, all three of us had become familiar with wrongness.

I had placed a framed photo of Holden on our tent platform, along with a candle in a glass holder. The wind picked up. Dark clouds boiled all around us, and needles of rain began ticking the tent fly. We climbed in for the night. I didn't want Holden's picture to get soaked, so I reached out through the tent flap and pulled it inside. But I couldn't bring myself to blow out his candle, so I just left it there, exposed. One year before, at that time, he had still been alive.

I tossed fitfully, my sleeping bag rasping against itself in the stillness, while memories of Holden swirled. I tried not to reenact his last moments, but rather, to see happier times. We'd had so many of those. Birthdays, holidays, conversations, dinners, walks, and swims. With Cam's steady breathing on one side and Lyla pressed against me for warmth on the other, I prayed to fall asleep and dream of Holden. Maybe something about this place and date, this ceremony, would bring him close, just for a moment. The rain pelted in rhythmic waves, and mountain winds rattled our cheap tent. The glow of the candle pulsed through the blue wall, its flickering warmth a comfort on this blackest of anniversaries.

Deep in the night, the rainfall increased, and the temperature dropped. Freezing pellets drummed the fabric above our heads. Lying in the blackness, I wondered what time Holden's soul had left his body. Would I somehow intuit the timing of his last breath, his final heartbeat, at the moment, a year before, he'd ceased to be?

I must have drifted off and awakened again. I could no longer detect the flame's golden bloom. The powerful mountain storm had dimmed his light. His darkness was complete.

He's gone, I thought. Gone, while I wasn't paying attention. I missed it. Again. And I cried softly in my sleeping bag, cold and empty. Husband to the left, daughter to the right.

The next morning, groggy and stiff from a night on hard ground, I pulled on my boots, unzipped the tent door, and crawled out onto the platform under a brilliant swath of blue. I extended my arms to the sky, then folded forward to stretch my legs and back. And there was the candle, its wick a neon point of stubborn orange at the centre of the tiniest flame, still burning, head above water in a pool of clear, melted wax, even after the powerful forces of nature had tried their best to extinguish it.

Afterword

When I first contemplated the idea of writing this book, I didn't know how to make all the chunks of my memory, and the many sections of Holden's life I didn't have access to, into some kind of cohesive fabric. So I began by writing what I knew, and when I arrived at a blank space, I let my imagination take the wheel. This story swerves back and forth between the known and the unknown. The dividing line between the two is often difficult to discern, and the grieving mind, faced with the absence of so many missing pieces, has a way of straddling that border, trying to integrate the parts into some kind of whole.

Throughout this process, I have come to realize that there are many notions of truth—emotional truth is one of them. Some call this auto-fiction. I prefer "informed fiction." Many of the characters are composites. Many scenes are conceptualized. Several people in Holden's life had bigger and more significant impacts on him, and he on them, than I could possibly portray here.

Why write at all? Why point a searchlight into the painful depths of my son's darkest moments? Because not talking perpetuates the suffering. More of the same silence that causes substance users to feel ashamed, judged, and isolated will not protect anyone, change anything, nor prevent any more deaths. When we remain quiet, the burden continues to be carried by those who cannot bear it. Through dialogue, we have the opportunity to open our minds and our hearts.

Acknowledgments

Early drafts of this work were completed while I was a student at the University of British Columbia, which is located on the traditional, ancestral, and unceded territory of the xʷməθkʷəy̓əm (Musqueam) people. This project was supported in part by funding from the Social Sciences and Humanities Research Council.

Holden's story has been nourished by a very long list of kind people to whom I will be forever grateful. I sincerely hope I don't forget anyone.

To my fellow non-fictioners at The Writers Studio at Simon Fraser University, where this book began with a few rough chapters: Diana Carter, Rebecca Fleck, Thi Tran, Daniela Cohen, Jo Dworschack, Barry Truter, Jenny Heron, Stephanie Candiago, Clara Cristofaro, and Katy Fedosenko. And of course to our mentor, J.J. Lee, who swore a great deal while telling me my own story had a place alongside Holden's. Special gratitude to TWS Founder Betsy Warland, in whose living room I saw a white feather on the windowsill and first imagined writing of Holden: thank you for your gentle and precise encouragement.

To the many engaged students/friends at the UBC School of Creative Writing who read early sections with care and insight: Molly Cross-Blanchard, Jasmine Sealy, Emma Cleary, Amy Higgins, Kate Grace Black, Sara de Waal, Stacy Penner, Napatsi Folger, Peter Takach, Cara Nelissen, Guy Hajaj (and bonus friends Avital + Lev ♡ Ness), Tania De Rozario, Loghan Paylor, Adrian Southin, Ray Clark, Tommy Partl, Ryan Kim, Erin Kirsh, Emily Chou, Jessica Lampard, Jamie Coda Canepa, Toby Sharpe, Charles Brown, Laura Anne Harris, Paloma Pacheco, Hina Iman, Spencer Oakes, Paul Whittle, Nicole Baute, Heather Debling, Ben Mussett, and Bree Galbraith.

To the dedicated faculty at UBC: Kevin Chong; Timothy Taylor; Nancy Lee; Ian Williams; Maureen Medved; Carol Shaben; Sheryda Warrener for the nouns; Amber Dawn, who deserves an extra-big thank you; John Vigna, who reminded me to revise relentlessly, then get out of the way; and Taylor Brown-Evans. And my enormous gratitude to the big heart and bigger mind of Alix Ohlin, who championed this project from the beginning and held it in her skilled hands for years.

To the brilliant team at Arsenal Pulp Press: Robert Ballantyne, Cynara Geissler, Jaiden Dembo, Jazmin Welch for the beautiful cover and interior design, editor Catharine Chen for her delicate touch and wise, thoughtful insights, and especially publisher Brian Lam, who saw and understood this book so clearly, then offered unlimited support, kindness, and respect. I couldn't ask for more.

To members of the writing community for the warm welcome: Becky Livingston, for your open-hearted friendship and conversations; Aislinn Hunter, a literary genius who understands witness from the inside; Erin Soros, the wildest, cleverest mind and gentlest heart; Cathie Borrie, you can just fuck right off; Lawrence Hill, for reading early essays and asking just the right questions.

To my agent, Marilyn Biderman at Transatlantic, for her confidence in me as a writer and her perseverance in finding Holden the perfect home, xo.

To the countless friends who stood close: Jo Burleigh; Margie Rosling; Andrea Gilmour; Heather Connelly Volpe; Leah Melenbacher; Lu Smith; Lianne and Andrew Britnell; Cindy and John Hird; Kathe Sanvido; Ian Wightman; Grahnia and Gareth McDonnell; Camille Picard; Terry Reid; Susan Edgecomb; Jennifer Hubbard; Ron Village; Warren Barrow; Coleen Denman; Heather Knowlden; Dale Wolfe; Ann Schretlen; George Orr; Jen Curleigh; Barbara, Gregg, Sal, Kate, and Jack Wiltshire; Mia Wood; and the many yogis who held space.

Love to my family: Mom, Dad, Laureen, Janet, Kevin, Marcia, Jack, Jeff, Christopher, and Lois, who would have been so proud.

My heart continues to hurt for: Becky Livingston (yes, I'm thanking you twice); Donna and Mike Striha; Bridget and Tony Malcolm; Wendy and Gord Catt; Kurt Trzcinski; and especially Bill, Liesl, and Sophia.

To Sarah Blyth and her tireless team at Vancouver's Overdose Prevention Society for their knowledge and compassion and for saving thousands of lives.

To Erin, Geoffrey, and Olivia Bird, who came to our door and never left.

To my dear, dear Squirrels—Laurel Spencer, Leslie Landell, Linda Warner, Hazel Park, Manami Hara, Marianne Thomson, Sandie Herunter, Shauna Markham—Friday coffee forever!

To Holden's friends, who miss him so: Hayden Eland, Filipo Intile, James MacFarlan, Miko Phillip, Marlow Nicols, Ariel Buxton, Kara Leigh Galloway, Alex Leeder, Sebastian Kovacs, Lauren Anthony, Emily Vineberg, Shane Baker Flood, Cory Einhorn, Jess Spears, Alex Sandoval, Kayla Brunke, Michelle Pihowich, Stan, Aidan, André … There are definitely more.

To the Vancouver Mural Fest community: David Vertesi, Scott Sueme, Andrea Curtis, Nick Colinet. And to all the talented graffiti writers who sprayed their talents at East 5th and Main: Oodles, Guph, Molar, Arise, Lunar, Mercy, Squid, Herah, Mable, Naks, Keep6, JNasty, Siloh, Take5, Vers, UncleO, Combo, Sleazy, Dyce Raw, KC Hall, Cobra, Soak, and all the rest.

To Scott Hull from ANb, who surprised and enlightened me.

To everyone who held us in their hearts, came to our door, delivered food or flowers, sent cards, texts, emails, and made other thoughtful gestures: We are ever grateful.

To Cam and Lyla, thank you will never be enough. I'm blessed to share this life with you. And finally, to Holden: I love you infinity.

Photo credit Jane Thomson Photography

Tara McGuire is a former broadcaster turned writer whose essays and poetry have appeared in several magazines, on CBC radio, and the anthology *Always With Me: Parents Talk about the Death of a Child* (Demeter Press, 2018). Her essays have been shortlisted for the Writers' Union of Canada Short Prose Competition for Emerging Writers in 2018 and 2020, and *Room* magazine's 2021 Creative Non-Fiction Contest. She is a graduate of The Writers Studio at SFU and has an MFA from the UBC School of Creative Writing. She lives in North Vancouver with her family.

taramcguire.com